CREATIVE
HOMEOWNER®

KITCHENS

DESIGN ■ REMODEL ■ BUILD

CREATIVE HOMEOWNER®, Upper Saddle River, New Jersey

Editorial Director: Timothy O. Bakke
Art Director: W. David Houser

Writers: James Hufnagel, Kathie Robitz, Barbara Sabella
Associate Editor: Patrick Quinn
Copy Editor: Beth Kalet

Graphic Designers: Michael James Allegra, Michelle D. Halko
Illustrators: Craig Franklin, Ed Lipinski, James Randolph,
            Frank Rohrbach, Paul M. Schumm, Ray Skibinski
Cover Design: Annie Jeon
Cover Photo: Melabee M Miller Photography
Photo Researchers: Kathie Robitz, Barbara Sabella

Printed in the United States of America

Current Printing (last digit)
10 9 8 7 6 5

Kitchens: Design, Remodel, Build
Library of Congress Catalog Card Number: 96-84687
ISBN: 1-880029-68-5
Web site: **www.creativehomeowner.com**

Photo Credits

Safety First

Though all the designs and methods in this book have been reviewed for safety, it is not possible to overstate the importance of using the safest construction methods possible. What follows are reminders; some do's and don'ts of basic carpentry. They are not substitutes for your own common sense.

- *Always* use caution, care, and good judgment when following the procedures described in this book.

- *Always* be sure that the electrical setup is safe; be sure that no circuit is overloaded, and that all power tools and electrical outlets are properly grounded. Do not use power tools in wet locations.

- *Always* read container labels on paints, solvents, and other products; provide ventilation, and observe all other warnings.

- *Always* read the tool manufacturer's instructions for using a tool, especially the warnings.

- *Always* use holders or pushers to work pieces shorter than 3 inches on a table saw or jointer. Avoid working short pieces if you can.

- *Always* remove the key from any drill chuck (portable or press) before starting the drill.

- *Always* pay deliberate attention to how a tool works so that you can avoid being injured.

- *Always* know the limitations of your tools. Do not try to force them to do what they were not designed to do.

- *Always* make sure that any adjustment is locked before proceeding. For example, always check the rip fence on a table saw or the bevel adjustment on a portable saw before starting to work.

- *Always* clamp small pieces firmly to a bench or another work surface when sawing or drilling.

- *Always* wear the appropriate rubber or work gloves when handling chemicals, doing heavy construction, or sanding.

- *Always* wear a disposable mask when working around odors, dust, or mist. Use a special respirator when working with toxic substances.

- *Always* wear eye protection, especially when using power tools or striking metal on metal or concrete; a chip can fly off, for example, when chiseling concrete.

- *Always* be aware that there is seldom enough time for your body's reflexes to save you from injury from a power tool in a dangerous situation; everything happens too fast. Be *alert!*

- *Always* keep your hands away from the business ends of blades, cutters, and bits.

- *Always* hold a portable circular saw with both hands so that you will know where your hands are.

- *Always* use a drill with an auxiliary handle to control the torque when large-size bits are used.

- *Always* check your local building codes when planning new construction. The codes are intended to protect public safety and should be observed to the letter.

- *Never* work with power tools when you are tired or under the influence of alcohol or drugs.

- *Never* cut very small pieces of wood or pipe. Whenever possible, cut small pieces off larger pieces.

- *Never* change a blade or a bit unless the power cord is unplugged. Do not depend on the switch being off; you might accidentally hit it.

- *Never* work in insufficient lighting.

- *Never* work while wearing loose clothing, hanging hair, open cuffs, or jewelry.

- *Never* work with dull tools. Have them sharpened, or learn how to sharpen them yourself.

- *Never* use a power tool on a workpiece that is not firmly supported or clamped.

- *Never* saw a workpiece that spans a large distance between horses without close support on either side of the kerf; the piece can bend, closing the kerf and jamming the blade, causing saw kickback.

- *Never* support a workpiece from underneath with your leg or other part of your body when sawing.

- *Never* carry sharp or pointed tools, such as utility knives, awls, or chisels, in your pocket. If you want to carry tools, use a special-purpose tool belt with leather pockets and holders.

CONTENTS

Introduction: Dreams & Schemes

Planning a new kitchen is a challenging, exhilarating, exhausting task. But it's well worth the effort. Although remodeling a kitchen is one of the most costly home improvements you can make, short of adding a whole new wing, it's also one of the most valuable—90-percent yield at resale within a year of completion is not uncommon.

When you do get around to building your new kitchen, make sure you get what you want because you'll likely live with it for a long time. You may envision a homey country look, or perhaps a sleek, spare design. Maybe you want to vary cabinet heights for different tasks, or replace your all-wood cabinets with laminated white that's decked out with a colorful stripe. Even if you've got a mental snapshot of what you want your new kitchen to look like, review the pictures in this book as well as those in manufacturers' literature and decorating magazines for additional inspiration and information. Study the decorative elements that make up various styles so you can make an intelligent decision about what appeals to you. Also, look at functional elements apart from style.

Then get to work—creating, scheming, planning, refining, and building.

Generous expanses of countertop, as well as lots of natural and recessed lighting, create an efficient and pleasant work space (above). Brick fireplace, glazed red tile, and ginger-bread details (opposite) evoke the charm of a bygone era.

Brass railings and wood bullnose countertop trim add rich details to this kitchen design.

Arched cabinet doors, stone flooring, and rustic wood surfaces combine with lace for an Old World ambience.

What Do You Want?

If you don't have a clear, comprehensive answer to the question of what you want, you should take a thorough inventory of the desires and needs of your household, including the opinions, likes, and dislikes of everyone in the family. Some questions to consider include:

- What do you like about your existing kitchen?
- What would you want to change?
- Is there enough accessible storage and countertop space?
- Do you need a "junk" drawer?
- What will you be doing in your kitchen apart from fixing meals?
- How do family members interact when they cook?

The answers to some questions will have a direct impact on outfitting the kitchen. An example of this kind of question is, Do you clean up as you go, or leave everything for later? Clean-as-you-go cooks need less counter space, but they benefit from a larger sink, where there's more room to stack dishes, pots, and pans.

All-white cabinets, a pair of skylights set into a wooden ceiling, canister lights, and a hanging fixture brighten this informal space.

Classical columns, furniture-quality cabinetry, and a candlestick chandelier bring formal flair to this kitchen.

The center island is a focal point in this traditional kitchen, where elements of white, wood, and light combine for a cozy ambience.

Colorful geometric shapes give a playful look to this simple kitchen design.

If you use a lot of fresh foods, you will appreciate a chopping block, and perhaps even a second sink for washing produce. If you rely mostly on packaged goods, abundant storage—perhaps in a full-height pantry—can minimize trips to the supermarket. Avid bakers probably will want a second oven, and perhaps a cool surface for rolling out pastry dough. People who follow recipes to the letter may require a cookbook holder raised above the counter to spare pages from spatters.

The list at right, modified from the National Kitchen and Bath Association, can help you organize your thoughts and get you to analyze what you want and need in a new kitchen—one that will work for you down to the last detail.

Organize Information

To keep track of all the decisions and details involved in planning and remodeling your kitchen, set up a scrapbook, folder, or file box. Keep kitchen photos clipped from magazines and newspapers, product brochures, articles about new

■ Kitchen Needs & Wants ■

Who uses the kitchen and for what?

• How large is your family?

• Does anyone else regularly cook or bake?

• Does anyone in the family have a special physical requirement?

• Is meal preparation most likely to be

   heat and serve?
   advance bulk preparation?
   full-course from scratch?
   something else?

• What is your style of entertaining, and how often do you do it?

• Is your kitchen a company gathering place, or is it off-limits to guests?

• Will you sort and store recyclables in the kitchen?

• Will your kitchen accommodate tasks besides food preparation and storage, such as

   laundry?   gardening?
   office?   something else?
   sewing/crafts?

• What "non-kitchen" items will need to be stored in the kitchen (casual jackets and mittens, for example, or a step-stool or vacuum cleaner)?

What feeling/tone do you want your kitchen to have?

Contemporary   Country
Traditional   Formal
Strictly functional
Family gathering center

What kind of products and features do you want in your new kitchen?

Cabinets	Countertop
Backsplash	Chopping surfaces
Flooring	Wallcovering
Microwave	Refrigerator
Freezer	Ice maker
Sink(s)	Faucet
Dishwasher	Trash compactor
Storage	Waste disposer
Pantry	Recycling area
Windows	Skylight
Outlets	Media center
Wet bar	Eating area
Desk	Washer/dryer

Light fixtures
Oven(s)/cooktop range
Under-cabinet appliances
Hot water dispenser
Something else

trends or products, physical samples and color swatches of surface materials, notes from visits to showrooms, and all your ideas and sketches. It might be helpful to sort your information into categories.

Paperwork. You should be able to put your hands on what you need:

• Calendar for scheduling and keeping a record of progress.

• Shopping lists with prices, warranties, serial numbers, receipts, etc.

• Telephone directory of all subcontractors, suppliers, and service representatives.

• Contracts, agreements, permits, and inspection approvals.

Layout and traffic patterns. The arrangement of work spaces and appliances, and the flow of traffic through the kitchen greatly influence how tasks are performed.

Appliances. Choose among a wealth of appliance styles and features. The choices you make will affect the entire plan, since appliances should be placed so they function most efficiently and conveniently.

Storage. You need enough and the right kind of storage to provide a place for dry goods, perishables, dishes and flatware, pots and utensils, linens, cleaning supplies, garbage, recyclables, and anything else you want to keep in the kitchen.

Lighting. You'll want good overall (general) light, but you also need to target particular areas or zones in the room (task lighting).

Surfaces. Colors and textures help define your style. However, a kitchen's walls, floor, and countertops are more than just decorative elements; they must be easy to clean and maintain, too.

Get It Done

How much does a new kitchen cost? Plan on spending about as much as you would for a new car. There is a broad range, of course, between the cost of a stripped-down subcompact

Frameless European-style cabinets with hidden hardware present a sleek, modern environment suggestive of speed and efficiency. Skylights and peak windows maximize light and invite nature into this controlled setting.

and a top-of-the-line luxury model, and so it is with kitchens.

By knowing what goes into each task when you talk to outside designers or contractors, and by doing work correctly when you do it yourself, you'll be able to control the cost of the kitchen without skimping on quality or convenience. Remodeling your own kitchen may seem daunting at first, but the project will begin to appear more manageable when you realize that it consists of a series of smaller projects. *Kitchens: Design, Remodel, Build* is intended to guide you through the entire process. The book will help you

• Analyze your existing kitchen and set your sights on the kitchen you would like to have.

• Choose the right materials, products, and appliances for your needs.

• Plan a layout that suits your lifestyle and the space available.

• Define your style with color, texture, lighting, and details.

• Decide what you can handle yourself, and where you might need help.

• Dismantle your old kitchen, remove and construct walls, install a skylight, run plumbing and electrical lines, and install a duct for a range hood.

• Finish the walls and ceilings, lay flooring, build cabinets or install stock types, and install counters, sinks, and appliances.

Before starting any project in the book, check with your local building inspector. Also consult national, state, and local codes for any restrictions or requirements.

Make safety a priority. Wear goggles, rubber gloves, and nose and mouth protection. When working with electricity, always turn off the power at the main service panel and be sure the circuit is completely dead before you begin.

Shaker-like simplicity and purity of design, along with well-defined task areas, create a milieu conducive to work.

This warm wood contemporary kitchen features varied counter and cupboard heights and creative use of cabinetry.

1

Function

Whether you typically prepare gourmet cuisine or simple fare, you'll want your new kitchen to allow you to function smoothly and at your best. At the same time, you'll want the kitchen to provide an atmosphere for enjoying the process. The following pages present ideas that will make putting together a meal easier, cleaning up the mess quicker, and storing equipment and supplies more efficient.

If you've ever become exasperated looking for the right pot in a crowded cabinet, you'll appreciate today's myriad cabinet and storage options. Along with new cabinets, you might want to match the right appliances to your family's needs and habits. If you can't make major changesin these two costly areas, you can improve the look of your old kitchen with new surfaces—countertops, flooring, and wallcovering. By selecting the right materials, you'll increase the efficiency of certain tasks and decrease time and energy spent on maintenance.

A common complaint about poorly designed kitchens is that they're too dark. Sometimes just installing a larger window or a skylight dramatically solves that problem. You can also supplement natural light sources with electric lighting to create a mood, highlight a work surface, or just brighten up the space.

Whatever the scope of your renovation, taking steps to improve your kitchen's working design will better the quality of the time you spend there.

Cabinets

While it's true that cabinets help define the style and create the environment of a kitchen, their main job is to store the many items involved in preparing, serving, and cleaning up food. They must be durable enough to withstand thousands of openings and closings for loading and unloading over years of use.

Regardless of the type and style of cabinets on which you decide, insist on quality construction. Good cabinets feature dovetail and mortise-and-tenon joinery and solidly mortised hinges. The interiors are well finished, with adjustable shelves that are a minimum $\frac{5}{8}$ inch thick to prevent bowing. The drawers in good cabinets roll on ball-bearing glides, and they support at least 75 pounds when open.

Construction Styles & Options

There are basically two construction styles for kitchen cabinetry: framed and frameless. You can buy inexpensive ready-made cabinets directly from a retailer's stock in finished form, in unfinished form, or as knockdowns. These will usually be framed cabinets. If you prefer, choose more expensive semi-custom and custom-made cabinets. You can get custom cabinets from a large manufacturer, or have them built to your specifications by a carpenter. Of course if you have the tools and the skill, you can always make your own cabinets.

Framed. Framed cabinets—or traditional-style cabinets—have a full frame across the face of the cabinet box. This provides a means of securing adjacent cabinets together and strengthens wider cabinet boxes with a center rail. Hinges may be either visible or hidden, and the front frame may or may not be visible around doors and drawers when they are closed.

Frameless. Frameless cabinets—also known as European-style cabinets—are built without a face frame. Close-fitting doors cover the entire front of the box, or they may be set into

Framed Cabinet. The frame across the face of the cabinet box may show between closed doors or be hidden in the case of full overlay doors.

Framed maple cabinets give this kitchen a warm feeling; special features like built-in wine racks and a cookbook holder add to its functionality.

stock cabinets may be fair, good, or excellent, depending on the manufacturer and price. Materials may be solid wood (hard or soft) and plywood, wood and particleboard, wood and hardboard, or all particleboard. They may be carefully jointed and doweled or merely nailed and glued together. Stock cabinets also come in steel and in several types of plastic, either in part or entirely. The quality of cabinets made from these materials also varies from exquisite to barely adequate. Stock cabinets range in price from inexpensive to moderately costly.

Unfinished and Knockdown. You can save some money by buying unfinished stock cabinets and staining or painting them yourself. You can save even more by purchasing knockdown cabinets, which are shipped flat to lower the costs of packing and delivery. Knockdowns are sometimes unfinished as well.

Semi-Custom. Like stock cabinets, semi-custom cabinets are available only in specific sizes, but they are not completed until they are ordered. These cabinets typically have many more finishes, colors,

the box opening. Hinges are typically hidden. Both domestic and European manufacturers offer frameless cabinets. Prices can be high and delivery times lengthy if you want features an import dealer does not have in stock.

Stock. Stock cabinets are literally in stock where they are sold or are quickly available by order. They are made in limited styles and colors, but in a wide variety of standard sizes that you can assemble to suit your kitchen space. The quality of

Frameless Cabinet. With these cabinets, also known as European style, note that there is no front frame on the cabinet box. Doors are mounted on the face or set into the box.

Frameless cabinets of different depths and heights, with varied door treatments and accessories, enhance form and function.

Open and closed shelving work together in this kitchen, which dramatically combines white-painted and dark-stained cabinetry.

Deep raised panels and glass doors with wood muntins are clues to the fine quality in this deceptively simple room.

Wall cabinets are angled around a corner, conforming to the elegantly curved base cabinet with tambour doors.

styles, options, and special features than stock cabinets. They will take longer for delivery because they are made to order.

Custom. Custom cabinets are built to the measurements of a particular project. Because custom cabinets are made from scratch, delivery may take from 4 to 16 weeks. The delivery delay rarely causes a problem because the preparation work for a new kitchen also takes time. But place your order well in advance of the date you will need your cabinets. Custom cabinets are almost always delivered completely finished, like fine furniture, whereas some stock cabinets may be bought unfinished. Prices for custom cabinets run from moderate to very expensive.

Carpenter-Built. If you have the time, some carpentry skills, and a work area, you can save money by constructing cabinets to your own specifications. Or you can hire a carpenter to build them. This, of course, won't be a money saver, but will give you great leeway in your design.

Storage

The type of storage in a kitchen is almost as important as the amount. Some people like at least a few open shelves for displaying attractive china or glassware; others want absolutely everything tucked away behind doors.

What are your storage needs? The answer depends partly on your shopping habits and partly on how many pots, pans, and other pieces of kitchen equipment you have or would like to have. A family that shops several times a week and prepares mostly fresh foods needs more refrigerator space, less freezer capacity, and fewer cabinets than a family that prefers packaged or prepared foods and makes only infrequent forays to the supermarket.

Planning

To help clarify your needs, mentally walk yourself through a typical meal and list the utensils used to prepare food, where the items come from, and your progress through the work area.

Food Preparation. During food preparation, the sink and stove come into use. Using water means repeated trips to the sink, so that area might be the best place to keep a steamer, salad spinner, and coffee and tea canisters, as well as glassware and cups. Near the

A curved end cabinet in a peninsula is a graceful way to round a corner between the dining and food preparation areas.

The built-in hutch is a fancy custom-look feature offered by many cabinet manufacturers today.

stove you may want storage for odd-shaped items such as a fish poacher or wok. You can hang frequently used pans and utensils from a convenient rack; stow other items in cabinets so they do not collect grease.

During the Meal. When the food is ready, you must transport it to the table. If the eating space is nearby, a work counter might turn into a serving counter. If the dining space is in another room, a pass-through facilitates serving.

After the Meal. When the meal ends, dishes must go from the table to the sink or dishwasher, leftovers to storage containers and the refrigerator. Now the stove and counters need to be wiped down and the sink scoured. When the dishwasher finishes its cycle, everything must be put away.

Open shelving is a common storage option, but it requires great attention to detail and tidiness to keep it looking attractive.

▪ Storage Checklist ▪

- **Do you like kitchen gadgets?** Plan drawer space, countertop sorters, wall magnets, or hooks to keep these items handy near the tasks they usually perform.

- **Do you own a food processor, blender, mixer, crockpot, electric can opener, knife sharpener, juicer, coffee maker, or coffee mill?** If you're particularly tidy, you may want small appliances like these tucked away in an appliance garage or cupboard to be taken out only when needed. If you prefer to have often-used machines sitting on the counter, ready to go, plan enough space, along with conveniently located electrical outlets.

- **Do you plan to store large quantities of food?** Be sure to allow plenty of freezer, bin, and shelf space for the kind of food shopping you do.

- **Do you intend to do a lot of freezing or canning?** Allow a work space and place to stow equipment. Also plan adequate storage for the fruits of your labor—an extra stand-alone freezer or a good-sized food safe in the kitchen or in a separate pantry or cellar.

- **Do you bake often?** Consider a baking center that can house your equipment and serve as a separate baking-ingredients pantry.

- **Do you collect pottery, tinware, or anything else that might be displayed in the kitchen?** Soffits provide an obvious place to hang small objects like collectible plates. Eliminating soffits provides a shelf on top of the wall cabinets for larger lightweight objects like baskets. Open shelving, glass-front cupboards, and display cabinets are other options.

- **Do you collect cookbooks?** If so, you'll need expandable shelf space and perhaps a bookstand.

Personal Profile

- **How tall are you and everyone else who will use your kitchen?** Adjust your counter and wall-cabinet heights to suit. Multi-level work surfaces for special tasks are an important trend in kitchen design.

- **Do you or any of your family members use a walker, leg braces, or a wheelchair?** Plan a good work height, kneeholes, grab bars, secure seating, slide-out work boards, and other convenience features to make your kitchen comfortable for all who will use it.

- **Are you left- or right-handed?** Think about your natural motion when you choose whether to open single cupboards or refrigerator doors from the left or right side, whether to locate your dishwasher to the left or right of the sink, and so on.

- **How high can you comfortably reach?** If you're tall, hang your wall cabinets high. If you're petite, you may want to hang the cabinets lower and plan a spot to keep a step-stool handy.

- **Can you comfortably bend and reach for something in a base cabinet?** Can you lift heavy objects easily and without strain or pain? If your range is limited in these areas, be sure to plan roll-out shelving on both upper and lower tiers of your base cabinets. Also, look into spring-up shelves designed to lift mixer bases or other heavy appliances to counter height.

- **Do you frequently share cooking tasks with another family member?** If so, you may each prefer to have your own work area.

Facilities

Storage facilities can make or break a kitchen, so choose the places you'll put things with care. Here's a look at a few alternatives:

Open Versus Closed Storage. Shelves, pegboards, pot racks, cup hooks, magnetic knife racks, and the like put your utensils on view, which is a good way to personalize your kitchen. Here's an area where you can save some money, too. Open storage generally costs less than cabinets, and because you don't have to construct, hang, and fit doors, it's easy for a do-it-yourselfer to build.

But open storage has drawbacks. For one thing, items left out in the open can look messy unless they are kept neatly arranged. Also, objects collect dust and grease, especially near the range. This means that unless you reach for an item almost daily, you'll find yourself washing it before as well as after you use it.

If extra washing and dusting discourage you from the idea of open storage but you'd like to put at least some objects on view, limit your displays to a few items. Another option is installing glass doors on wall cabinets. This handily solves the dust problem but often costs more than solid doors.

Pantries. How often you shop and how many groceries you typically bring home determine the amount of food-storage space your family needs. If you like to stock up or take advantage of sales, add a pantry to your kitchen. To maximize a pantry's convenience, plan shallow, 6-inch-deep shelves so cans and packages will never be stored more than two deep. This way, you'll easily be able to see what you've got on hand.

Specialty Cabinets. One of the greatest boons to modern kitchen cabinets is the availability of fitted and accessorized interiors. Among them are vertical drawers that hold

See-through cabinets mean stored items do not have to be hidden.

Fold-out pantry units allow single-depth, easy-access storage.

Slide-out trays add a great deal to base-cabinet convenience.

Tilt-out trays keep unattractive necessities handy and hidden.

canned goods, spices, and other standard-size containers. Some base cabinets have doors that open to shelves that pull out like conventional shallow drawers. Any of these may be fitted with dividers for large or small items, especially difficult-to-store utensils such as lids, trays, and cookie sheets. Another innovation is shallow interior shelves set back to allow space for racks on the door of the unit. This does not add shelf space, but it increases convenience and accessibility.

Specializing your storage greatly helps organize cookware and supplies. Even ready-made cabinets can be purchased with specialty inserts. You must calculate your storage needs ahead of time, though, so you'll know exactly what you want in the way of drawers, dividers, and bins. You can also specify esoteric fittings for spices, cutlery, linens, and other items.

• Slide-outs. Trays can hold small appliances, linens, small cans, and boxes. Bins are good for onions, potatoes, or large items.

• Carousel shelves. Circular shelves put dead corner space to use. Here two 270-degree shelves are attached to revolving right-angle doors. Single circular shelf units also are offered by some manufacturers.

Sliding multi-tiered racks make optimal use of often inaccessible space.

Appliance garages can be adapted for other items that often clutter a countertop, such as cookbooks and odds and ends.

Specialty Cabinets

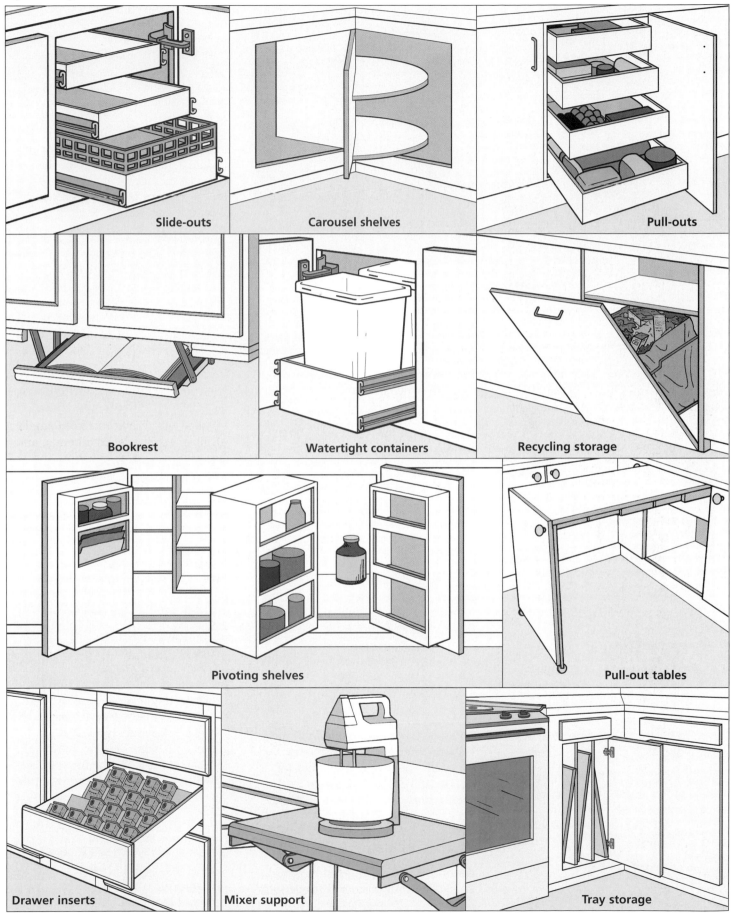

Slide-outs

Carousel shelves

Pull-outs

Bookrest

Watertight containers

Recycling storage

Pivoting shelves

Pull-out tables

Drawer inserts

Mixer support

Tray storage

Shallow cabinet shelves make room for handy spice shelves on the inside surface of the cupboard door.

A large island houses open shelves and wine racks that keep items easy to reach but away from splatter-prone work areas.

• Pull-outs. Door-fronted units have all-wood, old-fashioned drawers. This allows you to have drawers in a base cabinet where a door might look better.

• Bookrest. When closed, a drop-down bookrest blends in with the molding under a wall cabinet.

• Watertight containers. Empty cans are often messy. Lift-out plastic containers in a sliding rack are a good way to collect them.

• Recycling storage. A wire rack on a tilt-out door holds bags for sorting cans, plastic, glass. The shelf holds newspapers, extra bags.

• Pivoting shelves. Door-mounted shelves and in-cabinet swiveling shelf units offer easy access to kitchen supplies. Taller units serve as pantries that hold a great deal in minimal space.

• Pull-out tables. In tight kitchens, this is an excellent way to gain eating space or an extra work surface. Pull-out tea carts are also available.

• Drawer inserts. A drawer insert is a good way to keep packaged spices organized and easily accessi-ble. Inserts are made for flatware and other items, too.

• Mixer supports. A spring-loaded table swings up out of a cupboard for use and away again into the base unit.

• Tray storage. A narrow base cabinet with horizontal slots is perfect for storing cookie sheets and trays on edge. Locate this in a baking center.

Customized Organizers. If you de-cide to make do with your existing cabinets, consider refitting their in-teriors with cabinet organizers. These plastic, plastic-coated wire, or enameled-steel racks and hang-ers are widely available at depart-ment stores, hardware stores, and home centers.

Some of these units slide in and out of base cabinets, similar to the racks in a dishwasher. Others let you mount shallow drawers to the undersides of wall cabinets. Still others consist of stackable plastic bins with plenty of room to hold kitchen sundries.

Beware of the temptation to over-specialize your kitchen storage facil-ities. Sizes and needs for certain items change, so be sure to allot at least 50 percent of your kitchen's storage to standard cabinets with one or more movable shelves.

Herb and Spice Racks. Be aware that herbs and spices lose their fla-vor more rapidly when exposed to heat or sunlight, so don't locate a spice rack or shelving intended for storing herbs too close to the cook-top or a sunny window. Choose opaque containers, or keep season-ings in a cool, closed cupboard or in a drawer outfitted with a rack so you can quickly lay a hand on what you need.

Wine Storage. Some contemporary kitchens show off bottles of wine in open racks and bins that hold as much as a couple of cases. If you regularly serve wine with meals, by all means keep a few bottles on hand—but bear in mind that the kitchen is far from the ideal place to store wine for any length of time.

The problem is that heat and sun-light are two of wine's worst ene-mies, which is why fine wines are stored in cellars. The temperature in a wine cellar should be about 55 to 60 degrees F, so if you'd like to age new vintages for a year or two, keep

Tin panels are a folksy treatment for a modern appliance. Adjacent pantry and open shelves give the refrigerator a built-in look.

Cabinet panels and a hand-carved soffit imbue a large side-by-side refrigerator with the warmth of a country kitchen.

them in a cool, dark location, such as the basement or an attached climate-controlled garage, where the bottles won't be disturbed.

If you don't have a place or the need for a proper wine cellar, store bottles in a base cabinet set against an outside wall, well away from the oven, refrigerator, dishwasher, and hot-water pipes. Remember, too, that wine bottles should always be stored horizontally. This keeps the corks moist so they don't dry out and let air seep in, which could ruin the wine.

Food Preparation

Preparing food requires fire and ice. Luckily for us in the modern world, these are provided by a wide choice of functional and beautiful appliances: the ice by refrigerator/freezers, of course, and the fire by cooktops and ovens.

Refrigerators & Freezers

To estimate the refrigerator/freezer capacity your family needs, allow 12 cubic feet of total refrigerator and freezer space for the first two adults in your household, then add

2 more cubic feet for each additional member. Typically, a family of four would need a refrigerator/freezer with a capacity of 16 cubic feet. You must increase this capacity, however, if you prepare meals for the week in advance and keep them in the refrigerator or freezer. If your teenagers down a half-gallon of milk at a swallow, increase milk-storage capacity. If you freeze produce from your garden for use out of season, increase your freezer space or consider buying an additional stand-alone freezer.

As you make a selection, be aware that the fuller a refrigerator or freezer is kept, the less it costs to run. This fact is a compelling reason not to buy a refrigerator or freezer too large for your household or for the amount of food you normally keep on hand, especially where electricity costs are high.

Refrigerator sizes vary by more than capacity. Many require a space that extends out beyond

the full depth of a base cabinet and extends upward into the overhead cabinet space. In recent years, however, manufacturers have been offering 25-inch-deep freestanding models that do not protrude too far beyond the front edges of counters. Built-in 24-inch-deep designs further minimize the bulk of this massive piece of kitchen equipment. Shallower refrigerators and freezers are wider than standard models,

Modular refrigeration units, which can be located near work areas, expand functional design possibilities.

however, and often taller as well, so allocate kitchen space accordingly. Most conventional refrigerators come in one of three styles:

• Single door. This model usually has a manual defrost and a small freezer compartment on top. The freezer temperature usually is not low enough for long-term storage.

• Top freezer. The freezer and refrigerator sections are separate, usually with automatic defrosting. The separate freezer will maintain food for long periods of time.

• Side-by-side. This offers the greatest access to both compartments and requires the least door-swing clearance in front. Side-by-side models are wider than up-and-down versions, and their narrow shelves may not handle bulky items such as a large frozen turkey.

Under-counter-style refrigerators, freezers, and combination units may solve some design difficulties and provide for some specialized needs where tall units pose a problem. Typically, however, their capacity is quite small—around 5 cubic feet—and the small freezers in the combination units aren't satisfactory for much beyond short-term storage.

Modular refrigerators offer a departure from the vertical box we're used to. This concept allows refrigerator or freezer drawer units and cabinets to be located strategically throughout the kitchen—or house. The units are only 27 inches wide and are standard cabinet depth. They accept all types of paneling and handles, so they can blend in with cabinetry when closed. Drawer units and cabinets may be individually temperature-controlled for optimal food storage—32 to 34 degrees F for vegetables, 38 degrees for milk, and 30 to 32 degrees for meats. If you're considering modular refrigeration, get information from the manufacturer right from the start concerning installation specifications such as plumbing and electric requirements.

Refrigerator-Freezer Styles

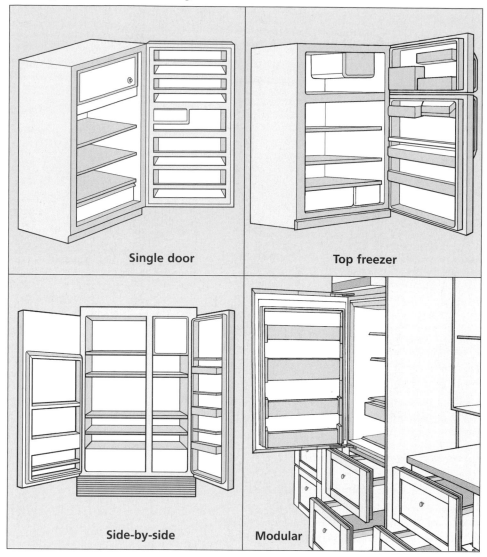

Single door

Top freezer

Side-by-side

Modular

■ Refrigerator Options ■

Here are some options and features you should investigate for your next refrigerator/freezer purchase:

• Adjustable/flexible shelving
• Automatic defroster
• Automatic ice maker
• Crispers
• Dairy compartment
• Deli drawer
• Egg tray
• Extra-tall bottle shelf
• Roller base
• Slide-out shelves
• Wine rack
• Zoned temperature control
• Decorator panel acceptance on the front door
• Door alarm (to warn when door is left open)
• Door racks sized to accommodate gallon milk containers
• Front venting (allows building into an enclosed space)
• See-through front panels on bins and drawers
• Spill-containment shelves (glass or plastic)
• Through-the-door cold water & ice dispenser

Equipment, utensils, cooktop, sink, and food basics are all at the chef's fingertips in this well-designed cooking center.

Inspired by the old-fashioned hearth, this cooktop alcove set apart from the rest of the room gives elbow room to the cook.

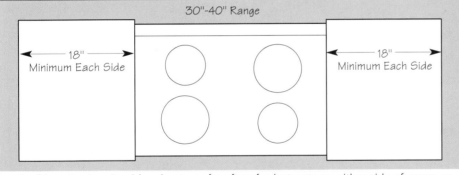

30"-40" Range

18"
Minimum Each Side

18"
Minimum Each Side

Cooking Center. Provide a heatproof surface for hot pots on either side of range or modular cooktop burners.

Cooking Center

The term "cooking center" may sound a bit grand, but with modular cooktops, microwave and convection ovens, gourmet menus (and the utensils to prepare them), and today's health-conscious emphasis on fresh-food preparation, many home chefs want more than just a set of burners with an oven underneath.

As you begin to plan your cooking center, take yourself through the process of meal preparation in your household. Make a mental inventory of the rangetop utensils you now have or plan to acquire:

• Will you be cooking with gas or electricity? Cooking equipment can be purchased in component parts as well as integrated ranges, which makes it possible to have a gas cooktop in conjunction with an electric oven, or vice versa.

• Do you want everything tucked away out of sight, or would you rather show off some of your favorite tools on an overhead or wall rack?

• Do you cook by inspiration and feel, grabbing ingredients from the pantry or refrigerator as you think of them, or are you methodical and orderly, needing a stand to hold an open recipe book in front of you and

a place to gather ingredients before you begin?

• How can you keep seasonings within easy reach? And which do you use most of the time?

• Where will you set hot pots and pans when they come off the burner or out of the oven?

• Will you clear your cooking mess to the same sink and dishwasher that the dinner dishes go to?

Your answers to these and other questions will help you design a cooking area that suits your needs, making meal preparation that much easier. Once you've decided on some design criteria, you'll need to look at specific equipment.

Ranges. Until the late 1950s, the heart of just about every American kitchen was a "stove" that stood off by itself so heat would not damage nearby cabinets and countertops. Today the closest successors to the stove are drop-in or slide-in ranges insulated at the sides and rear so they can fit flush against combustible surfaces. Like stoves, ranges include gas or

A drop-in range allows a smooth line where cabinets meet the floor, avoiding spaces that can collect dirt.

Stainless-steel commercial ranges have extra burners and multiple ovens perfect for large-group entertaining.

electric burners on top and an oven/broiler below. The four most common range styles are:

• Freestanding. Typical models are 30, 36, and 40 inches wide. Both sides are finished.

• High-low. A second oven, regular or microwave, on top provides extra cooking capacity compactly.

• Drop-in. These look the most built-in, but leave dead space beneath. They are usually 30 inches wide.

• Slide-in. The sides are not finished. Most are 30 inches wide; compact units are 20 or 21 inches wide.

Gas or electric? Whether you choose gas or electric to cook with depends in part on what's available locally. If natural gas is not available, appliance dealers can convert ranges to run on bottled liquid propane—but you'll need to arrange for regular delivery.

Many accomplished chefs prefer to cook with gas because gas burners heat up fast, cool quickly, and can be infinitely adjusted to keep food simmering almost indefinitely. Electric cooktops, on the other hand, are easier to clean. Also, new developments in cooktops, such as magnetic-induction cooking and

Range Styles

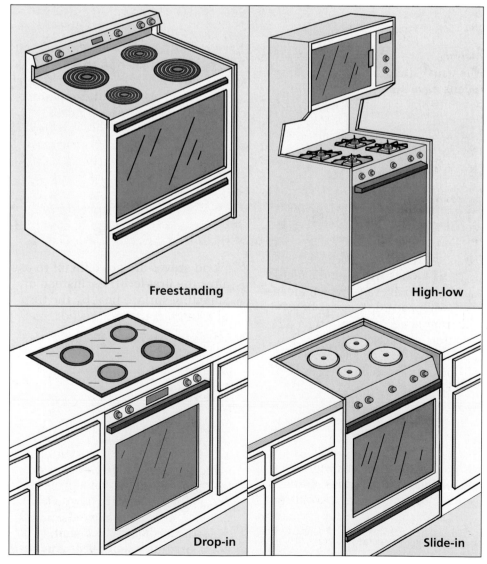

Freestanding

High-low

Drop-in

Slide-in

smooth-top surfaces, are designed for electricity, not gas.

Although many people prefer gas for surface cooking, ovens are a different story. Electric ovens maintain more even temperatures than gas units. Electric self-cleaning systems work better, too. "Self-cleaning" in gas ranges, with a few exceptions, means "continuous clean," which employs a special textured surface in the oven cavity to dissipate grime and prevent dirt from sticking. Electric ranges use a pyrolytic self-cleaning system that requires the oven to be turned to extremely high heat for a specified number of hours, reducing soil in the oven to fine ash. The residue can then be wiped away with a damp sponge. The cost of electricity may limit how often you use the self-cleaning feature.

Restaurant, or commercial-quality, ranges with heavy-duty burners deliver more heat more quickly than the usual kitchen range, and their ovens have superior insulation. Commercial-type cooking surfaces are made of cast iron, making them ideal for prolonged, low-intensity cooking. The sturdy appearance of a restaurant range appeals to serious cooks.

Measure space carefully before considering a restaurant range. While the average range is 30 inches wide, most restaurant ranges are at least 34 inches wide—and 6 inches deeper than average, which means they will protrude that far beyond the front edges of standard-depth counters. Also, restaurant ranges do not have self-cleaning ovens, although some have porcelain-finished interiors that can be washed easily. The ranges may come in colors, but are usually finished in commercial-looking stainless steel, matte black, or gray. Gadgets such as clocks, timers, glass doors, meat probes, and downdraft venting are unavailable.

Wood-burning ranges, which combine an economical heater with a

Wood-gas combination stoves may provide a comforting ambience, especially where firewood is plentiful and inexpensive.

cooking unit, used to be a staple in kitchens 50 or 60 years ago. Today the ranges are an exotic amenity. Modern versions will burn wood or coal, either as an adjunct to a conventional gas or electric range, or on their own. Some may include electric burners and an electric or combination wood/electric oven. Check first, however, whether wood- or coal-burning units are permitted in your locality.

Wood stoves are not difficult to use after the first few tries. Instead of adjusting surface heat by the turn of a knob, you move the pot to a cooler place. It's almost impossible to make a wood stove's oven perform as reliably as a gas or electric oven, however, though most have a temperature indicator.

Maintenance and safety can be big problems, too. You must keep the wood box filled with logs and kindling of the right size, shape, and quality. There must be a place outdoors or in a shed to stack wood. You must remove the ashes periodically. Most important, you must provide an excellent chimney

and keep it clean, without any creosote buildup.

Cooktops. A surface cooking unit has top burners only and fits into the countertop. Most of the space underneath can be used for convenional storage. Cooktops come in four varieties:

• Gas. Usually 30 or 36 inches wide, gas cooktops have brushed-chrome or porcelain-enamel finishes. Most feature electric ignition.

• Electric. Conventional electric cooktops have coil or cast-iron disk burners. Disks heat more evenly than coils and are easier to clean.

• Vented. Both gas and electric cooktops are available with downdraft venting.

• Smooth-surface. Electric or magnetic-induction cooking elements are concealed under a glass or ceramic surface.

Gas surface units differ from one another only in detail—one maker's burner may be easier to clean than another's or may have a different

Sleek lines, good looks, and easy cleanup are the chief attractions of smooth-top ceramic cooktops.

Heavy-duty gas burners flanked by a griddle provide wide options and instantaneous heat control to the chef.

spillover bowl. Gas cooktops are made in two- or four-section units, which may be located anywhere on a countertop where a gas connection can be provided. Some units come with a grill or a fifth burner. Other models offer a gas-fired broiler or barbecue.

Electric-coil or cast-iron disk units heat and cool much faster than they used to, although still not as quickly as gas. The burners come with 6- and 8-inch-diameter rings. Many people choose two of each because cooking on an electric ring with a pot smaller than the unit wastes electricity, while a pot larger than the unit will heat slowly. Special accessories such as pancake griddles and barbecue grills can also be built into countertops as surface units. Electric-coil cooktops cost about the same as gas units; cast-iron disk tops cost somewhat more.

Smooth-top units look easiest of all to clean, but you need to use a special cleaner promptly and regularly to maintain their appearance and even-heating capability. Some units require special flat-

Cooktop Styles

Gas

Electric

Vented

Smooth-surface

Wall units allow two ovens in the space of one and give equal access to standing and wheelchair cooks.

bottomed cookware; others take any type. They cost substantially more than conventional coil units.

Magnetic-induction cooktops magnetically transfer energy from below the ceramic surface into the cooking vessel. Because the burner does not get hot, it's easier to clean; spillovers and drips can be wiped away quickly. You can use only certain types of stainless-steel and cast-iron pots and pans on magnetic tops. Aluminum, copper, or glass cookware will not allow the necessary transfer of energy through the pot to the food. Magnetic surface units cost more than all the other types of cooktops.

Ovens. Ovens that are separate from cooktops can be located in a wall cabinet at a height that permits safe handling of heavy or awkward pans. The main features to consider, after making a choice between gas and electric, are the size of the oven's interior, whether you need one or two ovens, and what attachments are practical for your family. Most standard ovens, for instance, will hold a 20-pound turkey. But if your requirements are greater, shop for an oven that's more spacious.

You also may want to consider a convection oven. You'll pay more for a full-size convection oven, and because the heat source is outside the cooking cavity of a true convection oven, it won't broil. But here's

what a convection unit does: It circulates heated air around the food, pulls the air out of the cooking cavity, reheats the air over a hot element, and returns the reheated air to the cavity. Because the convection system is closed, moisture is retained in the unit and therefore in the food. Cooked meats tend to be juicier and baked goods moister. Convection ovens bake and roast faster than conventional models at temperatures that are 25 to 75 degrees F lower, which saves energy. Because superheating the air over hot elements burns off odors, it's possible to bake dissimilar items, such as an apple pie and an onion/garlic casserole, at the same time without corrupting each other's flavor.

An electronic timer can be a practical oven feature, especially for cooks who work at tasks outside the kitchen or away from home. Some timers can be set to turn ovens on and off at predetermined times. Some can also be set to keep food warm after the oven turns off. Other handy options include rotisseries, meat temperature probes, see-through doors, and electronic touch controls.

Microwave Ovens. Microwave units cut down cooking time for some foods to mere minutes, with more powerful units (750 to 1,000 watts) cooking faster than less powerful models (500 to 700 watts). However, food cooked in a microwave oven often demands a certain amount of coddling and doesn't turn out the same as with traditional methods. Roasts usually have to be turned at least once, and they don't brown well. Meat, fish, and fowl usually need to be covered during at least part of the cooking time to prevent overcooking. Cooking time increases with the amount of food, so conventional methods may be as quick with larger quantities. Even with

those drawbacks, though, microwave ovens offer a convenient and fast way to pop corn, defrost frozen food, reheat a plate of leftovers, heat a frozen dinner, and warm up a cup of coffee or tea.

Microwave ovens generally require cookware made of nonmetallic materials, including glass and certain plastics, many ceramics, porcelain, and pottery. Some metal cookware has been specially designed for use in microwaves, however.

Even if you're not hooked on microwave cooking but you want the convenience of quick reheating and defrosting, plan to get your microwave off the counter or cart and give it a place in the overall scheme of things. A microwave unit needn't be located in your primary cooking center, although some brands feature built-in range hoods that make them naturals for hanging over a range. For some cooks, it might make more sense to position a microwave near the refrigerator for quickly thawing frozen food. Whatever location you decide on, position the oven at about eye level, with 15 to 18 inches of counter space adjacent to or under it.

Ventilation. The aromas that emanate from your pots and pans during food preparation will get stale and unpleasant after they settle on your kitchen's surfaces.

A shelf positions a conventional microwave for eye-level monitoring.

Grease, smoke, heat, and steam should be removed routinely with a proper ventilating system.

The most common type of vent is an exhaust fan over the range or cooktop. It may be in a wall vented directly outside or in the ceiling directed through ductwork to the outside. Ductless models may be used where it's impossible or financially prohibitive to run a duct to the outside.

Ductless fans filter out particles and neutralize odors before sending the air back into the kitchen, but they have no effect on moisture or heat and tend to be less effective than models vented to the outdoors.

These kitchen fan units generally are housed in, or are an integral part of, a hood that's designed to capture and direct fumes toward the exhaust.

Cleanup Center

The kitchen sink is the focal point in the cleanup center. This includes the sink, 18 to 24 inches of counter space on either side for dishes and food you need to wash, a dishwasher, a waste disposer (where local codes permit), and storage for glassware, frequently used utensils, detergents, colanders, and other sink accessories. The trash recep-

tacle and recycling bins are also in the cleanup center; a trash compactor may be included here as well.

Because it's often located under a window, and always tied to the plumbing system, the sink is one of the most fixed of kitchen fixtures. If you're thinking about moving your sink and dishwasher more than 48 inches from the current location, you'll probably have to rework vent and drain lines, and you might have to move a window as well. If cost containment is important to you, it's wise to begin your kitchen plan by seeing whether you can locate a sink at or near the place the old one occupies.

Where there's no window behind the sink, decide what you'll do with the wall space there. One choice is to integrate the space into a run of cabinets with units that are shorter than those on either side, so you'll have headroom. Another possibility is to install full-height cabinets only six inches deep. Whatever treatment you select, be sure your cleanup center includes adequate daytime and nighttime light falling directly onto the sink and adjacent counters.

A great window improves the atmosphere of a cleanup center.

Sinks & Faucets

Sinks come in a wide variety of sizes and shapes. Materials include stainless steel, pressed steel, cast iron, and the same solid-surfacing material used for countertops. Sinks of each material come in single-, double-, and triple-bowl models. A single-bowl sink is large enough for soaking big pots and pans. Two-bowl sinks may have identical-size basins, or one may be smaller or shallower than the other. Three-bowl sinks include a small disposal basin at one side or between the larger bowls.

A faucet may come as part of your sink, or there may be openings for a faucet and sprayer.

Spinning trash bins provide convenient, out-of-sight recycling receptacles.

A pull-out trash drawer gives you a place to hide kitchen waste and recyclables.

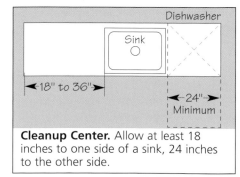

Cleanup Center. Allow at least 18 inches to one side of a sink, 24 inches to the other side.

• High gooseneck. These spouts facilitate filling tall pitchers and vases and make pot cleaning easier when the sink bowl is shallow. This is great at a bar sink or auxiliary food preparation sink for cleaning vegetables.

• Single lever. One lever turns on and mixes hot and cold water. Styles range from functional to sleek.

• Double-handle faucet. Temperature may be easier to adjust with separate hot and cold controls. Most contain washers and seals that must occasionally be replaced.

• Single-handle faucet with pull-out sprayer. Allows single-handed on, off, temperature control, and spraying.

Stainless-Steel Sinks. Stainless steel, made with nickel and chrome to prevent staining, continues to be a popular choice for sinks, although some homeowners complain about spotting. This kind of sink offers the greatest selection of bowl sizes and configurations. Choose 18-gauge stainless for a large sink or one with a disposer, lighter 20-gauge material for smaller sinks. Stainless steel also differs in grade, depending on the amount of nickel and chrome it contains. The more of both, the better.

Pressed-Steel and Cast-Iron Sinks. Both of these sinks have porcelain-enamel finishes. Cast iron is heavier and less likely to chip than pressed

A small bowl in a double sink is perfect for washing veggies.

Sink Styles

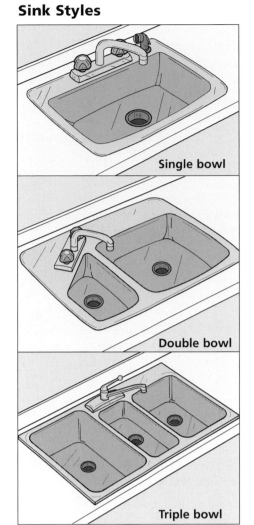
Single bowl

Double bowl

Triple bowl

steel. Cast iron is also quieter than both stainless and pressed steel when water or a disposer is running.

Solid-Acrylic Sinks. Acrylic sinks can be molded directly into a solid-surface countertop, creating a seamless unit that is especially easy to keep clean. Separate drop-in models are also available. Sinks of this material are even quieter than cast iron, but costly.

All these sinks generally come in three styles:

• Single bowl. This sink is economical, but difficult for hand washing and rinsing cookware and glassware.

• Double bowl. There are many configurations, some with optional cutting boards and corner faucets.

• Triple bowl. This unit needs about 12 inches more counter space than a double-bowl unit.

Faucet Styles

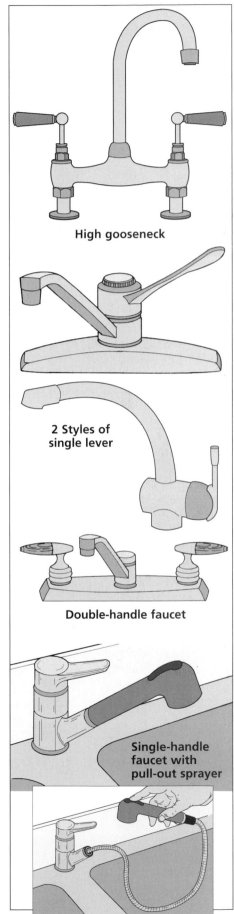
High gooseneck

2 Styles of single lever

Double-handle faucet

Single-handle faucet with pull-out sprayer

Besides the common kitchen varieties, there are sinks for virtually every practical and aesthetic need—perfect circles, sinks that turn corners, deep farm-style kitchen sinks, and so on. They can range from a simple necessity to a costly extravagance.

Near-the-Sink Appliances

Dishwashers. Dishwashers have become a standard item in new and remodeled kitchens. Even though it consumes energy in the form of hot water and electricity, a unit that is used properly may require less energy than washing dishes by hand.

Typically, dishwashers are 24 inches wide and are installed below the counter right next to or very near the sink. If space is scant, consider an under-sink dishwasher, which can be installed under the shallow bowl of a special sink designed for this purpose and available from a variety of sink manufacturers.

If you wish to locate a dishwasher next to a sink in a corner, be sure to put a cabinet at least 12 inches wide between the sink base and the dishwasher. This cabinet will serve as a spacer when the dishwasher door is open, so you'll have room to stand at the sink while loading the dishes.

Dishwashers are priced according to the number of cycles and other features they offer. Most have rinse-

A cleanup center generally includes a sink flanked by water-related appliances. It can have auxiliary stations like the island sink in the foreground.

and-hold, soak-and-scrub, and no-dry options. More costly machines feature additional cycles: preheating, which lets you turn down the setting on your water heater, soft-food disposers, delay-start mechanisms, and solid-state control panels.

Waste Disposers. These convenient appliances shred organic wastes and send them down the drain. Some communities require waste-disposal units; others ban them—so check with your local building authorities before deciding whether you want the convenience of one.

A continuous-feed disposer allows you to feed waste into the disposer as it operates. A batch-feed disposer grinds up $1\frac{1}{2}$ to 2 quarts at a time. Continuous-feed disposers are controlled by a wall switch, batch-feed models by a built-in switch activated by replacing the drain lid. Local codes often have much to say about which type you can use.

Trash Compactors. Compactors are available in slide-out or drop-front models in sizes ranging from 12 to 18 inches wide. Some models stand on their own, but a well-planned kitchen can incorporate a model that is designed to fit under a countertop like a dishwasher.

Compactors do not use much electricity, but most require special heavy-duty bags. Inside a trash compactor, a screw-driven ram compresses inorganic debris such as cans, boxes, and bottles to about one-fourth the original volume. Many compactors have a device that sprays deodorizer each time the compactor is operated. Recycling programs may restrict

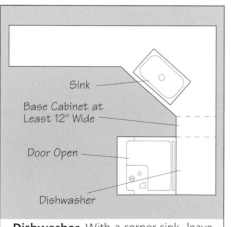

Dishwasher. With a corner sink, leave enough room to stand in front of the sink while loading the dishwasher.

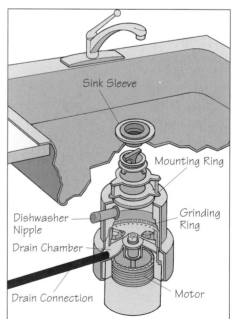

Sink Sleeve

Mounting Ring

Grinding Ring

Dishwasher Nipple

Drain Chamber

Motor

Drain Connection

Waste Disposers. A disposer can eliminate most organic garbage handling. Check whether the continuous or batch-feed type is allowed in your area.

what can be compacted, so check with local authorities.

Water Filters. Whether freestanding, countertop, or built-in models, water filters are designed to purify drinking water so it will look and taste better.

Filters for clarifying cloudy or silt-laden water come with a cellulose element, which can be replaced as necessary. Filters with replaceable carbon elements remove chlorine and other additives that affect taste or odor. Unfortunately, some filters, regardless of claims, do little of anything. Before selecting

a unit, have a reputable water-conditioning specialist analyze your water to identify its problems and suggest solutions.

Hot-Water Dispensers. These handy units heat $\frac{1}{3}$ or $\frac{1}{2}$ gallon of water and hold it at a bubbling 190 degrees F, an ideal temperature for making tea, drip coffee, and instant coffee or soup. Some units are said to be more energy-efficient than boiling water on an electric range.

The main components of a hot-water dispenser fit under the sink. The dispenser tap may attach to the hole in the sink intended for a spray hose or through a hole in the countertop with lines running through any cabinet wall. The dispenser heating element requires access to an electrical line under the counter. A vent and an expansion chamber are safety features.

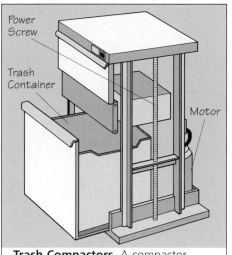

Trash Compactors. A compactor efficiently handles inorganic waste that does not have to be recycled. Pull-out and drop-front models are available.

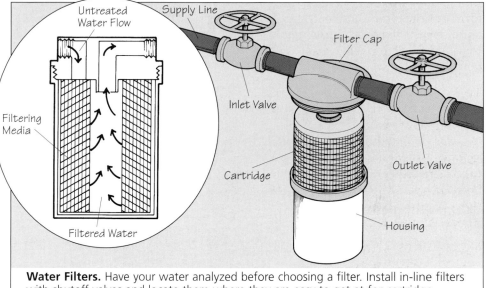

Water Filters. Have your water analyzed before choosing a filter. Install in-line filters with shutoff valves and locate them where they are easy to get at for cartridge replacement; under the sink is not always the best spot. Water for a dishwasher or clothes washer seldom needs to be filtered.

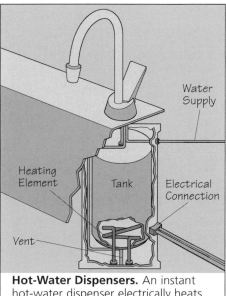

Hot-Water Dispensers. An instant hot-water dispenser electrically heats and holds water for use at 190 degrees F. A vent and an expansion chamber are safety features.

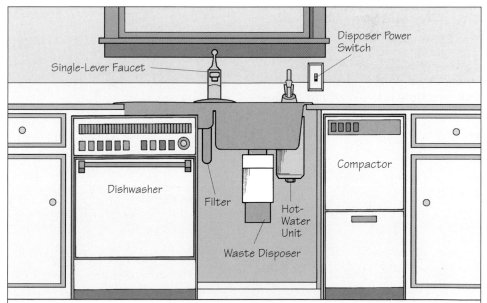

Full-Service Installation. This efficient installation includes a dishwasher that fits under the shallow half of a double-bowl sink. In-line filters treat the water supply; the dishwasher is connected to the hot-water line ahead of the filter. A hot-water dispenser, garbage disposer, and trash compactor complete the installation.

Laminate countertops can be defined with contrasting edge trim or bullnoses.

Routed edges are a special touch that's possible when you use solid-surfacing material.

Surfacing Materials

The surfaces of your kitchen help define how it looks and determine how well it cleans up and withstands wear and tear. Choose countertops, wallcoverings, and flooring to suit your style and lifestyle.

Countertop Materials

The market offers lots of countertop materials, all of which are worth consideration. Many are practical for all countertop needs. Sometimes, however, the most practical type for someone else is not the most suitable for you. You can dress up plain counter materials with front-edge enhancements, or you can combine different materials on the same surface.

Tile provides a beautiful, durable, heat-proof countertop.

Plastic Laminate. This thin, durable surface comes in hundreds of colors, textures, and patterns. The material is relatively easy to install; its smooth surface washes easily, and it's heat-resistant, although very hot pots can discolor or even burn it. Laminate stands up well to everyday wear and tear, but it can be easily scratched with knives and other sharp utensils, and surface damage is difficult to repair.

Ceramic Tile. Glazed tile can be magnificently decorative for counters, backsplashes, and walls, or as a display inset in another material. Tile is smooth, easy to wipe off, and can't be burned by hot pots. However, ceramic is not forgiving to dropped glassware, and it's subject to breakage itself from a heavy or glancing blow. Ceramic tile costs more than laminate, but you can save money by doing the fairly simple installation yourself.

Solid-Surfacing Material. Also called solid acrylic, solid surfacing comes in ½-inch and ¾-inch thicknesses. Acrylic resists moisture, heat, stains, and cracks. The surface becomes scratched fairly easily, but the scratches are not readily apparent. Serious blemishes can be removed by sanding or buffing. Acrylic can be fabricated to resemble marble and granite, or

Granite countertops are dramatic, durable, and pricey.

Well-sealed wood may be used in a serving area.

it can be a block of solid color. Either way, the material can be carved or beveled for decorative effects just like wood. Manufacturers recommend professional installation.

Marble, Slate, and Granite. These natural materials are beautiful but heavy and expensive. Marble scratches and stains easily, even if waxed. Slate can be easily scratched and cracked and cannot take a high polish. Granite, which is more expensive than slate, cannot be hurt by moisture or heat, nor does it stain if finished properly. Granite can take a high polish. Installation is a job for a professional.

Wood. Butcher block consists of hardwood laminated under pressure and sealed with oil or a polymer finish. Because it's thicker than other materials, butcher block will raise the counter level about ¾ inch above standard height. Also, wood is subject to damage by standing water or hot pans. Butcher-block tops are moderately expensive but can be installed by amateurs.

Other kinds of wood counters may be used, especially in serving areas rather than food-preparation or cleanup centers. Well sealed hardwoods such as maple are best for this.

Concrete. Thanks to new staining techniques, concrete can be saturated with color all the way through, thus making it a stylish countertop option. It can be preformed to any shape and finished to any texture. Set stone or ceramic tile chips into the surface for a decorative effect. Route it to drain off water at the sink. be cautious, however; a concrete countertop must be sealed, and it may crack

Wall Treatments

It's hard to beat the ease of a coat of paint for adding a fresh face to a kitchen. But there are other ways to finish off the walls, too, such as vinyl wallcovering and paneling. You can go with one, two, or all three of these options in several combinations.

Paint. Basically, there are two kinds of paint: latex, which is a water-based formulation, and oil-based products. You can buy latex and oil paint in at least four finishes: flat, eggshell, semi-gloss, and gloss. In general, stay away from flat paint in the kitchen. Any of the other finishes, which are easier to clean

Latex is recommended for most surfaces, in general, including un-primed walls, bare masonry, and fresh plaster patches.

Wainscoting warms the room and contrasts with wallpaper.

Oil-based paint is tougher and wears better on surfaces that come into contact with moisture. This kind of paint is especially good for use over bare wood and surfaces that have been previously painted. (If you plan to use it on new wallboard, you'll have to apply a primer first.)

Wallcovering. Vinyl wallcoverings and coordinated borders offer an easy, low-cost way to put style into your new kitchen. Practical because they are nonporous, stain-resistant, and washable, vinyl coatings are available in a wide variety of colors, textures, and patterns. Prepasted, pretrimmed rolls are the easiest for a novice to install. Just remember to remove any old wallpaper before applying new covering to walls.

Overall patterned wallpaper makes the white wall cabinets appear to float above the counter.

Wallpaper borders help clarify and define space, creating the impact of an architectural element.

Paneling. If you're looking for a simple way to camouflage a wall's imperfections, paneling is it. Today's paneling options include prefinished softwood- or hardwood-veneered plywood, simulated wood-grain on plywood or hardboard, prehung wallpaper on plywood, simulated wood-grain or decorative finish panelboard, tileboard or other decorative hardboard paneling, and solid pine or cedar plank paneling. For a versatile look, panel only part of the wall, going halfway or three-quarters of the way up. Top it off with molding, then paint or wallpaper the rest of the wall. Depending on how you install it, you can create horizontal, diagonal, or herringbone patterns.

Flooring

Floor coverings fall into two broad categories: resilient flooring, which has some resiliency, or bounce, and hard flooring, with no flex whatsoever. Resilient floors are less tiring to stand on than hard-surface floors and less likely to produce instant disaster for dropped glasses or chinaware.

Before replacing an old surface, make sure the subfloor is in good condition. Subflooring that is in need of repair will eventually ruin any new flooring material that you install.

Resilient Vinyl Sheet Flooring and Tile. Vinyl flooring wears fairly to very well, needs only occasional waxing or polishing (in some cases none at all), and is easy to clean. In addition, vinyl comes in a wide variety of colors and patterns. Cost is inexpensive to moderate compared with other flooring materials. Installing vinyl tile is a popular do-it-yourself project. Installing sheet goods is a bit more complex but well within the skills of an experienced do-it-yourselfer.

Vinyl does have disadvantages, however. It dents easily when subjected to pressures such as high-heel shoes or furniture legs. Vinyl surfaces may also scratch or tear

Easy-care vinyl flooring, available in lots of patterns and colors, can be used to highlight the decor or fade into the background.

Hardwood floors are durable, especially those with factory-applied coatings that are impervious to moisture, and may be appropriate for modern kitchens.

easily, and high traffic areas are likely to show wear. You can control some degree of wear by the type of vinyl flooring you choose:

Composition flooring combines vinyl resins with filler. This least expensive vinyl flooring may show signs of wear in five years.

Photovinyl covers photographic images with clear urethane. The thickness of the urethane layer determines how long the floor will last. You should buy minimum 10-mil-thick up to the most expensive 25-mil-thick flooring.

Inlaid vinyl flooring is solid vinyl with color and pattern all the way through to the backing. This most expensive vinyl flooring is designed to last upward of 30 years.

Laminate. Basically the same in composition as countertop material, laminate flooring looks just like wood. It comes in tongue-and-groove planks or squares, is durable, and holds up well in high-traffic, humid kitchens. Installation is fairly easy, and the material can go right over an existing tile, vinyl, concrete, or wood floor, as long as the old floor is level (These floors are installed similar to laminated wood floors. See page 142.)

Wood. Thanks largely to polyurethane coatings that are impervious to water, wood flooring has made a comeback in kitchens. You already may have a wood floor buried under another floor covering. If this is the case, consider exposing it, repairing any damaged boards, and refinishing it. Or install an all-new wood floor. Wood can be finished any way you like, though much of the wood flooring available today comes prefinished in an assortment of shades.

Hardwoods like oak and maple are popular and stand up to a lot of abuse. Softwoods like pine give a more distressed, countrified look. Flooring comes in 2¼-inch strips as well as variable-width planks. Parquet flooring, another good option for the kitchen, consists of wood pieces glued together into

One of the most enduring materials, but one of the most unforgiving, is ceramic tile. Consider colored grout for easy care.

a geometric pattern. These prefinished squares can be installed in a way similar to that used for vinyl tiles.

Carpeting. Kitchen carpeting is not widely used these days, but it still offers certain advantages. Of all the available types of flooring, carpeting is the quietest and most resilient—and one of the least expensive. Because it's made of synthetic materials and backed by waterproof latex or foam, kitchen carpeting is washable. On the negative side, kitchen carpeting is vulnerable to wear and thus is relatively short-lived. And although it's washable, carpeting is not as easy to clean and keep sanitary as smooth flooring.

Hard-Surface Flooring. Ceramic tile, stone, and slate floors are hard, durable, and easy to clean, especially when you use grout sealers. Because these floors are so inflexible, anything fragile dropped on them is likely to break. Also, they are tiring to stand on and noisy, and they conduct extremes of temperature. For those who love

the look of this kind of flooring, however, the drawbacks can be mitigated with accent and area rugs that add a cushion.

Ceramic tile makes an excellent kitchen floor when installed with proper grout and sealants. The tiles range from the earth tones of unglazed, solid-color quarry tile to the great array of colors, patterns, and finishes in surface-glazed tiles. Grout comes color-keyed so it either can be inconspicuous or add design interest. Ceramic and quarry tiles are best suited to a concrete subfloor, though you can lay them over any firm base. Cost ranges from moderate to expensive. Installation is hard work, but not complex if the subfloor is sound. This is a great project for do-it-yourself remodelers who want to create special designs with the tiles.

Stone and slate are cut into small slabs and can be laid in a regular or random pattern. Materials are inexpensive or costly, depending on quality and local availability. Even if you find these materials more expensive than other floor coverings, don't dismiss them solely on price. They will never need to be replaced, making your initial investment your final one. Because stone and slate are laid in mortar and are themselves weighty materials, a concrete slab makes the ideal subfloor. In other situations, the subfloor must be able to carry a significantly heavy load. Installation is a complex do-it-yourself job.

Lighting

Good lighting plays a key role in efficient kitchen design—and goes a long way toward defining the personality of the room. With the proper fixtures, in the proper places, you can avoid working in shadows. Install several different lighting circuits, controlled by different switches, and you can change your kitchen's atmosphere easily. Lighting falls into three broad categories:

General, or ambient, lighting illuminates the room as a whole and helps to create a mood.

Task lighting focuses on work surfaces like sinks, countertops, ranges, eating areas, and other places where you need to get a really good look at what you're doing.

Accent lighting brings drama and architectural flavor to a

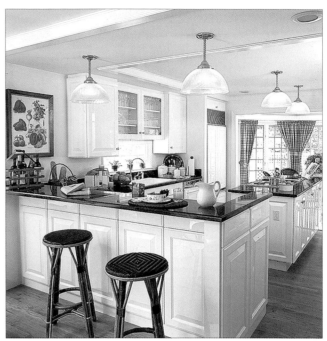

Drop-down glass-shaded fixtures provide elegant task lighting in this formal kitchen.

An abundance of recessed canister lights, cove accent lighting, and under-counter task lighting enhances this room's design and function.

kitchen. Accent lighting controlled with a dimmer switch can also serve as general lighting.

For an effective lighting scheme, plan a mix of these three types, in the amounts specified in the chart. Bear in mind, though, that several factors affect how much general and task lighting a given kitchen needs. Dark surfaces soak up more light than lighter ones. Glossy surfaces reflect more light (and glare) than matte finishes. And, as summarized in the chart, different fixture types do different lighting jobs.

Fluorescent Versus Incandescent

The type of light you choose—fluorescent or incandescent—also affects lighting quality. Fluorescent tubes give off two to three times as much light per watt as incandescent bulbs, cost two-thirds less to operate, and last far longer. The size and shape of fluorescent fixtures limit design possibilities, however, and the direction of fluorescent lighting is difficult to control.

For years, critics charged that fluorescent lighting produced colors that were too cold and added a greenish-purple cast to the room. In response, manufacturers developed "warm white deluxe" tubes that approximate the color range of incandescent lighting and are more flattering to food. Choosing incandescent and fluorescent lighting needn't be an either-or decision. You might use fluorescent lights above or below wall-hung cabinets, for instance, and one or more incandescent fixtures for ambient or task lighting.

Windows & Doors

Sunlight brings cheer and sparkle to any kitchen. All you have to do is welcome it inside with windows, glass doors, or a skylight. When you shop for window and door units, make energy conservation a prime consideration. Double glazing is

How Much Light Do You Need?

	Incandescent	Fluorescent	Location
General (ambient) lighting	3½—4 watts per square foot of area. Double this if counters, cabinets, or flooring are dark.	1½ watts per square foot of floor area	90 inches above the floor
Task lighting			
Cleanup centers	150 watts	30—40 watts	25 inches above sink optimal
Countertops	75—100 watts for each 3 running feet of work surface	20 watts for each 3 running feet of work surface	14—22 inches above the work surface
Cooking centers	150 watts	30—40 watts	18—25 inches above burners. Most range hoods have lights.
Dining tables	150—200 watts	X	25—50 inches above the table
Accent lighting	Plan flexibility into accent lighting so you can vary the mood with the flick of a switch or the twist of a dimmer. Suspended, recessed, track, and cove fixtures all work well.		

Fixture Types

Surface-mount	Attached directly to the ceiling, it distributes very even, shadowless general lighting. To minimize glare, surface-mount fixtures should be shielded. Fixtures with sockets for several smaller bulbs distribute more even lighting than those with just one or two large bulbs.
Suspended	Globes, chandeliers, and other suspended fixtures can light a room or a table. Hang them 12 to 20 inches below an 8-foot ceiling or 30 to 36 inches above table height.
Recessed	Recessed fixtures, which mount flush with the ceiling or soffit, include fixed and aimable downlights, shielded fluorescent tubes, even totally luminous ceilings. Recessed fixtures require more wattage—up to twice as much as surface-mount and suspended types.
Track	Use a track system for general, task, or accent lighting—or any combination of the three. You can select from a broad array of modular fixtures, clip them anywhere along a track, and revise your lighting scheme any time you like. Locate tracks 12 inches out from the edges of wall cabinets to minimize shadows on countertops.
Under-cabinet	Fluorescent or incandescent fixtures (with showcase bulbs) mounted to the undersides of wall cabinets bathe counters with efficient, inexpensive task lighting. Shield under-cabinet lights with valances and illuminate at least two-thirds of the counter's length.
Cove	Cove lights reflect upward to the ceiling, creating smooth, even general lighting or dramatic architectural effects. Consider locating custom cove lights on top of wall cabinets, in the space normally occupied by soffits.

If you can't afford true divided-light windows for your remodeling, optional pop-in grilles let you create the look without the cost.

These awning windows installed into the soffit area admit light for an expansive feeling and may be opened for ventilation.

now the norm, and some manufacturers offer triple-glazed panes. Since a house loses more heat at night than during the day, movable insulated shutters and drapes can provide privacy and minimize nighttime heat losses from windows. Make sure exterior doors are well insulated and weatherstripped.

Window Types

Before you decide that your kitchen needs more or bigger windows, take down the curtains from your existing windows—the change in light levels may amaze you. If that's not the answer, consider adding or enlarging the windows. Place them wherever they work best. Sometimes an above-cabinet soffit space provides an excellent site for awning-type windows, which can add ambient light and extra ventilation. Or you may install additional traditional-style windows. These needn't be the same width as the old ones, but they usually look better and involve fewer installation problems if the top edges line up with other windows in the room.

If you want a window to provide natural task lighting for a kitchen sink or work surface, its sill should be 3 to 6 inches above the countertop. For safety reasons, most building codes don't permit windows over ranges or cooktops.

Don't overlook style when selecting a window. If your house is a colonial, for example, stick with a traditional double-hung window instead of the contemporary casement type that may not blend with your home's overall architecture. Also check for other desirable features. A tilt-in unit, for instance, makes cleaning easier. Optional grilles simply pop in and let you create the look of a divided-light window. For purists, manufacturers fabricate true divided-light windows in standard sizes. There are five common types of windows. They can be used individually, or combined in various ways.

Fixed Windows. These are the simplest type of window because they do not open. A fixed window is simply glass installed in a frame that is attached to the house. Fixed windows are the least expensive, admit the most light, and come in the greatest variety of shapes and sizes. But, of course, they can't be used for ventilation.

Double-Hung Windows. Perhaps the most common kind used in houses, double-hung windows consist of two framed glass panels that slide vertically, guided by a metal, wood, or plastic track. One variation, called a single-hung window, is made using an upper panel that cannot slide and a lower, sliding panel.

Insulated window treatments will keep out heat when sunlight is too strong and will retain warmth at night.

Casement Windows. Casements are hinged at the side and swing outward from the window opening as you turn a small crank. Better casement windows can be opened to a 90-degree angle for maximum ventilation.

Awning Windows. These generally swing outward like a casement window, but are hinged at the top. Awning windows can be left opened slightly for air even when it rains.

Sliding Windows. Sliders are similar to a double-hung window turned on its side. The glass panels slide horizontally, and are often used where there is need for a window that is wider than it is tall.

Skylights. In a single-story house or one with a vaulted ceiling, a properly planned and located skylight can provide five times more natural light than a window of equal size located in a wall. It's important to plan for the seasonal angle and path of the sun to avoid unwelcome heat

A skylight can be the ideal solution to introducing natural light to a kitchen with few or no windows.

gains and losses from skylights. It's usually better to locate a skylight on a north or east-facing surface, for example, to prevent overheating and provide diffuse light. Venting

models, placed near the roof ridge, can also greatly improve natural ventilation. Seek advice from an architect or designer if you're not sure how a skylight will affect your kitchen's climate.

Door Types

Interior and exterior doors are offered in dozens of shapes, sizes, and materials. Most units are made of wood or wood byproducts, but many are made of metal and stamped or embossed to look like wood. Exterior doors often incorporate glass panels. French and sliding patio doors are almost all glass. Most interior wood-based doors are fabricated in one of three ways: as individual panels set in a frame, as a hardboard facing molded to look like a panel door and secured to a frame, or as a thin sheet of plywood secured to each side of a wood framework.

Panel and Panel-Look Doors. These door styles offer a variety of choices. They can be constructed with as few as three to as many as ten or more solid panels, in all sorts of shapes and size combinations. Sometimes the bottom is made of wood and the top panels are glass.

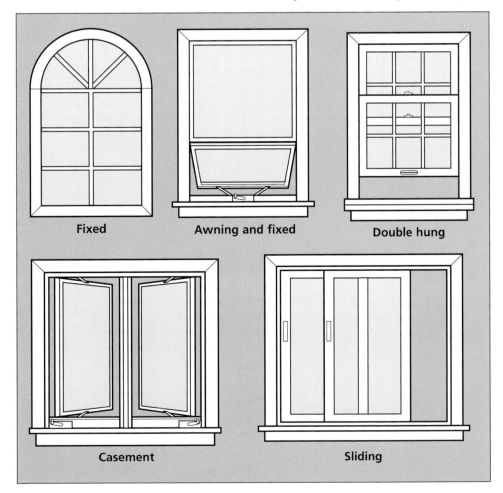

Fixed   Awning and fixed   Double hung

Casement   Sliding

■ Which Way Should Windows Face? ■

Orient a door, window, or skylight to take best advantage of breezes and seasonal sunlight. Also take into account trees, neighboring structures, and the potential view.

• South light will pour into windows with a southern exposure in winter because the sun's path is low in the sky. But in the summer, when it rides high in the sky, the sun will beat down on the southern roof instead. Southern exposure is an ideal placement for a window because it gains heat through the window in winter, but not in summer, especially if it's shielded by a deep overhang. A skylight on a southern or western exposure will capture solar heat during the winter—and the summer, too. Be careful about this placement.

• East light brightens the morning yet rarely heats up the room. Skylights on north- and east-facing roofs lessen heat gain in the summer.

• West light subjects a kitchen to the hot, direct rays of late-afternoon sun, which can make a room uncomfortable until far into the night. If a west window is your only option, shade it with overhangs, sun-stopping blinds, or broad-leaf plantings.

• North light has an almost consistent brightness throughout the day. Because it's from an open sky, without direct sun, the light doesn't create glaring hot spots or deep shadows in work areas. North light lacks the drama of other exposures, but kitchen design and colors can compensate for that.

Summer Sun

Winter Sun

W N S E

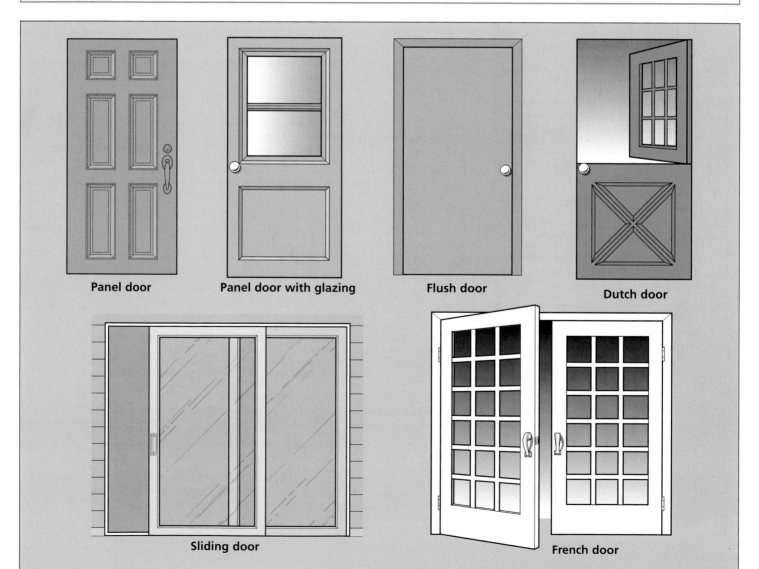

Panel door

Panel door with glazing

Flush door

Dutch door

Sliding door

French door

Thanks to improved glazing technology, a greenhouse addition can enhance a kitchen remodeling.

A bay of windows offers a charming way to create a dining area in a room.

Flush Doors. Generally less expensive, flush doors come in a more limited range of variations. You can enhance their simple looks with wood molding for traditional appeal.

Sliders. Sliding doors consist of a large panel of glass framed with wood or metal. Usually one of the doors is stationary while the other slides. Replacing an existing wood door with one that's all or mostly glass can double its natural lighting potential. For safety and security, be sure that the new door has tempered glass or shatterproof plastic. Enlarge an existing door or window opening, or cut a new one, to gain access to a deck or patio outside. The frame may be wood, aluminum, or wood covered with aluminum or vinyl.

French Doors. These traditional doors are framed glass panels with either true divided lights or pop-in dividers. Usually both doors open. Manufacturers also offer units that look like traditional hinged doors but operate like sliders.

Dutch Doors. Made in two parts, Dutch doors have independently operating sections, top and bottom. Locked together, the two halves open and close as a unit. Or you can open just the top for ventilation.

Sunrooms, Greenhouses, & Bays

If a full-scale kitchen addition just doesn't make sense for your house, you might wish to enhance your existing kitchen, at less cost, with a "mini-addition," in the form of a sunroom or greenhouse-like bump-out.

Prefabricated Sunrooms. These add-ons usually have double- or triple-glazed glass panels and come in prefit pieces that can be assembled by amateur carpenters, although this isn't a simple project by any means. For a sunroom you'll need a foundation, usually a concrete slab with an insulated perimeter that goes below the frost line. A sunroom should face within 20 degrees of due south to take greatest advantage of solar heating in colder climates.

Window Greenhouses. Also called box windows, these units provide a site for year-round kitchen gardening. All you need to do is remove a window and hang a prefabricated unit or a home-built greenhouse outside. Fill it with flowering plants or greenery, grow herbs or vegetables, or use it to give your outdoor garden a jump on spring. This window treatment is also an excellent way to replace a poor outside view with your indoor garden while keeping the window open to light.

As with sunrooms, window greenhouses work best with southern exposures. You might also have sufficient light from an eastern or western exposure if no trees, buildings, or other obstructions cast shadows. You might as well rule out a northern exposure; a north-facing greenhouse loses great amounts of heat in winter, and many plants don't grow well in northern light.

Bay Windows. Bay units allow you to add a foot or two of sunny space without having to construct a foundation. In this case, you would cantilever the bay window from your home's floor joists. Most window manufacturers sell bays in a variety of widths and configurations, ranging from simple boxes to gentle bows. Installing one is a job best left to a skilled carpenter.

Lifestyle

The kitchen is a hot-ticket item in the real estate market today, and no wonder: More and more, family life is centered around this room. It's not unusual to find most of the family in the kitchen, even when they're not eating. It's the place to do homework, pay the bills, play games, and even entertain company.

A thoughtful look at your lifestyle will help you discover if you want the open design of a great room, which integrates areas for cooking, dining, and relaxing. If your approach is more formal, you may prefer the traditional arrangement that keeps the kitchen and its cooking clutter off-limits to dining and living areas. In this case, a small table or eating bar for casual family meals and snacks may suit you better.

Whether or not you go for the open-plan kitchen, you may still want to include activity centers in the remodeled kitchen's design. If you love to bake, sew, or create crafts, or you need a space to organize a home office, think of making a secondary work center part of the kitchen.

Whatever the scope of your new kitchen, plan it as much as possible with a barrier-free design. This simply means taking measures to make the space comfortably accessible to all who will need to use it, including those who walk, reach, and lean, or sit and wheel. Barrier-free design follows the same tenets as all good design: Form follows function.

Great Rooms

Kitchens to live in have become popular in home design. The large rooms combine separate but open-

A vaulted ceiling and an open plan for cooking, dining, and lounging define today's popular great room.

to-one-another spaces for cooking, dining, relaxing, and entertaining. Such spaces are often called great rooms. Families with young children, for example, will love a kitchen that is part of an open-room plan. This open design allows cooking parents to keep an eye on kids who may be watching TV.

Dinner guests tend to congregate here, too, because they like to stay in touch with the cook. This informal great-room arrangement suits casual contemporary lifestyles, as well as changing attitudes about food. For many families, cooking has evolved from a necessary chore to a creative event where everyone gets involved, guests as well as family members.

Getting Space

You can create a great room by building an addition to your present home or by combining space from existing adjacent rooms. If you choose the latter, make sure you don't knock down any load-bearing walls, and be mindful of any other structural elements, such as a chimney, that may interfere with your design.

One benefit of combining two or more smaller spaces into one is that the sum of the parts is often greater than the whole. Not only is total floor space combined, but so is light and ventilation. Traffic options and floor plans are opened up, too, and focal points such as worktables or counters can do multiple duty for different tasks.

When considering the floor plan, remember that the kitchen is the key element. Traffic must be diverted away from the task areas. One way to manage traffic is to incorporate an island or peninsula into the layout. An island will keep the kitchen open to other areas while closing off the cooking zone to anyone who doesn't have to be there. A large island or peninsula with an eating bar also offers a handy place to set up a buffet, serve a snack, or let the kids do

The kitchen area of a great room has to be attractive since it is open to other public spaces where guests are often entertained.

homework. An island also provides a convenient spot for guests to gather while dinner is in the works.

Unifying Space

Because a great room is an open plan, you'll want a cohesive decor to flow throughout the spaces. Coordinated fabrics and wallcoverings will help you do this, as will installing the same flooring material throughout. Also, some manufacturers produce furniture-quality cabinet designs, as well as matching units to house media equipment, bookcases, desks, and the like, which can dress up the space with a custom-built appearance.

Even appliance manufacturers are great-room conscious. When

To unify the look of separate but incorporated spaces, select common fabrics and colors.

shopping for a typically noisy appliance, such as a dishwasher, range hood, or waste disposer, ask about low-noise or noise-free models.

Lastly, take advantage of any scenic views you may have by installing

Always take advantage of a beautiful view of the outdoors, if you are lucky enough to have it, with lots of windows and French doors.

family could gather to savor a good meal together. These days, removing the wall that separates a kitchen and dining room creates somewhat less than a great room, but much more than a food preparation laboratory. Though this kind of arrangement can make everyday meals especially convivial occasions, such togetherness may not be everyone's cup of tea.

If you do a lot of formal entertaining, prefer to be left alone while you cook, or just don't relish a meal served within sight of the pots and pans, consider pocket doors, sliding panels, or accordion-fold doors to close off the dining and food-preparation areas from each other when desired.

Table Talk

There are minimum clearances you'll need to accommodate a table and chairs in your kitchen. In general, a family larger than five or six should look for sit-down space elsewhere. Still, you may want to provide an in-the-kitchen eating spot where you can serve snacks and off-hour meals to just a few people. In terms of dimensions and other basics, here's how to allocate the floor space you'll need for the furniture and for the people who sit around it.

lots of windows. If you have an adjacent deck or patio, consider large patio doors.

Eating Areas

Most of us want a table or eating counter in the kitchen that's within easy reach of food-preparation and cleanup areas. If you live in a house that's more than 50 years old,

chances are you have a formal dining room you rarely use. You may already have ideas about combining underused spaces like this to create one large room for cooking as well as enjoying meals.

Family Kitchen

The concept of the "heart of the home" or "family kitchen" recalls an earlier time when cooking was done over an open hearth and the entire

Eat-in kitchens are more popular today than ever. Try to incorporate this element in your plan.

If you don't have room for a table and chairs, reserve a section of the kitchen island for informal meals.

A kitchen island or peninsula can be a suitable place for enjoying a quick meal. When planning, be sure to include knee room underneath the countertop.

Seating Allowances

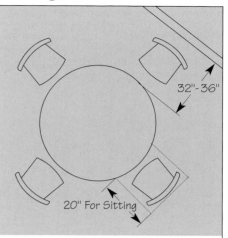

Space Requirements. A seated adult occupies a depth of about 20 inches, but needs 12 to 16 inches more to pull back the chair and rise.

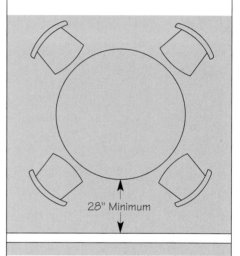

Space Saver. Placing chairs at angles to the wall can save a few inches. This strategy works with either a round or a square table.

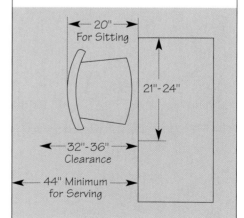

Rectangular Tables. Provide for 21 to 24 inches per person and 32 to 36 inches of clearance between the table and wall. Increase the table-to-wall distance to at least 44 inches on the serving side.

Seating allowances. Because you must have room to sit down and get up, tables, chairs, and access room require a surprising amount of space. Figure on 12 to 15 square feet per person. A family of four will need at least 48 square feet of space for in-the-kitchen dining. To size a round table, figure that a 36-inch diameter can seat four adults and a 48-incher will seat six. For a square or rectangular table, calculate 21 to 24 inches of table space for each person.

When space planning, you must pay attention to the distance between the table and any nearby walls and cabinets. A seated adult occupies a depth of about 20 inches from the edge of the table, but requires 12 to 16 inches more to pull back the chair and rise. This means you'll need 32 to 36 inches' clearance between the wall and the edge of the table. You can get away with a minimum 28-inch clearance if you place chairs at angles to the wall.

On any serving side, plan a 44-inch clearance to allow room to pass.

Also, as you plan a spot for your table, make sure that it doesn't intrude into the kitchen's work triangle or interfere with traffic routes. Don't put the eating area too far away, however. The closer you are to cooking and cleanup centers, the easier serving and clearing will be.

Booths

Not quite enough room for a table and chairs? Take a tip from diners and restaurants, and plan a booth with bench or banquette seating. Booths conserve floor space because you don't need to slide chairs back. And if you box in the benches and fit them with flip-up seats, you gain valuable storage for linens and other table items. If you box in the benches, be sure to provide heel space underneath.

A kitchen alcove or bay window is a natural place for a booth, or

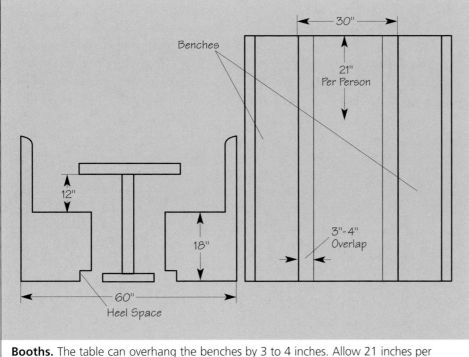

Booths. The table can overhang the benches by 3 to 4 inches. Allow 21 inches per person at a 30-inch-wide table. Benches, fixed or movable, must have heel space beneath.

30 inches across. Because you slide into and out of a booth, the table can overhang the benches by 3 or 4 inches. Total floor space required for a four-person booth, then, would measure only 5 feet across, compared with a minimum of about 9 feet for a round or square table with chairs.

Counters as Eating Bars

If you're planning to incorporate a peninsula or island in your new kitchen, you're probably already eyeing its potential as a counter where you can serve a quick meal. What dimensions do you need for a good fit?

First, how many people do you hope to seat? Remember, each adult requires 21 inches of table space. This means a counter that's 63 inches long can accommodate three stools at most.

How high the bar should be depends on the kind of seating you prefer. A 28- to 32-inch-high counter requires 18-inch-high chairs with

you can back one up to an island, peninsula, or wall. Also, you can construct seating units with backs that are high enough to serve as walls of their own.

Plan 21 inches of table space for each person, with at least 15 inches of knee space underneath. This means that a family of four needs a table that's 42 inches long and

If your kitchen will include a square or rectangular table, calculate at least 21 inches of table space for each person.

The table in the photo at left can be pulled up to a built-in banquette, above, to maximize seating and to conserve floor space.

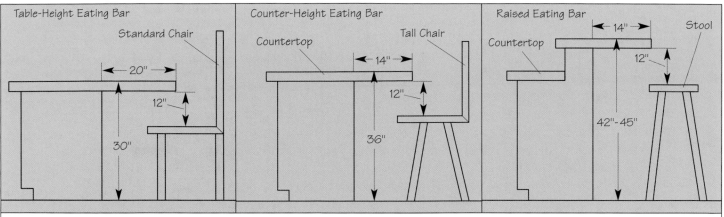

Counters as Eating Bars. Leave 12 inches between the seat and the underside of the counter. Eating bars 28 to 32 inches high require 20 inches of knee space. Bars 36 inches and higher need 14 inches of knee space. Use 18-inch-high seats at a 30-inch counter, 24-inch-stools for a 36-inch counter, and 30-inch stools for a higher counter.

A small semicircular snack counter finds an unobtrusive niche at one end of a long rectangular island.

20 inches of knee space. If you make the counter the same height as any others in the kitchen (standard 36 inches), you'll need 24-inch-high stools and 14 inches of knee space. Go up to bar height—42 to 45 inches—and you'll need 30-inch-high stools with footrests.

One problem with snack bars is that everyone faces in the same direction. Dining at a counter may be fine for breakfast or a quick lunch on the run, but you'll want a table for more sociable meals like dinner. Another problem is orienta-

tion. A counter that faces a blank wall is undesirable as an eating place, so try to orient yours facing into the kitchen or out a window.

Secondary Work Centers

If your new kitchen will be the hub of the household, it's going to be more than a place to cook and eat a meal. Depending on your family's needs, habits, and hobbies, you may want to incorporate a home

office, gardening center, laundry, baking center, sewing and craft area, or entertainment bar into your design. Sometimes a corner or spare countertop will suffice.

Home Office

A desk-height surface with a knee-hole provides a place in the kitchen to draw up lists, make phone calls, pay bills, leave messages for family members, look up recipes, and organize home management in dozens of other ways. This kind of planning center easily expands into a home office that can be used to do homework or run a cottage industry when you add a computer, printer, and fax and answering machines.

Whether the space is as modest as a small countertop and a shelf for cookbooks, or a complete work station with a full-size desk, file cabinets, and electronic equipment, decide on a spot early in the planning stage so you can run any electric, telephone, and intercom wiring you need. Situate the area outside the kitchen's work triangle, and provide adequate lighting for the kinds of activities you'll be doing there.

You may want to locate other electronic components in the office space, too. Your home's "command central" can be as sophisticated as you can afford: It may include an intercom; a security system with separate controls for window, door, and smoke alarms; a programmable

A built-in desk provides a perfect spot for paying bills, organizing household paperwork, and doing homework.

thermostat; timers; TV, VCR, and stereo equipment; and perhaps a closed-circuit-TV system for monitoring children's play areas.

Baking Center

Serious cooks, especially those who enjoy baking, will appreciate a well-appointed baking/mixing center. Allocate at least 36 inches of counter space near the oven or refrigerator—ideally between the two. To make mixing and kneading less tiring, drop the counter height 6 or 7 inches by using 30-inch-high base cabinets. Plan a countertop that is extra deep, too—30 inches or more—to provide plenty of room for rolling out dough. The surface should be heat- and moisture-proof. A countertop made of smooth stone will provide a cool surface that keeps rolled-out dough from sticking, but a smooth laminate will work, too. You'll also want counter space for setting up a mixer or blender, laying out ingredients, and loading cookie sheets or baking pans and a cooling rack. Include good fluorescent under-cabinet lighting so you're not working in your own shadow.

Give special thought to where you want the mixer. Some manufacturers offer mixer platforms that rise up out of a base cabinet, eliminating the need for awkward tugging and lifting to reach or replace the appliance before and after use. In addition, you'll want to keep small tools within hand's reach. Provide enough places to store the rolling pin, mixing bowls, and flour sifter, as well as cake, pie, muffin, and bread tins. Extra-deep cabinet drawers are handy for this use, as are carousel or slide-out trays. Items like cookie sheets and rectangular cake tins are best stored on edge in vertical compartments so you don't have to stack them.

Lastly, consider all of the ingredients you want to keep on hand. Large pull-out or tip-out bins are ideal for flour and sugar. Smaller containers can hold baking powder, nuts, raisins, vanilla, chocolate, and other spices and decorations.

Gardening Center

If you're an avid gardener, what better place to nurture new or ailing plants than a sunny kitchen window or greenhouse window unit? A full-scale kitchen gardening center might include a counter for cutting and arranging flowers, starting seeds, and potting plants; a separate deep utility sink; a faucet

In a baking center, drop the counter height to a comfortable level for mixing and kneading dough. Include a cool-surface countertop, too.

Gardeners will love a space in the kitchen for potting plants. Use a deep sink and arched faucet with sprayer.

If your hobby is sewing or crafts, plan an ample work surface as well as suitable storage for materials in your design.

Guests love to congregate in the kitchen, so entertain the notion of a bar sink in an island that doubles as a buffet.

attachment for watering; grow lights; and storage for pots, soil, plant food, and other supplies. Your center could also be as simple as a deep window sill surfaced with ceramic tile to stand up to water.

Laundry

If your current laundry facilities are in the basement, finding a place for a washer and dryer near your remodeled kitchen will save a lot of steps. There are a number of design criteria to keep in mind for a laundry center. A side-by-side pair of full-size appliances measures 48 to 58 inches wide. To conserve floor space you might consider stackable laundry machines, which are about half as wide as conventional machines but usually have smaller tubs. Full-size units are also 42 or 43 inches high, which is 6 to 7 inches taller than standard kitchen counter height so you can't run a countertop over them. And because standard-size washers are top-loading, you can't put a dryer or cabinet above them.

If you want to fit laundry appliances under a counter, consider installing a set of front-loading stackable units side-by-side. The convenience of being able to do laundry while cooking dinner may more than compensate for their smaller capacities. If you have a two-bowl sink, you can reserve one side for laundry when necessary. Don't forget a cabinet for storing detergent, fabric softener, and any other laundry supplies. It's also a good idea to plan for a built-in ironing board that folds up inside a cabinet when not in use.

Sewing & Crafts

A few cupboards and drawers positioned well outside the work triangle near a peninsula, island, or table make an excellent station for sewing or crafting. A roll-top counter appliance garage with an electrical outlet might be just the thing to store a portable sewing machine so you don't have to lift it onto a counter. Depending on the overall feeling in your kitchen, you might even keep some materials such as dried flowers, raffia bows, or spools of thread on open shelves or pegs so they are available for a quick mend or a moment of inspiration.

Entertainment Bar

People who entertain a lot, especially in a great-room kitchen, will appreciate an area well stocked with glassware and equipped with trays and plates suitable for serving hors d'oeuvres and desserts. An area such as this can be quite simple: a short length of counter and cabinets, for example. However, a bar sink, a second dishwasher, an auxiliary refrigerator, and a warming drawer are helpful in this setting to keep pre- and post-meal clutter away from the main preparation and cleanup areas of the kitchen.

A wheelchair-bound individual should be safely able to use this range, which is significantly lower than a standard cooktop.

The low position of one of these wall ovens makes sense for persons who cannot reach high levels.

Universal Design

Have you ever had an accident that made even simple kitchen tasks temporarily difficult, or perhaps impossible? Do you live with an elderly parent or very active young children? Does a member of your household suffer from arthritis or use a walker or wheelchair?

Perhaps now, while you're still in the planning stages of your new kitchen, you should consider the principles of universal, or barrier-free, design. This means making your kitchen safe and accessible for all members of the family, regardless of any physical challenges. You won't have to compromise the room's appeal in the process; good design naturally lends itself to safety and convenience.

Design Criteria

Here are some guidelines for making your kitchen efficient and functional under any circumstances:

• Design a floor plan that incorporates wide aisles (at least 42 inches) around the work triangle. Also, plan 60-inch-diameter turning circles at strategic places.

• Make doorways a minimum of 32 inches wide to accommodate wheelchairs and walkers. Avoid swinging doors and specify pocket or sliding types whenever possible. If you must use swinging doors, levers are easier to use than doorknobs.

• Plan lots of counter space near the food-preparation and cleanup areas. This space will allow the quick release of hands from heavy pots and objects.

• Install a variety of counter heights in addition to the standard 36 inches to serve different needs. A 31-inch-high counter with a knee-hole provides workspace for wheelchair-bound persons and can serve double duty as a baking center, which calls for the same height. A 45-inch-high eating bar can provide a place for a person with back pain to work without bending over. An alternative to fixed-height counters is adjustable counters. Another flexible counter option is a slide-out surface, similar to a breadboard, with reinforced tracks capable of bearing weight.

• Install wall cabinets lower on the wall and with shallow shelves so they can be reached easily by most people.

• Equip base cabinets with more-convenient pullout bins and swivel trays. Mixer platforms that rise up out of a base cabinet can be used for any heavy items, eliminating the need for awkward tugging and lifting.

• Make sure electrical outlets and TV and phone jacks are no less than 18 inches from the floor. Light switches should be 42 inches from the floor—6 inches lower on the wall than standard installations. All of these should be easily reached by someone in a wheelchair or walker.

• Try out the controls and knobs when shopping for appliances to ensure easy manipulation. Labels should be easy to read.

• If possible, buy cooking units with front-mounted knobs, which are easier to access. However, they may be unsafe for use where there are young children.

• Be sure the cooktop has staggered burners, which allow the cook access to the back without reaching over hot pots in the front.

Modular refrigeration units provide flexible placement around the floor plan and at points where they are most needed.

• Install wall ovens and cooktops at heights geared to the specific needs of the cooks in your kitchen. Also, there are special 30-inch-high slide-in ranges that are designed for the wheelchair-bound cook but are convenient for anyone to use.

• As for a refrigerator, choose a side-by-side model for universal access, or use a modular unit that allows custom placement of individual units at locations most suited to specific workers and their tasks.

• Install a single-lever faucet with a programmed temperature-control valve. These faucets are easy to use and protect against scalding accidents.

• Use nonslip cushioned flooring.

• Attach brass rails as a countertop edging to serve both as a design statement and as a grab bar.

• Install a chair rail to save walls from wheelchair gouges and to add interest as well.

• Try to find room for a half-bath adjacent to the kitchen area.

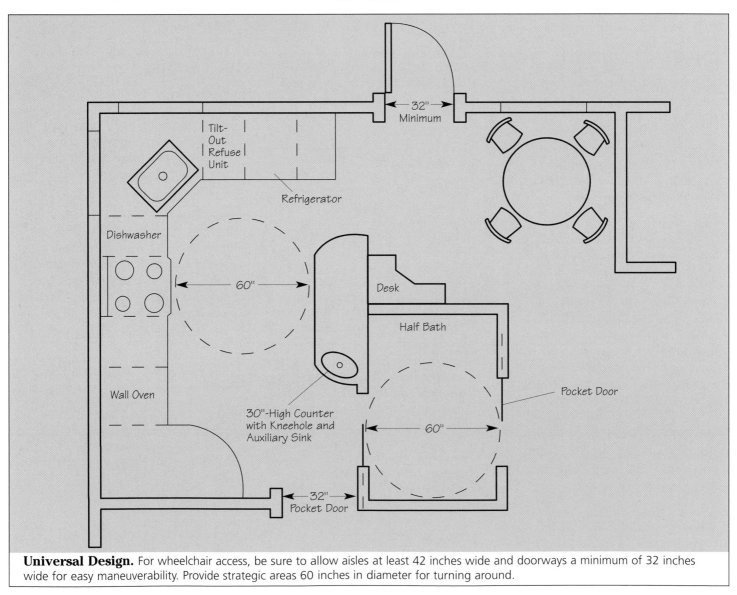

Universal Design. For wheelchair access, be sure to allow aisles at least 42 inches wide and doorways a minimum of 32 inches wide for easy maneuverability. Provide strategic areas 60 inches in diameter for turning around.

3

Design

Your kitchen's style is influenced by the cabinets, the layout, the appliances, the countertop material, the color of the walls, the texture of the floor, and the shape of the windows. After you have considered all these elements and how they can enhance your lifestyle, you must design them into a cohesive whole that serves your purpose and shows off your personality.

Your renovation plans might include adding on square footage or incorporating space from an adjacent room or closet. Regardless of the kitchen's ultimate size, the work flow should fall into the classic work triangle, which divides the kitchen into three main task areas. The layout will likely fall into one of several basic kitchen shapes that have been proved over time: U-shaped, L-shaped, G-shaped, galley, or one-wall. You can use an island or peninsula to modify these configurations and to provide additional storage and work surfaces.

You may decide to stay with the layout you have and simply replace all or some of the elements in it. If traffic flow and the arrangement of appliances or doorways makes work inefficient, however, you can play with alternative ideas provided in the section on do-it-yourself floor plans.

Style

No matter what your taste—country, traditional, contemporary, eclectic— as you work on your basic layout you should think about the details that will make your new kitchen suit your way of life.

Architectural Style

A kitchen's design is distinguished more than anything by the style of the cabinets. Assisted by decorative details like the wall and floor treatments, window style, and accessories, the door fronts of the cabinets will put a face on the kitchen's architecture. There are many variations on the following three themes,

but most of the differences are in the details.

Contemporary. Sleek and unadorned, contemporary-style cabinets consist of plain panel doors and hardware that's hidden or unobtrusive.

Traditional. This style is more formal and elegant. Look for raised-panel cabinet doors or clear-glass panels separated by thin strips of wood called muntins. Rich wood finishes or painted white wood may be accented with sparkle from brass or brass-tone hardware.

Country. A simple door style, a light stain or a distressed-color finish, and unpretentious wood or ceramic knobs and handles pull the country look together.

Color Basics

Of all the ways to personalize a kitchen, color is the most magical. In fact, the dominant color of a room can actually affect the mood of those within. Red is stimulating, and in its vibrant forms is usually reserved for accents. Yellow and orange are welcoming and happy, but strong forms can also promote subtle feelings of unrest; pastel creams, peaches, and corals are good alternatives for large expanses. Blues and greens are restful and calming: Warm up blue with a touch of yellow or coral, and mix almost any color with green, the background color of nature. The brightness of your kitchen colors should be measured against the intensity of light. Evaluate color swatches in morning, afternoon, and evening light to determine what will work best under all lighting conditions.

Color Schemes. Color can be used in many ways. The method of choosing colors to convey a desired overall effect is called creating a color scheme.

Monochromatic color schemes vary a single hue. You might use only shades of blue, for example, or

keep everything within the gray to black range. Some beautiful kitchens have been done in one shade of one color, with variety supplied by the gleam of stainless steel or copper or the texture of tile or marble.

Related schemes consist of a range of colors in the same family—all the tones of autumn leaves, for example, or the various greens of spring, lightened with touches of yellow.

Complementary color schemes use opposites on the color wheel, such as reds and greens or blues and yellows.

A generous use of glass lets the homeowner incorporate a fabulous view or lush garden into the interior design of a room. In this kitchen, rustic beams, natural stone, and the green wallcovering reinforce the country theme, while furniture-quality cabinetry refines the look.

Neutral colors such as beige, gray, white, and black mix well with most colors or work well on their own.

Adding white to any color lightens its value, so white added to red produces pink. Black darkens its value, so black added to red produces a shade of maroon. Remember this point when you devise complementary or mono-chromatic schemes: Once you establish your color scheme, different intensities of the same color will serve to vary and fortify the effect.

Color and Space. Color can expand or contract a room. A general principle is that dark colors and finishes make a room look smaller, while light ones do the opposite. Strong contrasts, such as light cabinets and dark wallpaper, visually take up more space than if these two elements were of the same color and intensity.

Color Trends. The cabinets, tiles, counters, and appliances you select will be with you for a while, and in trendy colors they can become dated quickly. There are certain limitations, too, on the colors you can choose: Most appliances come only in white and a limited range of neutral hues. One way to cope with both the dating and color-matching problems is to select appliances with changeable front panel inserts. You simply remove a piece of trim

Artful effects like the painted vine that encircles this window are finding their way into kitchens.

from the door, slip in the color panel of your choice, and replace the trim. Another option is to go with appliances that accept external door panels that match your cabinetry. Lastly, a time-honored and economical solution is to stick with a neutral or white palette for appliances—and introduce color on wall, floor, and countertop surfaces that can be replaced or changed inexpensively.

Texture

Brick, vinyl, slate, wood, stone, tile, fabric, and other materials bring texture to your kitchen. A glossy plastic laminate countertop, for example, has a shine quite different from the gleam of a satiny stainless-steel sink. By varying textures you can enhance your color scheme.

Details

You might want to express your individual style using design elements like tile backsplashes with scenes of nature, refrigerator panels of punched tin, burnished copper range hoods, brick-faced cooking alcoves, exposed ceiling beams, or crown moldings. Maybe you have a treasured plate collection you want to mount on a soffit or display on wall-hung shelves. Perhaps you'll create an interesting vignette with a hand-painted motif, or spice up the room with a wallpaper border or stenciled design. The shape and color of your kitchen gains depth and distinction from the details that reflect your tastes and interests.

Strong geometric shapes like the square cutouts used to display china and pottery make a bold modern statement in the architecture of this kitchen. The wine rack in the left foreground is at once practical and decorative.

Layout

What if your existing kitchen is critically cramped, and no amount of rearranging is going to make it much better? Should you dig deep into your finances, call in an architect or remodeling contractor, and plan a kitchen addition? The answer is a qualified "maybe."

Adding Space

Full-scale additions almost always cost more per square foot than new construction, so you should realistically expect to recover only part of your remodeling investment— say 75 to 90 percent—when you sell your home. Also, lot-line restrictions may limit the amount of new space you can add, especially at the sides or front of your home. Before you add square footage with new construction, consider some alternatives:

Conversion. One option is to convert a covered porch or entryway into kitchen space. If it's constructed on good footings and has a roof that's in good shape, you may be able to enclose, wire, and insulate the space for considerably less than a full addition would cost.

Annexation. Also, look to adjacent areas for a few square feet you might annex. Often, it's as simple as relocating a closet or removing a non-bearing wall.

Transposition. If your kitchen is not only too small but also inconveniently located, you might be able to switch it with another room, such as a bedroom or dining room, as long as plumbing changes are not too extreme.

Addition. If none of the mini-addition ideas will solve the space problem, there are good reasons to go ahead with an addition:

• Besides providing the larger kitchen you want, an addition can provide you with a family room, expanded dining facilities, a sunroom, deck, or other desirable living space.

Finding More Room

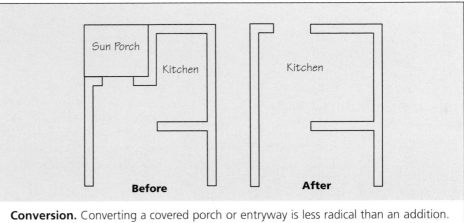

Conversion. Converting a covered porch or entryway is less radical than an addition.

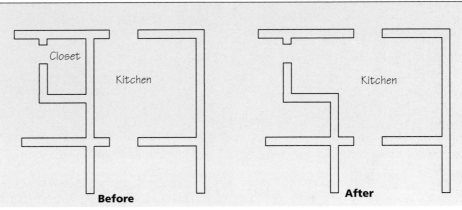

Annexation. Annex an adjacent closet as the simplest solution.

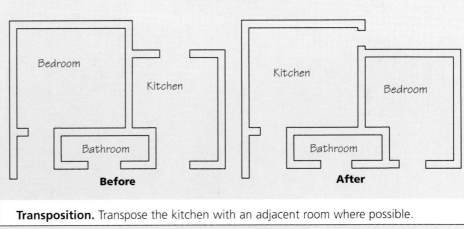

Transposition. Transpose the kitchen with an adjacent room where possible.

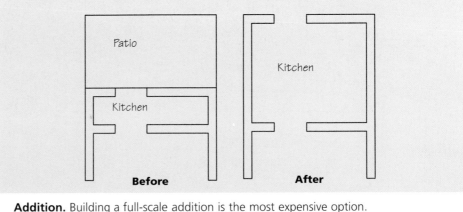

Addition. Building a full-scale addition is the most expensive option.

Adding on can provide the solution to a kitchen that offers no room for formal dining.

An addition can be the answer to converting a dark, cramped space into an open, airy one.

• If your kitchen is not only too small, but also inconveniently located, an addition may enable you to move it and convert the existing space to some other use, such as a new bedroom.

• A skillfully designed addition may also improve your home's exterior appearance, as well as its views and outdoor living areas.

Planning a kitchen addition starts the same way as any remodeling plan— with graph paper, appliance and cabinet templates, and so forth. But before you break ground, check out your ideas with a knowledgeable contractor, architect, or designer. He or she can tell you whether your scheme is feasible and what building permits you may need, and might suggest refinements that will save money, add value, or do both.

Work Triangle

The so-called work triangle seems to be a mantra chanted over and over by anyone talking, writing, or thinking about a kitchen's function. There's a good reason for this. Kitchen efficiency experts have determined that the kitchen's three necessities—sink, range, and refrigerator—should be arranged in a triangular pattern whose three sides total 12 to 26 feet. The mini-

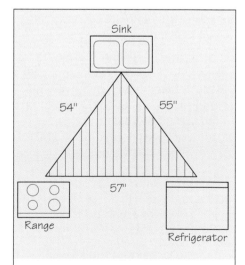

Work Triangle. This design shows good distance limits. A larger triangle would require too much walking; a smaller one would create a cramped kitchen.

mum and maximum distances conserve walking distance from point to point without sacrificing adequate counter space between work stations. These dimensions are to some degree arbitrary, and the sides of the triangle needn't be exactly equal. You'll discover that many efficient work triangles have unequal sides, yet each pattern can be the basis of an excellent kitchen.

Traffic Patterns

Pay special attention to the way traffic moves through and in your existing kitchen and any new layout you may be considering. You should be able to move easily from one place to another in the kitchen and from the kitchen to other rooms in the house, as well as outdoors.

It's also important that through-traffic doesn't interfere with the work triangle. Otherwise, carrying a hot pot from the range to the sink could put you on a collision course with youngsters heading for the back door.

Often, you can cure a faulty traffic pattern simply by moving a door or removing a short section of wall. Another way to improve the way a kitchen functions is to experiment with basic layouts.

Basic Layouts

Most kitchen layouts fall into some variation of the following configurations: one-wall, galley (corridor), L-shaped, U-shaped, and G-shaped. These layouts have come into common use because they lend themselves to efficient interpretations of the work triangle. The one exception—the one-wall kitchen—has qualities that make it a perfect fit in special situations.

One-Wall Kitchen. A one-wall kitchen lines up all its cabinets, counter space, and equipment along one wall. This arrangement flattens the work triangle to a straight line. Try to locate the sink between the range and refrigerator for maximum accessibility.

Traffic Problems and Solutions

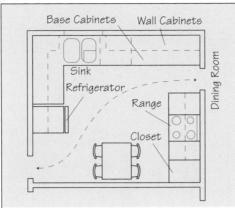

Before. Doors at opposite corners created diagonal traffic that cut off the range from the sink and refrigerator areas.

After. Moving both doors pulls traffic out of the work zone. The U-shaped layout puts the refrigerator, sink, and range in a good working arrangement.

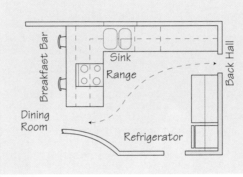

Before. Open kitchens can also have traffic problems. Here the refrigerator is isolated and the work area sprawls over a kitchen with too many doors.

After. Moving one door and closing another gets traffic out of the work area. Relocating the range makes the breakfast bar at the left much more usable.

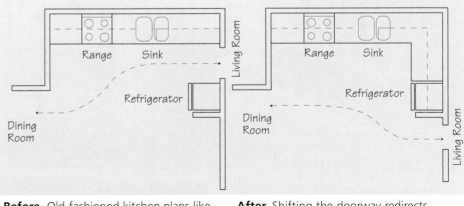

Before. Old-fashioned kitchen plans like this often provide no place to set food down near the refrigerator. Again, traffic passes through the work area.

After. Shifting the doorway redirects traffic and adds more counter and storage space. The new layout arranges the work area in an efficient L-shape.

One-wall kitchens make the most sense in tiny, single-room apartments or in a narrow space. They are sometimes used in a larger, multifunctional area to minimize the kitchen's importance and maximize the room's open space. In this context, the kitchen wall could be closed off from the rest of the room with sliding doors, screens, or shutters when not in use.

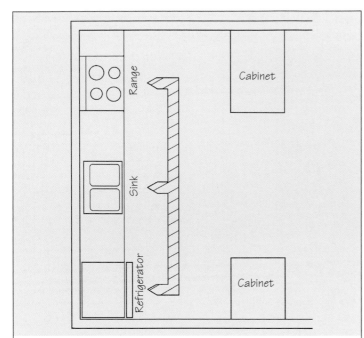

One-Wall Kitchen. A one-wall design requires the least amount of kitchen space.

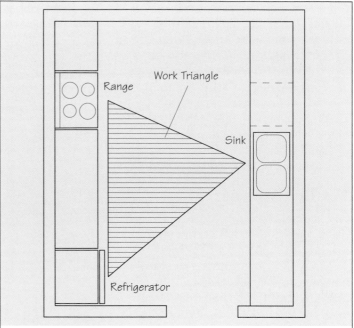

Galley Kitchen. This kitchen layout works best for one cook at a time.

Designing this kitchen against one wall makes an efficient use of space, which must also serve as a dining room and hallway.

To keep appliance doors from colliding in a single-cook galley kitchen, the aisle must be a minimum of 36 inches.

Galley Kitchen. A galley, or corridor, kitchen places appliances, cabinets, and counters along opposite walls. This scheme enables you to establish a good work triangle, but it works best as a one-cook kitchen.

Try to allow a 48-inch-wide aisle between the facing base cabinets. This makes it possible to open cabinet and appliance doors easily, with space left over for an adult to maneuver around them. Since base cabinets are 24 inches deep, you need a minimum width of 8 feet for a galley kitchen. If space is really tight, you can cut down the aisle to a bare minimum of 36 inches—but watch that appliance doors don't collide with each other when they're opened. Think twice, too, about a corridor arrangement that has doorways at both ends. This promotes traffic from outside passing through the work triangle.

L-Shaped Kitchen. An L-shaped kitchen lays out the work centers along two adjacent walls. L-shaped layouts typically have one long and one short leg. Although L-shapes require more space than galleys, they permit an efficient work triangle that discourages through-traffic. Try to place the sink at the center of the work triangle, ideally under a window.

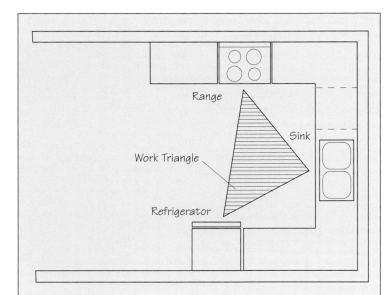

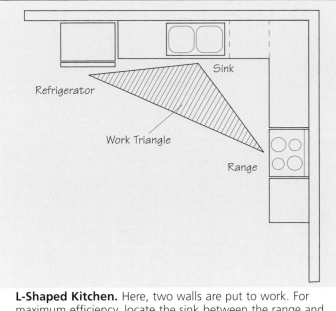

L-Shaped Kitchen. Here, two walls are put to work. For maximum efficiency, locate the sink between the range and the refrigerator.

U-Shaped Kitchen. This design is highly efficient and provides the greatest amount of counter space between the sink and appliances.

This L-shaped kitchen, with the added bonus of a work island with a grill/griddle, is a model of efficiency.

A properly planned U-shaped design maintains ideal distance between the work centers, but the overall plan requires lots of space.

One advantage of an L-shaped layout is that you can often fit a kitchen table or booth into the corner diagonally opposite the L. Planned with care, an L-shaped kitchen can accommodate two cooks with ease. One can prepare food on counters adjacent to the sink while the other works at the range.

U-Shaped Kitchen. A U-shaped kitchen arranges cabinets, counters, and appliances along three walls,

making it highly effective. Some plans open up one or more walls to an adjacent area like a family room or informal dining space. An extra dividend is freedom from through-traffic.

A U-shaped plan incorporates a logical sequence of work centers with minimal distances between them. The sink often goes at the base of the U, with the refrigerator and range on the side walls oppo-

site each other. The U-shape takes up lots of space, at least 8 feet along both the length and width of the kitchen. Corners are a problem, too, because access to storage can be a challenge. Lazy-Susan shelving helps make use of this otherwise dead space.

Neither L- nor U-shaped layouts need to be absolute. An L-shape that continues beyond a peninsula could turn into an F- or even an E-shaped kitchen. And with both types, don't rule out creating a third or fourth "wall" with an island or peninsula.

G-Shaped Kitchen. A G-shaped plan is ideal for providing room for two cooks to operate independently or in concert without interfering with each other. The plan defines two separate work triangles that usually, but not always, share the refrigerator.

Often there's a second sink and separate cooktop and oven areas in a G-shape. With this arrangement, one cook moves between the refrigerator, sink, and cooktop while the other moves between the refrigerator, second sink, and oven. Sometimes both work triangles can share two points, like the sink and refrigerator, and diverge at the cooktop and ovens. With modular refrigeration units and warming drawers, as well as microwave ovens and specialized countertop appliances, it's possible to separate the two work triangles from each other completely.

Off-the-Wall Space

If you've run out of wall space but have floor space to spare, consider

If you and your partner enjoy cooking together, consider a G-shaped design, which incorporates two work triangles into its scheme.

improving your kitchen's efficiency with a peninsula or island.

Peninsulas. Properly sized and properly placed, peninsulas cut down on steps and increase counter space. Peninsulas also offer flexible storage because you can get to them from either side. The peninsula base and ceiling-hung cabinets become convenient places to keep tableware and other dining-area supplies.

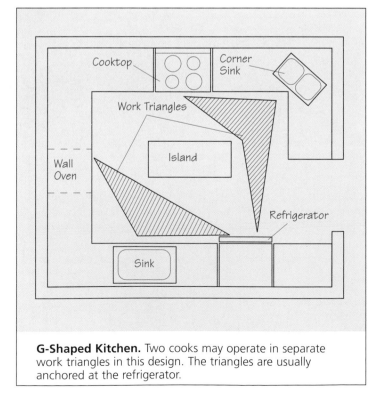

G-Shaped Kitchen. Two cooks may operate in separate work triangles in this design. The triangles are usually anchored at the refrigerator.

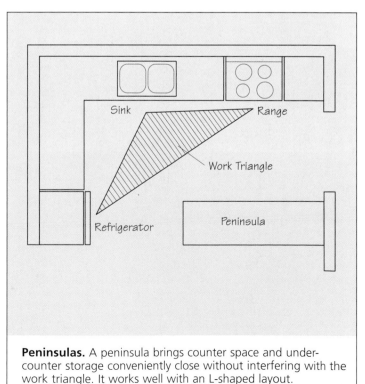

Peninsulas. A peninsula brings counter space and under-counter storage conveniently close without interfering with the work triangle. It works well with an L-shaped layout.

To prevent doors from colliding, allow a minimum of 48 inches of floor space between a peninsula and the counter opposite it. If plumbing and ventilation hookups permit, you might choose to place the range or sink in the kitchen side of a peninsula. On the other side you might choose to install an elevated eating counter.

Islands. In a big L- or U-shaped kitchen, you can shorten the dis- tance between the sink, range, and refrigerator with a center island. This arrangement works especially well in the large kitchen of an older home, visually breaking up open floor space, increasing efficiency, and sometimes providing eating space.

Some homeowners choose to install a range or cooktop in the island; others use it for the sink and dish- washer. Either way, allow for adequate counter space on either side of the sink or cooking unit. As with a peninsula, make sure you'll have at least 48 inches of space between an island and any other counter. Consider using a different surface here, too, such as butcher block for chopping or marble for rolling pastry dough.

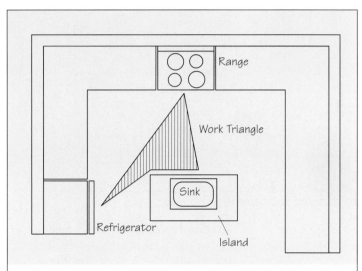

Islands. An island can reduce the size of the work triangle in a U- or L-shaped kitchen, provided you have adequate floor space all around it. Depending on the location of utility lines and venting possibilities, either the sink or a cooktop/range can be put into an island.

Kitchen islands can come in all sizes and shapes. This one is angled to maximize traffic flow in a small room.

A stepped-down snack counter can be situated on the other side of a work counter to make the most of kitchen space.

If square footage is no problem, your kitchen island can include the works, from cooktop and sinks, to an eating area.

This high-tech peninsula with a refrigerated wine rack faces into the family room and serves as a media center with a TV, VCR, and stereo.

The additional kitchen sink located in this work island is ideal for rinsing produce and preparing vegetables.

The overhead cabinet for glasses enhances this peninsula's use when entertaining.

Measurements for Planning

With a pencil, graph paper, measuring tape, ruler, eraser, and scissors, you can draw an outline of the space you have and try out different arrangements of appliances, counters, and cabinets. There are also commercial planning kits that have a floor-plan grid and cutouts of standard-size cabinets and appliances.

Careful Measuring

Start by making a rough floor plan of your existing kitchen. Include doors and windows, obstructions, breaks in the wall, outlets and switches, and any other pertinent information.

Measure accurately, all in inches, so you don't confuse 5'3" with 53"—a significant difference. Write measurements on the rough sketch as you go. Start at any corner of the room and measure to the first break or obstruction—a window or range, for instance. Note this measurement on your sketch. Measure from that point to the next break or obstruction, and so on around the room. Also measure the height of doorways and windows from the floor up, and from the ceiling down.

Measure the vertical and horizontal location of electrical outlets, light switches, and lighting fixtures. Show the rough locations of gas and plumbing lines, as well as ducts and vents.

Measure around the room at two or three heights: floor level above the baseboard, counter height (36 inches), and with arms stretched high (6 or 7 feet). Add up the measurements recorded along the walls for overall measurements. Now measure the overall length and width of your kitchen at the floor and note this on your sketch. These should equal the corresponding overall measurements. If there's a significant difference in the measurements at different heights, your room is out of square and it could be tricky to get a snug fit for your cabinets, which are square. If the difference is too great to be masked by molding and caulk, say ½ to ¾ inch, you may need the help of a professional.

Scale Drawings

You can use each square of ¼-inch graph paper to represent 6 inches of actual floor space. Lay out the room's four walls to scale, referring to your rough sketch. Draw all irregularities on your scaled plan, being sure to account for the thickness of any walls that project into

the room. Draw the existing doors and windows to exact scale, even if you expect to change them when you remodel. Also indicate existing utility lines and electrical connections.

Don't bother with appliances, cabinets, counters, or any other elements you plan to rearrange. These are best dealt with by cutting scaled templates from graph paper. Then you can move the templates around to experiment with any layout that occurs to you.

Cabinets. Assembling a run of kitchen cabinets and appliances requires fitting a series of standard-size components into a space that's probably not an exact multiple of any dimension. The job isn't difficult, however, because custom and stock cabinet widths progress in increments of 3 inches. By juggling sizes you can usually put together a series of cabinets that ends up

just shy of the total distance from one wall to another. You'll make up the difference with filler strips at one or both ends.

The drawings on these pages depict typical cabinet dimensions, but if you're taller or shorter than average you may want to alter the heights at which your cabinets will be installed. You also may mix and match installation heights to create specialized work sites. Most base cabinets are 30½ inches high. Toe space and the base on which they rest bring them up to 34½ inches. Add another 1½ inches for the countertop, and the total counter height comes to 36 inches.

Adjusting Heights. Some studies indicate that the standard 36-inch counter height is too low for most people and that 37½ inches is better. If you want to elevate your counters an inch or so, increase the height of the toe space.

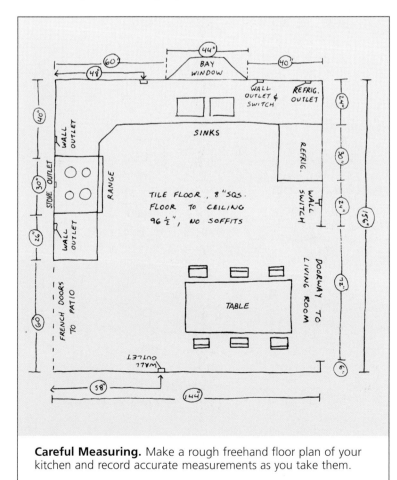

Careful Measuring. Make a rough freehand floor plan of your kitchen and record accurate measurements as you take them.

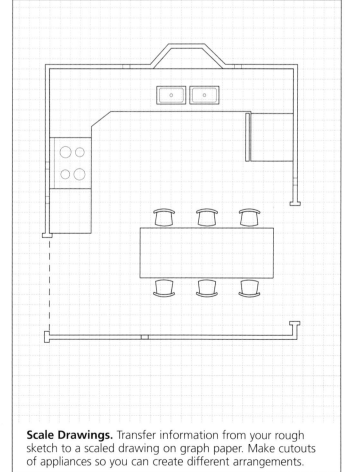

Scale Drawings. Transfer information from your rough sketch to a scaled drawing on graph paper. Make cutouts of appliances so you can create different arrangements.

The distance between the counter-top and the bottom of the wall cabinets typically measures 14 to 18 inches. The 18-inch height allows room for tall appliances on the counter, or for a microwave oven installed under the wall cabinets. The 14-inch height makes upper shelves in the wall cabinets more accessible to shorter people.

Preparing Your Plan. Use the dimensions for cabinets, appliances, and sinks in the charts at right when you draw and cut out templates for your scaled kitchen plan. There's not much you can do about appliance dimensions, of course, but most manufacturers can modify stock or semi-custom cabinets to your order for special equipment or space needs.

Preparing Your Plan. You can adjust these typical cabinet installation dimensions to suit the physical needs of those using the kitchen.

■ Typical Base Cabinets ■

- **Sink Bases.** A "dummy" drawer front covers the bowl. Wide doors provide access to the plumbing and disposal unit underneath.
- **Drawer Cabinets.** Think of the items you want to store before deciding whether to order a three- or four-drawer base unit.
- **Base Cabinets.** Typical units have one or two doors and drawers, in a variety of widths. Door and drawer front sizes also vary.

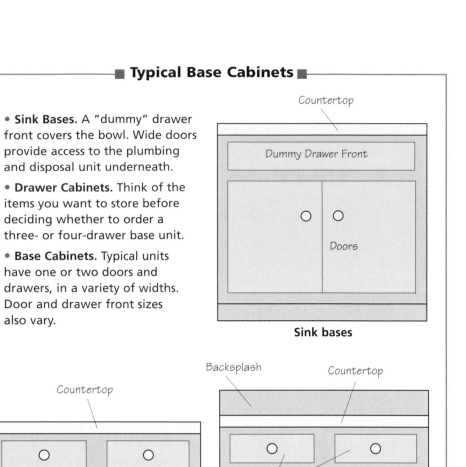

Sink bases

Drawer cabinets

Base cabinets

Cabinet Dimensions (in inches; ranges in 3-inch increments)

Cabinet	Width	Height	Depth
Base unit	9–48	34½	24
Drawer base	15–21	34½	24
Sink base	30, 36, 48	34½	24
Blind corner base	24 (not usable)	34½	24
Corner base	36–48	34½	24
Corner carousel	33, 36, 39 (diameter)	X	X
Drop-in range base	30, 36	12–15	24
Wall unit	9–48	12–18, 24, 30	12, 13
Tall cabinet (oven, pantry, broom)	18–36	84, 90, 96	12–24

Appliance Dimensions (in inches)

Appliance	Width	Depth	Height
Cooktop	15, 30, 36, 42, 46 (with grill)	22	X
Wall oven	24, 27, 30	24	24—52
Range	24, 30, 36	24, 27	36, 72 (oven above)
Commercial range	36—68	30—36	37—60
Vent hood	30, 36	18—20	7—9
Refrigerator	28—36	28—32, 24 (built-in)	58—72
Modular refrigerator/freezer	27	24	$34\frac{1}{2}$, 80
Upright freezer	28—36	28—32	58—72
Chest freezer	40—45	28—32	35—36
Dishwasher	18, 24	24	$34\frac{1}{2}$
Compactor	15	24	$34\frac{1}{2}$
Washer and dryer	27—30	27—30	36, 72 (stacked)
Grill	18—36	21—22	X
Microwave oven	18—30	12—16	10—16

Sink Dimensions (in inches)

Sink Type	Width	Front to Rear	Basin Depth
Single-bowl	25	21—22	8—9
Double-bowl	33	21—22	8—9
Side-disposal	33	21—22	8—9, 7
Triple-bowl	43	21—22	8, 6, 10
Corner	17—18 (each way)	21—11	8—9
Bar	15—25	15	$5\frac{1}{2}$—6

Corners. One of the trickiest parts of planning a run of cabinets and appliances comes when you arrive at a corner. Storage here tends to be inefficient, especially in the deeper recesses of base cabinets, where things sneak out of sight, out of reach, and soon out of mind as well. There are a variety of alternatives, thanks to specialty cabinets.

The two most popular ways to turn a corner are with blind bases, straight units that have a door on only one side and overlap the beginning of the next run, and corner bases, which integrate two cabinets into a single L-shaped unit. With blind bases you usually need a filler so doors will clear each other. Wall cabinets also come in blind and corner units. When ordering blind cabinets, you must specify whether you want a left- or right-hand version.

Another way to negotiate a turn is to situate a sink, refrigerator, or range there. Corner sinks may arrange basins at right angles to each other and fit into a standard corner base. Be sure to allow adequate counter space on either side of a sink or appliance. Use the small triangle of counter space in the corner to hold useful or decorative items, or make it a raised platform for plants.

A peninsula offers an excellent opportunity to take advantage of dead corner space inside cabinets. Items that can't be easily reached from the kitchen side can be stowed on the opposite side. Like blind bases, peninsula corner cabinets come in left- and right-hand configurations.

Corners also waste countertop space, because the area under wall cabinets makes an inconvenient work surface. One solution is an angled appliance garage that fits between the counter and wall cabinets and houses a mixer or food processor.

Eight Ways around a Corner

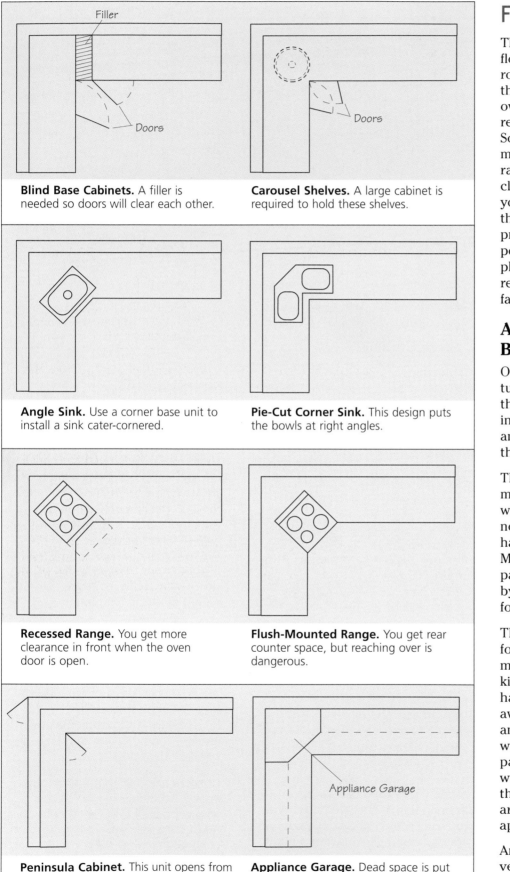

Blind Base Cabinets. A filler is needed so doors will clear each other.

Carousel Shelves. A large cabinet is required to hold these shelves.

Angle Sink. Use a corner base unit to install a sink cater-cornered.

Pie-Cut Corner Sink. This design puts the bowls at right angles.

Recessed Range. You get more clearance in front when the oven door is open.

Flush-Mounted Range. You get rear counter space, but reaching over is dangerous.

Peninsula Cabinet. This unit opens from both sides to solve the corner problem.

Appliance Garage. Dead space is put to use; install an electrical outlet inside.

Do-It-Yourself Floor Plans

There are many ways to revise the floor plan of an existing kitchen. The room's peculiarities, combined with the special desires of the home-owners, lead to solutions that other remodelers might never consider. So why bother to study how others might do things? With a little inspiration from one project here, a clever idea from another there, you'll be attuned to the possibilities that exist in your own remodeling project. To acquaint you with some possibilities, we've prepared floor plans for four existing kitchens, then redesigned them to better suit the families that live there.

Annexing a Butler's Pantry

Our first remake comes from a turn-of-the-century home. Back then, few components were built in. Instead, cabinets and appliances were treated like furniture that could be moved about.

The original kitchen supplemented meager counter and storage space with an adjacent "butler's pantry," not a bad feature if you happen to have a butler or other live-in help. Meals, even breakfast, were prepared in the kitchen and pantry by servants, then carried to a formal dining room.

The typical modern family of four has no servants and would much rather eat light meals in the kitchen, where anything they might have forgotten is just a few steps away. To make space for a table and four chairs, we removed the wall between the kitchen and pantry. Then, to create an efficient work triangle, we also relocated the door to the dining room and arranged cabinets, counters, and appliances in an L-shaped layout.

An angled range with an overhead vent hood occupies dead corner space, with a microwave oven and tall storage cabinet to the left.

Annexing a Butler's Pantry

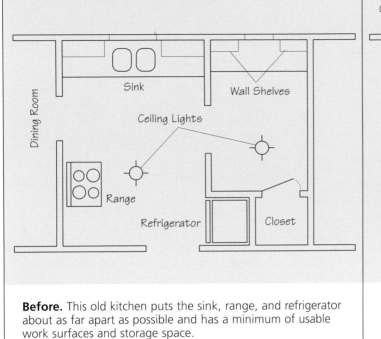

Before. This old kitchen puts the sink, range, and refrigerator about as far apart as possible and has a minimum of usable work surfaces and storage space.

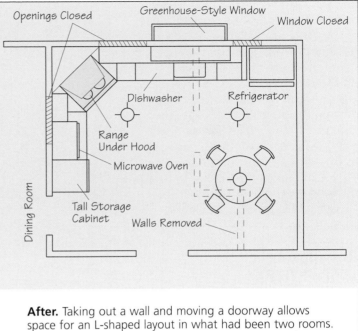

After. Taking out a wall and moving a doorway allows space for an L-shaped layout in what had been two rooms. Two windows have been replaced by a greenhouse bay.

There wouldn't have been enough space for a sink under the original window to the right of the range's new location, so we closed up that window—in the old pantry—moved the sink a couple of feet, and installed a greenhouse bay behind it. Now the refrigerator ends the run of cabinets and counters.

Reorganizing Wasted Space

The builder of this family-style kitchen meant well, but failed to achieve a layout that worked smoothly. Lack of floor space is no problem here. In fact there seems to be way too much of it. Imagine repeatedly taking a dozen or more steps back and forth from the refrigerator to the sink, or carrying hot, heaping plates to a table stranded in the middle of nowhere.

Counter space is also poorly allocated. There's too much next to the refrigerator and none at all to the right of the burner top. Also, every time the wall-oven door is opened it blocks traffic from the adjacent doorway.

Shrinking the Kitchen. The redesign cuts the working and dining areas down to size and adds some new angles. We moved the sink to an angled peninsula, making room for a compactor to the left of the sink. At the end of the peninsula, a custom-made, movable octagonal table is within easy reach of the refrigerator and cleanup center. Pull the table away from the peninsula, and it can seat up to eight.

Reorganizing Wasted Space

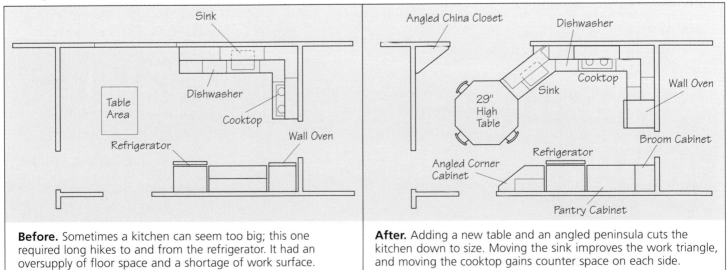

Before. Sometimes a kitchen can seem too big; this one required long hikes to and from the refrigerator. It had an oversupply of floor space and a shortage of work surface.

After. Adding a new table and an angled peninsula cuts the kitchen down to size. Moving the sink improves the work triangle, and moving the cooktop gains counter space on each side.

The angles of a new china closet and the counter space next to the relocated refrigerator parallel those of the table and peninsula. Now the refrigerator has a handy "landing" counter, where groceries can rest on their way from store to storage, either in the refrigerator or the new pantry next to it. Moving the cooktop to the sink's former site provides generous counter space to the left and right of the burners. This also makes it possible to bring the wall oven closer to the other appliances, out of the through-traffic lane.

Revamping a 1950s Kitchen

As kitchens from the 1950s go, this one worked reasonably well. The range was a long hike from the sink, but otherwise the L-shaped layout defined a manageable work triangle and there was space left over for a table, chairs, and extra storage near the dining room.

However, as you'd expect in a house of this vintage, the cabinets, counters and equipment were almost worn out—providing a splendid opportunity either to remedy the layout's minor flaws or to create a dynamic new layout.

Fine-Tuning. Besides suffering from a somewhat awkward work triangle, this kitchen lacked counter space for today's blenders, food processors, coffee brewers, toasters, and other countertop appliances.

In our first tune-up redesign, moving the range to the corner

Ways to Shrink a Kitchen

Break up the wasteland of floor space in the center with an island. Islands work especially well in two-cook kitchens. Consider other jobs your kitchen might accommodate. Devoting leftover space to a laundry, sewing center, home office, or planting area might take some pressure off some other rooms.

Revamping a 1950s Kitchen

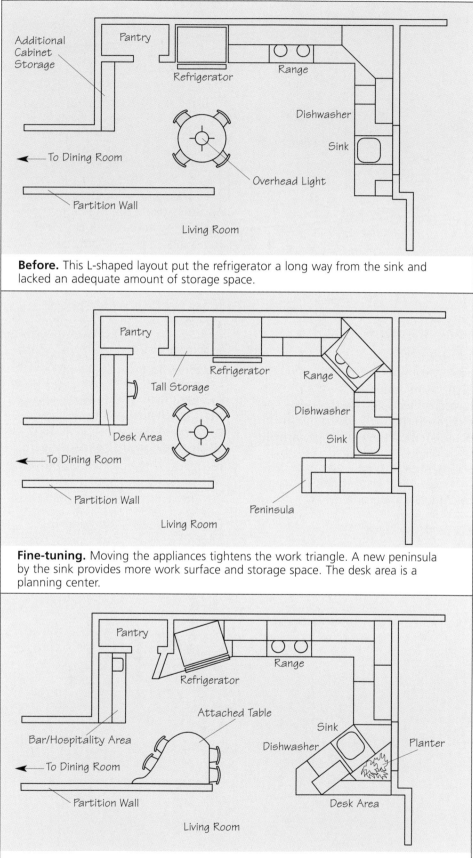

Before. This L-shaped layout put the refrigerator a long way from the sink and lacked an adequate amount of storage space.

Fine-tuning. Moving the appliances tightens the work triangle. A new peninsula by the sink provides more work surface and storage space. The desk area is a planning center.

Splurging. Angled placement of the refrigerator and sink, and addition of a free-form table, add interest to the design. Moving the desk to the triangular sink peninsula makes room for a bar/hospitality area.

helps solve both problems: The triangle's legs are shorter, and the counter space next to the refrigerator is increased by more than a foot. Adding a peninsula next to the sink further increases usable counter and cabinet space. With more storage in the kitchen proper, we decided to replace the extra floor-to-ceiling cabinets at the left with a planning center. Wall-hung cabinets and built-in desk make a handy new place to conduct family business.

Splurging. Now look what could happen to our ho-hum 1950s kitchen if we spent a bit more. Our second redesign moves the sink, not the range. A triangular peninsula accommodates the sink, dishwasher, a planter, and a planning desk.

To further tighten the work triangle, we angled the refrigerator slightly. This move cramped the space formerly occupied by the table and chairs, so they were replaced by a piano-shaped table jutting out from the wall. Lastly, the space next to the dining room has become a

hospitality center, complete with a bar sink.

Stretching into a Porch

Older homes often have kitchens that are tiny by today's standards, but many open to a side or back porch that begs to be brought in from the cold. Enclosing a porch is an obvious way to add kitchen space. If your porch has a solid foundation and a sound roof, enclosing it is a feasible project for even a beginning do-it-yourselfer. And because a porch is already part of the house, you needn't worry about setback and lot-line ordinances that affect additions.

Case Study. This small kitchen stranded a range at one end of a compact L and positioned the refrigerator as a roadblock to traffic passing to and from a back porch. Using the porch's existing roof and floor enabled the owners to triple their kitchen space, at a fraction of what an all-new addition would have cost. At first, what to do with all that new-found space posed a problem. The plan on the bottom

right shows the homeowners' well-thought-out solution.

A kitchen eating area was one priority, so about half of the old porch now provides a delightful place for family meals, with big windows offering views of the back and side yards. Converting the dining room window into a doorway provides access to the eating area and back door without passing through the kitchen's work zone.

In the kitchen area, elongating the old L more than doubles cabinet and counter space. Baking, cooking, and cleanup centers are well defined but still convenient to each other. A new sink fits into dead corner space, with a planter behind it that thrives in the light streaming in through the windows in both walls.

Now the refrigerator stands against the new back wall, handy to the eating area. In the refrigerator's old location the owners have stacked a washer and dryer, with adjacent counter space for sorting and folding laundry and a pantry for foodstuffs.

Stretching into a Porch

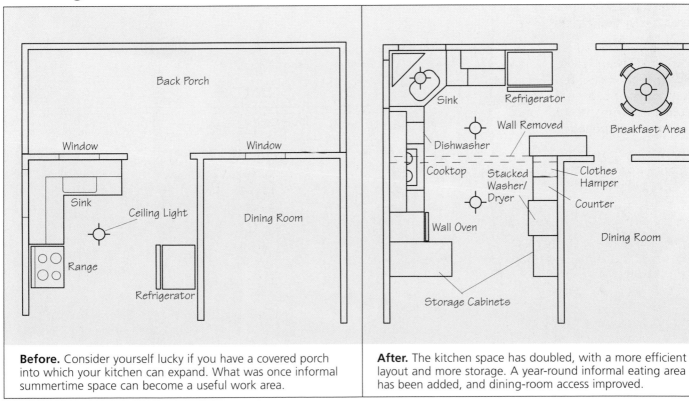

Before. Consider yourself lucky if you have a covered porch into which your kitchen can expand. What was once informal summertime space can become a useful work area.

After. The kitchen space has doubled, with a more efficient layout and more storage. A year-round informal eating area has been added, and dining-room access improved.

4

Finances & Contracting

The best laid plans can come to a screeching halt when you sit down and add up the price of new cabinets, appliances, fixtures, and other materials like countertops, flooring, and wallcovering. So unless your source of funds is unlimited, you'll have to develop a budget carefully before making any purchases.

Sometimes, financing a new kitchen is simply a matter of compromise, knowing what you need and choosing to wait for what you'd like. Believe it or not, professional advice from an architect or certified kitchen designer can help trim the fat from the tab, too. These trained professionals know more than one way to solve a problem. The contractor can also help you save money by suggesting economical shortcuts or alternatives in building techniques and materials.

Lastly, decide on the scope of your participation in the job. Obviously, any work you can do yourself will save you money.

Budget

Kitchen remodeling costs can run from a few thousand dollars to a hundred thousand or more. Where your project falls in this broad spectrum depends on the most basic question: How much can you afford?

■ Kitchen Makeover Planner ■

Need	Want	CONSTRUCTION	Need	Want	WALLS	Need	Want	FITTINGS
☐	☐	Add-on space	☐	☐	Paint	☐	☐	Single-lever faucet
☐	☐	Move/remove walls	☐	☐	Wallcovering	☐	☐	Center set faucet/spray
☐	☐	Replace/add window(s)	☐	☐	Paneling	☐	☐	Center set faucet
☐	☐	Replace/add door(s)	☐	☐	Ceramic tile	☐	☐	Widespread set
☐	☐	Modify plumbing lines	☐	☐	Wallboard	☐	☐	Separate sprayer
☐	☐	Modify electrical lines			**FLOORS**	☐	☐	Bar faucet
☐	☐	GFCIs	☐	☐	Vinyl sheet	☐	☐	Garbage disposal
		CABINETRY	☐	☐	Vinyl tile	☐	☐	Water filter
☐	☐	Replace/reface units	☐	☐	Ceramic tile			**HARDWARE**
☐	☐	Island/peninsula	☐	☐	Wood	☐	☐	Doorknobs
☐	☐	Pantry			**LIGHTING/VENTILATION**	☐	☐	Cabinet drawer pulls
☐	☐	Planning center	☐	☐	Ceiling fixture(s)	☐	☐	Cabinet door pulls
☐	☐	Bake center	☐	☐	Hanging fixture(s)	☐	☐	Switch plates
☐	☐	Media center	☐	☐	Recessed lights			**PROFESSIONAL SERVICES**
		COUNTERTOPS	☐	☐	Track lights	☐	☐	Architect
☐	☐	Plastic laminate	☐	☐	Wall sconces	☐	☐	Kitchen designer (CKD)
☐	☐	Ceramic tile	☐	☐	Ceiling fan	☐	☐	Interior designer
☐	☐	Solid-surfacing	☐	☐	Dimmers			**FURNISHINGS**
☐	☐	Wood	☐	☐	Range hood	☐	☐	Table
☐	☐	Marble	☐	☐	Exhaust fan	☐	☐	Chairs
☐	☐	Granite			**MAJOR APPLIANCES**	☐	☐	Stools
☐	☐	Faux stone	☐	☐	Refrigerator	☐	☐	Hutch
		FIXTURES	☐	☐	Cooktop/oven/range	☐	☐	Desk
☐	☐	Single-bowl sink	☐	☐	Microwave	☐	☐	Phone
☐	☐	Double-bowl sink	☐	☐	Dishwasher	☐	☐	Media equipment
☐	☐	Bar sink	☐	☐	Trash compactor	☐	☐	Computer

Budget. To make shopping easier, this checklist is organized to separate needs from wants. After you've filled it out, you may be able to figure out what your budget can handle and where you can make compromises, if necessary.

A major kitchen remodeling is one of the better home improvement investments. At the time of resale it can return 75 to 90 percent of the amount invested. But you should also consider how much you want to spend in relation to the total value of your home. Family budget advisers suggest that this figure should be no more than about 10 to 15 percent.

Allocating Costs

Before you solicit bids from architects or contractors, you should determine a preliminary budget. After you've worked out a plan, visit several kitchen showrooms in your area. Choose some cabinet styles you like and ask the dealer to give you a ballpark figure for what you have in mind. Then go to appliance and plumbing suppliers. Choose two or three models of each piece of equipment you'll need. Jot down the price and list of features each model has. At a building-supply dealer, do the same for flooring and countertop materials, as well as any windows, doors, and skylights you'd like. A visit to an electrical supplier and a lighting showroom will give you an idea of those costs.

Next, make up lists of various possible equipment combinations and the prices. Add up the totals. Double each estimate to account for labor and additional materials, and you'll have an approximation of what the project will cost.

Getting Bids

Once you have a rough estimate that falls within your budget, you're ready to proceed with soliciting bids. This can only be done when you, an architect, or a kitchen designer have prepared final building plans.

This kitchen says "upscale." Before talking to contractors, make a list of what you would like to use in your new kitchen, then visit showrooms and home centers to get a handle on prices.

Request bids from more than one and preferably three contractors to get the best possible price. Provide each bidder with a complete set of plans. You can expect to wait two to four weeks to receive your bids. A contractor needs to assess the project properly, based on plans, in order to draw up all anticipated costs.

The usual method of bidding on remodeling projects and new construction is fixed-price bidding, rather than cost-plus estimates. With a fixed-price bid, the contractor studies your construction plans, estimates the costs to do the work, adds in a profit, and comes up with a price for the job. Once the contract is signed, the contractor is obligated to perform the work specified in the contract for the sum agreed upon. If, however, you decide on any changes after the contract is signed, the contractor is given a chance to alter the estimate. Stay away from cost-plus estimates, where you agree to pay the contractor any costs he incurs plus a profit margin. That kind of estimate is too open-ended.

You may receive widely varying bids. The most expensive does not guarantee the best work. That contractor may have high overhead, or the job may come at a busy time, which may involve hiring extra workers or paying overtime. Conversely, a low bid could be submitted by someone who needs the work at the moment or who will do some of the work personally. If you feel bids are out of line, ask the contractors for the reasons. Often, relatively small changes in your design or requirements can produce significant savings.

Financing

Many families can't afford to pay cash for a major remodeling. If you've lived in your home a number of years, the money for a new kitchen could come from the equity you've built up as a result of appreciation and mortgage amortization. Refinancing an old mortgage spreads the cost over 15 to 30 years—and the interest on a home mortgage is tax deductible.

Personal and home-improvement loans are two other sources of cash. Shop carefully for interest rates. With personal loans, you may have to pledge an asset as security and pay the principle and interest back in three to five years.

Home-improvement loans are generally based on the equity you've built in your house. They typically have lower interest rates and longer terms than personal loans. Home-improvement loans come in two types: home-equity lines of credit and lump-sum loans. With a line of credit, you receive—and pay for—money only as you need it. The advantage of a line of credit is that you can draw money

gradually and pay for the project as it proceeds. As its name implies, a lump-sum loan is disbursed in its entirety at one time, so you start paying interest on the whole principle from day one. Terms for both loans generally range from 5 to 20 years.

Architects & Designers

If you plan to make major structural changes, you'll need an architect. An architect's job is to prepare floor plans and specifications for the construction phase. The architect also can be hired to supervise the entire job, from planning through construction. If you don't contemplate structural changes or if your kitchen will be installed in a newly constructed house, consider turning to a kitchen designer for assistance instead.

Hiring an Architect

When hiring an architect, you'll sign a contract that sets forth the services to be performed and the fees to be paid. If you've hired your architect to work on your project from start to finish, expect to pay this professional a fee of somewhere between 8 and 15 percent of the total construction cost.

If you decide to hire an architect only to prepare floor plans and working drawings, a flat fee can be determined. The fee will most likely be calculated on an hourly basis. Expect to pay $50 to $75 an hour for an architect's time. A typical fee might range from $500 to $1,000.

When choosing an architect, look for the letters A.I.A. after the name. This acronym indicates membership in and accreditation by the American Institute of

Don't be afraid of hiring an architect to draw up plans. These professionals can save you money in the long run by solving tricky design problems that might otherwise thwart your aims.

Architects, the professional association of architects in the United States.

Hiring a Kitchen Designer

Kitchen designers plan out the functional details of a kitchen and often work in conjunction with cabinet dealers or design-and-build firms. If you plan to purchase your

---

■ **Professional** ■
Organizations

Here is a list of professional organizations that may be of help to you in planning your kitchen. The organizations provide referrals or written materials that can help make your kitchen remodeling a success.

American Institute of Architects
1735 New York Ave., N.W.
Washington, DC 20006
202/626-7300

American Society of Interior Designers
608 Massachusetts Ave., N.E.
Washington, DC 20002
800/775-ASID

Kitchen Cabinet Manufacturers Association
1899 Preston White Dr.
Preston, VA 22091
703/264-1690

Major Appliance Consumer Action Panel
20 N. Wacker Dr.
Chicago, IL 60606
312/984-5858

National Association of the Remodeling Industry
4301 N. Fairfax Dr., Suite 310
Arlington, VA 22203
800/440-NARI

National Kitchen & Bath Association
687 Willow Grove St.
Hackettstown, NJ 07840
800/FOR-NKBA

---

cabinets from one of these sources, the design fee will be included in the price of the cabinetry package.

If you plan to buy the cabinets from another source, you can negotiate a flat fee with a designer for just the design work. A designer will charge $25 to $50 an hour. Average fees range from $250 to $1,000. Either way, the designer will provide you with exact floor plans and elevations that you can give to your contractor.

When choosing a kitchen designer, look for the initials C.K.D. after his or her name. These letters indicate that the designer has been tested and certified by the National Kitchen and Bath Association (NKBA).

Working with Contractors

When it comes time to start construction, you'll have to decide who's going to going to do the work. You can hire a general contractor, who will take the entire job from start to finish. Or you can hire individual contractors, such as a plumber, an electrician, a carpenter, and the like, to do separate parts of the job until the kitchen is done. If you're handy with tools, you may want to save money or gain a feeling of accomplishment by doing some or all of the work yourself. Before you decide on this option, though, be realistic about what you can expect to accomplish.

General Contractors

A general contractor takes responsibility for all construction phases of your job. He or she will supply the labor and materials, schedule and coordinate the various trades, contract with and pay subcontractors, obtain any necessary building permits, arrange for required inspections at different stages of the work, and generally see that your plan is brought to fruition.

The contractor may hire subcontractors to do all or parts of the job, or hire workers directly. Often subcontractors will have to return at different stages of the work. Efficient scheduling to minimize delays is one of the most important aspects of a contractor's job. A good general contractor with organizational and construction expertise can save you time and many sleepless nights. But of course, you'll have to pay for this service. Ask for bids from several contractors (three is a good number). Be sure you give them all the same information to work with if you want to compare their quotes legitimately.

Be certain that the contractor you choose is an established member of the business community in your area. Ask to speak to past customers. Find out whether they were satisfied with the contractor's performance in terms of both quality and schedule. You'll also want to know that your contractor is in good financial shape, since any default on materials or subcontractor payments may end up as a lien on your kitchen. Talk to local building-trade suppliers (lumberyards, concrete companies) to find out whether your contractor has a good reputation within the industry. You can also check with the local Better Business Bureau or Chamber of Commerce to see if there's an adverse file on record, but bear in mind that they can report only on complaints.

You'll sign a contract with your general contractor setting forth all responsibilities, including a list of materials the contractor is expected to supply, specifying grades of materials, brands, or stock numbers where appropriate. The contract will also include a payment schedule and the total price of the job. You can typically expect to pay 20 to 25 percent down and 15 to 20 percent when the job is satisfactorily completed. The balance might be divided into two or three payments, to be made every three to four weeks during the interim. Make sure that all of the work is guaranteed and that the terms of the guarantee are spelled out.

Subcontractors

To save money you can act as your own general contractor and subcontract the job yourself. But first ask yourself how much time you're willing to devote to the project. All of the subcontractors will have to be evaluated and hired separately, and will require their own contracts and sets of working drawings.

Each subcontractor must be supervised and scheduled around the work of others. If you're tackling a major remodeling and no one will be home during working hours, you'll definitely need a general contractor to coordinate construction.

Doing It Yourself

Before doing any of the remodeling work yourself, honestly evaluate your abilities. Perhaps you have the knowledge to accomplish some tasks, but no reliable helper for two-handed chores. Some other things must be left to professionals, regardless of the help available to you.

Depending on where you live, an architect may have to file your building permit. In some municipalities, *only* licensed electricians may be permitted to handle jobs related to wiring. There's a good reason for this stipulation: Some projects are too dangerous for the amateur to attempt, and this is not the time for on-the-job training.

If you decide to do some of the work yourself, plan on working at the beginning or end of the construction process. This way you can move at your own pace without holding up the subcontractors you've hired, which could increase the expense. For instance, do some of the demolition work, such as removing old cabinets and appliances, or some of the preparatory work, such as installing and taping drywall. Finishing work you should consider

might include painting and wallpapering, staining, or laying down vinyl tiles. Even some new kinds of hardwood flooring are designed for do-it-yourself installation.

If something is beyond your reach, either for lack of funds or lack of experience, put it off until you can handle it. Try to remodel the kitchen in stages. The project will take less of a bite out of your pocket this way, and in the end, you'll get the results you really want.

Each project begins by rating the level of difficulty of the task at hand. The level of difficulty is indicated by one, two, or three hammers:

Easy, even for beginners

Moderately difficult, but can be done by beginners who have the patience and willingness to learn

Difficult. Can be done by a do-it-yourselfer, but requires a serious investment in time, patience, and specialty tools. Consider hiring a specialist.

A list of tools and materials required for the work is also provided with each project. Certain tools are basic to most of the remodeling tasks described:

Basic Carpentry Tools

- Combination square
- Flat-bladed screwdriver
- Hammer
- Handsaw
- Measuring tape
- Pencil
- Phillips screwdriver
- Pliers
- Plumb bob
- Pry bar
- Spirit level
- Utility knife

To work on plumbing systems, you'll need other basic tools:

Basic Plumbing Tools

- Adjustable pliers
- Emery cloth
- Hacksaw

- Leather gloves
- Measuring tape
- Propane torch
- Round file
- Tubing bender
- Tubing cutter
- Wet towel

Almost all electrical work can be accomplished with the following assortment of tools:

Basic Electrical Tools

- Cable staples
- Hacksaw
- Hammer
- Electric drill and assorted bits
- Electrical tape
- Fish tape (for running cable through finished walls)
- Needle-nose pliers
- Plastic wire connectors
- Screwdrivers (flat-bladed and Phillips)
- Measuring tape
- Utility knife
- Voltage tester
- Wire stripper
- End nippers

Immediately following the tools and materials list for each project, step-by-step instructions show how to execute the work. Follow the directions to complete the project successfully.

Before starting any project in the book, check with your local building inspector. Also consult national, state, and local codes for any restrictions or requirements.

Make safety a priority. Wear goggles, rubber gloves, and nose and mouth protection. When working with electricity, always turn off the power at the main service panel and be sure the circuit is completely dead before you begin.

5

Projects:
Construction Basics

Your plans are set. Appliances, cabinets, and other components are on order. Now it's time to tear out your old kitchen and prepare for a new one.

If the kitchen is the heart of a home, remodeling might be compared to open-heart surgery. Prepare to live with dust, noise, and disorder for some time. Rather than go hungry or go broke on restaurants, you might set up a temporary kitchen, in the dining room, for example. Move the refrigerator there, and set up a cooking station with a microwave and toaster oven. Use a nearby bathroom as a water supply. Of course, you'll have to adjust your menu accordingly.

Kitchen Deconstruction

Removing the Sink

Shut off the water supply and open the faucets to drain residual water in the supply lines. Use a wrench to disconnect the trap from the sink tailpiece. Loosen nuts on supply lines with an adjustable wrench. Unscrew the sink-mounting lugs, if there are any, and lift up the sink, faucets and all.

Removing Counters & Cabinets

Once they're empty, you'll be surprised at how easily counters and cabinets come out. In most cases you simply unscrew counters from underneath, lift them off, then remove screws that hold the cabinets to each other and to the wall, as shown at right.

If a long counter proves unwieldy, cut it in two with a reciprocating saw or saber saw. Once the old cabinets and counters are free, get them out of the way, then attack the flooring.

Removing Flooring

Forget about trying to salvage old flooring. Break up hard-surface tile by whacking it with a heavy hammer

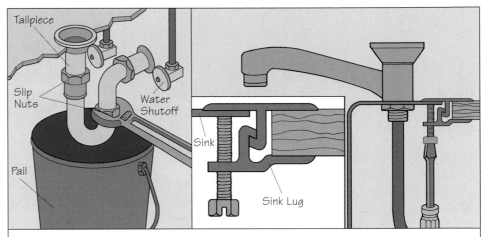

Removing the Sink. Close the shutoffs; disconnect the water supply lines (left). Remove the trap (tape the wrench jaws to avoid marring the slip nuts). Many sinks clamp to the counter with lugs, as shown. Unscrew any lugs (right), lift the sink clear, and remove it entirely.

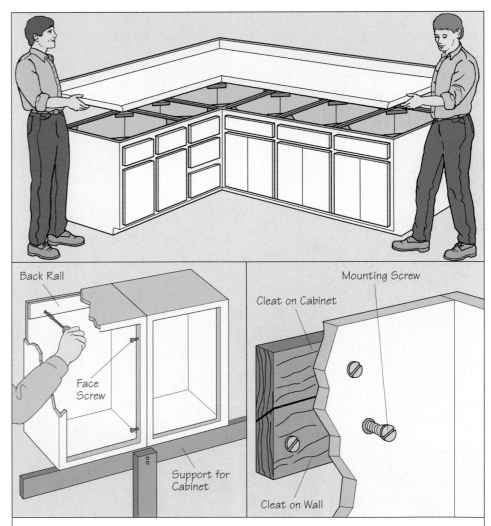

Removing Counters and Cabinets. Look up from underneath and you'll find screws holding a countertop to the corners of base cabinets. Remove the screws and maneuver the countertop free (top). Remove any screws that hold the base cabinets to the walls. Support the wall cabinets as you remove screws that fasten the sides together and hold the back to the wall (above left). Some cabinets hang on cleats (above right). Remove the mounting screws and lift the cabinets free. If there is a filler (soffit) above, remove it first.

or sledge, then scrape the pieces from the subfloor with a garden spade. Slit linoleum and resilient sheet goods with a utility knife, work a spade underneath, then peel up the flooring.

Old asphalt tile can be especially tenacious. If you can't work a chisel or spade underneath a tile, soften it with a heat lamp or electric iron.

CAUTION: Don't use a torch; you might set fire to subflooring.

Removing Framing

There are two basic types of walls in every house, and it is essential that you identify each one before attempting to remove it. If you skip this step you risk injury to yourself and serious damage to your house.

Bearing Walls. A wall that supports structural loads (such as a floor, a roof, or another wall above) and helps to transmit those loads to the foundation of the house is a bearing wall. Except for gable walls, most exterior walls are bearing walls. Usually a wall that runs lengthwise through the center of a house is a bearing wall and joists along each side of the house rest on it. Bearing walls sometimes can be spotted from the attic; they are the ones

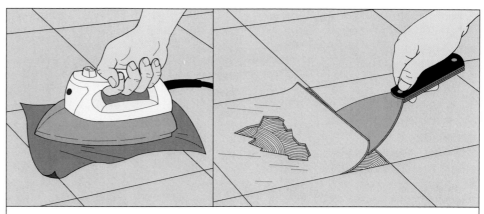

Removing Flooring. Use a hot iron to soften adhesive under resilient tiles or sheet flooring (left). Remove damaged tile with a putty knife (right). Break up hard-surface floor coverings with a sledge and chip away pieces with a spade or chisel.

holding up the ends of joists (particularly where two sets of joist ends overlap). You may also be able to identify bearing walls from the basement. Look for walls that rest atop a beam or a basement wall. If you are not sure about the kind of wall you are dealing with, the safest thing to do is assume that it is a bearing wall. In order to remove bearing walls safely, you have to identify all the loads involved and provide alternate support for them. Seek professional advice from a builder or engineer when a bearing wall must be removed.

Non-Bearing Walls. Non-bearing walls, also called partition walls,

support only the wall covering attached to them. Usually a non-bearing wall can be removed without affecting the structural integrity of the house. If a wall does not support joist ends and does not lie directly beneath a post, it may be a non-bearing wall. Walls that run parallel to ceiling joists usually are non-bearing walls.

Wiring and Plumbing. Before removing a wall, check the area immediately above and beneath it from the attic and basement, if possible. Look for wires, pipes, or ducts that lead into the wall. There is no way to tell for sure how big the job is until the drywall or plaster is

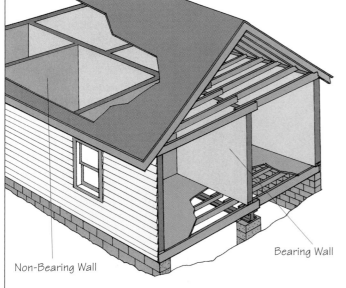

Bearing Walls. Before removing a wall, determine whether or not it is a bearing wall. Look for clues such as lapped joists above. Walls that are parallel to the attic joists usually are not load bearing.

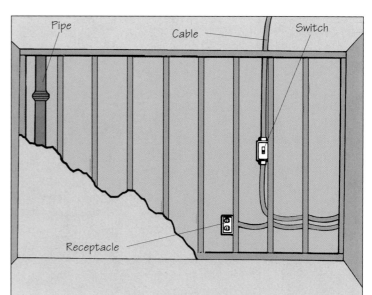

Wiring and Plumbing. Plumbing and wiring are two commonly encountered obstructions within a wall. Examine the wall from the attic and the basement to get a clue as to the utilities' locations.

pulled from at least one side of the wall. Wiring is easy to relocate, but plumbing supply piping (hot and cold water pipes) is more difficult. Plumbing vent pipes are trickier still, primarily because of code requirements that restrict their placement. Heating ducts and drainpipes are the toughest of all to relocate. Consult a professional if you are unsure of what to do. With luck, the wall you open up contains nothing but dust.

1. Pry off all wood trim with a pry bar. If you want to salvage the trim, insert wood shims as you move along the length of each piece to keep the trim from breaking in two.

Gutting a Wall or Ceiling

Think twice before you tear into a wall or ceiling. The work almost always adds up to more than you bargained for at the outset, and the dust and debris somehow finds its way into all corners of the house—even if you take heroic measures to contain it. Still, there are many unavoidable conditions that necessitate pulling off the tile, plaster, or drywall, if not over the entire wall, at least in the area of operation. New fixtures may require new piping. Extensive rewiring may be called for. You may want to insulate the wall and install a vapor barrier. Finally, the old substrate may be showing the effects of years of dampness.

Before you begin, take measures to protect yourself and the house from the stuff that will come loose. Wear gloves, protective eyewear, heavy shoes, and a hard hat. If you buy a hard hat, look for one with built-in eye and ear protectors. Ear protectors can prevent hearing loss caused by exposure to noisy power tools.

Keep the door to the area of operations closed. Line the path to the outdoors with tarps. If the room has an outside window, set-ting up a chute leading from the window into a dumpster or trash can will save you from carting the debris out through the house.

Difficulty Level: ⚒ ⚒ *to* ⚒ ⚒ ⚒

Tools and Materials
- [ ] Basic carpentry tools
- [ ] Adjustable pliers
- [ ] Adjustable wrench
- [ ] Masonry chisel (for plaster)

1 **Prepare the Work Site.** Turn off the circuit breaker that controls the room's power. If you will be relocating plumbing fixtures or working on walls containing pipes, make sure the water supply has been shut off before proceeding. Take down any pictures, mirrors, plants, switch plates, outlet cover plates, and heating grilles. Remove any cabinets mounted in or on the wall. Pull off door and window trim and baseboards with a pry bar. Tap the short end of the bar under the trim with a hammer, then push the bar to lever the trim away from the wall.

2 **Remove the Drywall or Plaster.** Bang a starter hole through old drywall with the claw end of a hammer or the pry bar tapped with a hammer. Use the

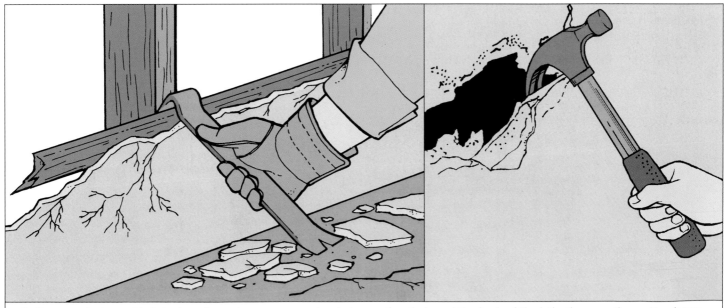

2. Remove plaster and lath by inserting a hammer or pry bar between the studs and the back of the lath; then pry the section loose (left). Tear out drywall by using the claw end of a hammer; remove all nails as you go (right).

claw of the hammer or pry bar to pull off one large chunk at a time. Remove all nails as you go. Protect your hands with gloves when removing the metal trim edges.

Break plaster walls apart with a hammer. Whack a hole through the plaster, to begin, then pull out a piece of lath near the top. Insert the claw of your hammer or a pry bar between the lath and studs near the top, and pry away lath and plaster pieces in one operation. Finally,

1. Use a sledge hammer to loosen one stud at a time. Use light force; you will not be able to reuse the lumber if it becomes damaged.

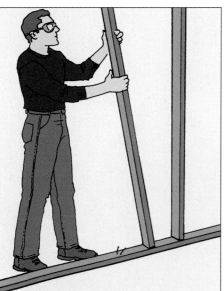

2. Twist each stud away from the top wall plate. Be careful not to step on nails that protrude through the bottom plate.

remove all nails, leaving the studs exposed and clean.

CAUTION: You risk damaging pipes and electrical wiring when you poke into walls and ceilings, so take extra care around areas where you suspect these items might exist. Also cover openings in heating ducts and exposed drains to keep chunks of debris from falling into them.

Removing a Non-Bearing Wall

Difficulty Level:

Tools and Materials
- [ ] Basic carpentry tools
- [ ] Sledge hammer
- [ ] Wrecking bar

1 **Loosening the Studs.** After stripping the wallcovering from both sides and relocating utilities, use a sledge to force the bottom of each stud away from the nails that hold it in place. Proceed cautiously until you get the feel for how much force is required.

2 **Removing Studs.** Once the bottom is loose, grasp the stud and push it first sideways, and then outwards and back and

3. Use a wrecking bar to lever up the bottom plate. Remove all debris promptly to avoid tripping over it.

forth to work the top nails loose until you can remove the stud. Cut and remove one stud at a time or you will find yourself assaulted by a dangling row of severed 2x4s. As you work, hammer over nails that protrude from the bottom plate. This way they cannot puncture your foot as you work on the next stud.

3 **Prying off Plates.** Use a wrecking bar to remove the end studs, and then the top and bottom plates. Nails may be located anywhere along the length of each end stud.

Building Partition Walls

You may need to build a wall or walls to separate certain areas in a kitchen, say for dining. A partition wall extends to the ceiling, dividing the room space. It does not, however, play a role in the sturctural integrity of the house. Usually any walls used in a kitchen are not large, so they can be built one at a time on the subfloor and tipped into place. If space is limited, though, you may have to piece the wall together in place.

Difficulty Level:

Tools and Materials
- [ ] Basic carpentry tools
- [ ] Framing square
- [ ] Chalkline
- [ ] Framing lumber
- [ ] Circular or power miter saw
- [ ] 10d, 12d, 16d nails
- [ ] 4-foot level

Using the Tip-Up Method

Most partition walls are built with 2x4 lumber and most have a single top and bottom plate. If a wall contains the drain line for plumbing fixtures, however, you might want to use 2x6s to frame it. Build the wall just short of the floor-to-ceiling height so you can tip it into place, then shim it at ceiling-joist locations when it's in position.

1 **Mark the Location.** Use a framing square to ensure square corners, and a chalkline to mark the exact location of the wall on the subfloor. If you are working alone, drive a nail partway into the subfloor to hold one end of the chalkline as you snap it. (Or, if you have one, have a helper hold one end.)

2 **Lay Out the Plates.** Cut two plates so that they are the same length as the wall. Align the plates and measure from one end, marking for studs at 16-inch intervals on center, the standard spacing for studs. Continue to the other end of the

plates even if the last stud is less than 16 inches from the end. To check your work, mark a point exactly 48 inches from the end of the plates. If done correctly, the mark will be centered on one of the stud locations.

3 **Cut the Studs.** Wall studs are cut to the height of the wall less ¼ inch twice the thickness of the lumber (to account for tip-up space and the thickness of the plates). Count the number of layout marks to get an estimate of the number of studs needed. Then cut the studs square.

4 **Build the Frame.** Separate the plates by the length of a stud and set them on edge with the layout marks facing each other. Lay all the studs in approximate position, then drive a pair of 16d nails through each plate into the ends of each stud. Use the marks to align the studs precisely.

5 **Form a Corner.** To provide a nailing surface for the drywall, add an extra stud to each end of the wall that is part of an outside corner. One method of building the corner involves nailing spacers between two studs, then butting the end stud of the adjacent wall to this triple-width assembly. Another method is to use a stud to form the inside corner of the wall. Use whichever method you find most convenient.

6 **Raise the Wall.** Slide the bottom plate into approximate position according to the subfloor layout lines. Then lift the wall upright. With a helper to prevent the wall from toppling over, align the bottom plate with the layout lines made in Step 1. When you are satisfied with the location of the wall, shim the top plate and nail a pair of 16d nails every 24 inches or so through the bottom plate into the subfloor (into joists wherever possible). If the ceiling in the room

1. Lay out the position of the walls using a framing square and a chalk-line. Mark an X on the side of the line that will be covered by the plate.

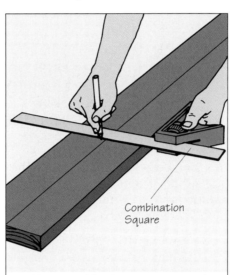

2. Use a combination square to mark the position of each stud on the plates. By marking the plates simultaneously, you can be sure the layouts match.

3. Use a circular saw to cut each stud to fit exactly between the plates. Stud length is the wall height minus 3¼ in.

4. Using 16d nails, attach the studs and plates, keeping them aligned and flush. Blunted nail tips will not split the plate.

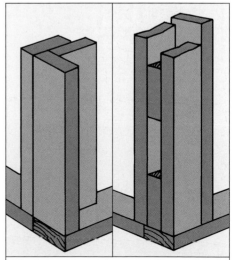

5. Corners must have a nailing surface for drywall. The left method requires less lumber; the one on the right uses up scraps.

6. When raising a wall, tip it fully upright and slide it into position according to layout marks.

7. Use a level to plumb the wall. Check several places on the wall as you nail the top plate.

8. As you join walls, consider how the drywall will be installed. Add extra framing or blocking if necessary.

below is made of plaster, use long screws rather than nails to fasten the plate. Using screws prevents the ceiling from cracking.

7 **Plumb the Wall.** Use a carpenter's level to ensure that the wall is plumb. Adjust the frame as necessary, and nail through the top plate and shim into the ceiling framing or into blocking if the wall is running parallel to the ceiling framing.

8 **Join Intersecting Walls.** In the places where walls intersect, you will need additional studs to provide support for drywall. Add a single stud to the end of the intersecting wall and a pair of studs on the other wall.

Building a Wall in Place

When there is not enough room to assemble a complete stud wall in the confines of the subfloor, the wall must be built in place. Slip each stud between the top and bottom plates.

1 **Install the Top Plate.** Cut both plates to the length of the wall and mark them for the position of the studs (16 inches on center). Determine the location of the top of the wall and hold the top plate up there, making sure the stud layout faces down so you can see it. Then use a 16d nail to attach the top plate to each intersecting joist.

2 **Locate the Bottom Plate.** To transfer the location of the plate to the subfloor, hang a plumb bob from the top plate in several successive locations, marking them as you go. Align the bottom plate with the layout marks, adjusting it until you are sure that it is directly below the top plate. Then use pairs of 16d nails to nail it to

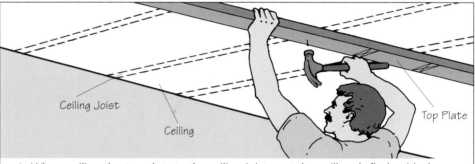

1. When nailing the top plate to the ceiling joists, set the nailheads flush with the surface of the plate; otherwise, you may have trouble fitting studs into place. Check that the plate is straight as you work.

2. Use a plumb bob to position the bottom plate, then nail it to the subfloor. Transfer stud locations from the top plate to the bottom plate in the same way.

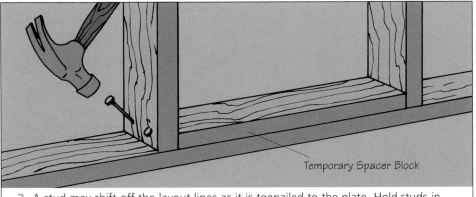

3. A stud may shift off the layout lines as it is toenailed to the plate. Hold studs in place with a temporary spacer block. Make sure the nail does not poke through the other side of the stud.

the subfloor. Keep the nails away from the stud locations already marked on the plate.

3 **Install the Studs.** Measure between the plates at each stud location and cut studs to fit. Place a stud in position against the layout marks and use 12d nails to toenail it to each plate. Make toenailing a bit easier by using a spacer block to keep the stud from shifting. Cut the block to fit exactly between studs. If the stud spacing is 16 inches on center and the studs are 1½ inches thick, the block will be 14½ inches long. Remove the spacer as successive studs are toenailed.

Installing Doors & Door Framing

The framing around doors in partition walls is fairly simple to build because the partitions are not load bearing and there is no need for a structural header above the door. Many do-it-yourselfers find prehung doors easiest to install; they can be installed whether or not a structural header is in place. These factory-assembled units eliminate some rather fussy carpentry work. Because the size of the rough opening depends on the size of the door and its frame, however, purchase the door before you frame the wall. The rough opening generally is ½ inch wider and ¼ inch taller than the outside dimensions of the jamb.

Installing Drywall

Drywall, also called wallboard, is an amazing material that largely replaced plaster in houses built after World War II. It has a core of gypsum plaster that is sandwiched between two layers of paper.

Drywall comes in sheets that are 48 inches wide. Sheets are available in lengths from 8 to 16 feet in 24-inch increments. Sheets come in thicknesses of ¼, ⅜, ½, and ⅝ inch. For studs spaced 16 inches apart or less, use ½-inch drywall. Use ⅝-inch thickness if the studs are spaced 24 inches. In some old houses, studs are spaced still wider or are irregular. In that case, support the drywall by 1x3 or 2x4 furring strips, nailed horizontally across the studs at 16- or 24-inch spacing.

Before you begin, make sure the framing is straight and rigid. You can attach wood shims to concave sections of framing to bring the framing out to the desired line. Studs that can't be corrected with shims should be pulled out and replaced. Mark stud locations on the floor, so you will know where to sink nails or screws.

Difficulty Level: 🔨🔨

Tools and Materials

☐ Basic carpentry tools
☐ Keyhole saw
☐ 48-inch aluminum drywall T-square (or straightedge)
☐ Electric drill with screwdriver bit (if you use screws)
☐ Drywall nails or galvanized drywall screws long enough to penetrate at least ¾ inch into the framing

1 **Mark and Cut the Drywall.** Measure the height of the wall and width of the stud bays you want to cover with a single sheet. You can install drywall vertically or horizontally. Vertical installation may be easier to install if you are working alone. To prevent cracks, avoid making joints directly next to doors and windows. Mark the sheet with a straightedge. Draw the utility knife against the straightedge to score the paper facing, being careful to keep your other hand out of the path of the knife.

2 **Snap the Joint in Two.** Slip a length of lumber under the cut line and gently push down on

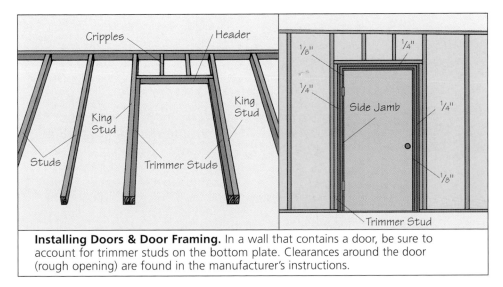

Installing Doors & Door Framing. In a wall that contains a door, be sure to account for trimmer studs on the bottom plate. Clearances around the door (rough opening) are found in the manufacturer's instructions.

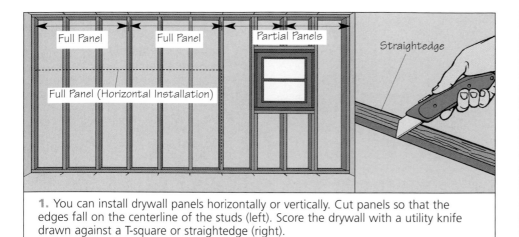

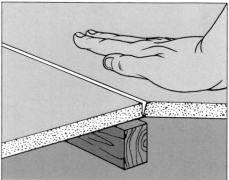

1. You can install drywall panels horizontally or vertically. Cut panels so that the edges fall on the centerline of the studs (left). Score the drywall with a utility knife drawn against a T-square or straightedge (right).

2. Insert a piece of lumber below the scored line and push down to snap the joint in two.

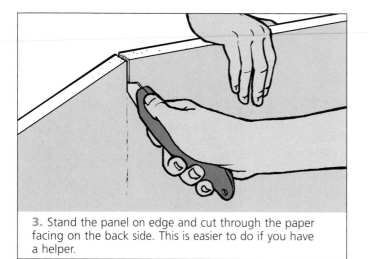

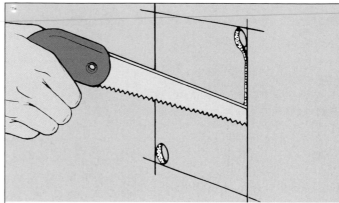

3. Stand the panel on edge and cut through the paper facing on the back side. This is easier to do if you have a helper.

4. Bore holes at opposite corners of each cutout and cut the piece out with a keyhole saw. You can avoid drilling the corners by making several passes along each edge with a utility knife.

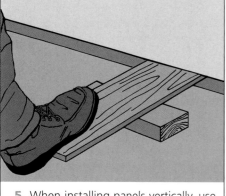

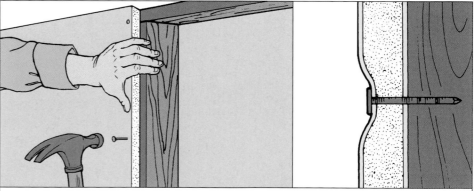

5. When installing panels vertically, use two pieces of wood, set up as shown, to lever the panels against the ceiling.

6. Nail or screw the drywall to the framing at 6-inch intervals around the edges and at 12-inch intervals in the center (left). Drive fasteners just enough to dimple the facing paper (right).

one side to snap the drywall panel apart, separating the cut through the thickness, but not through the backing paper.

3 **Cut through the Backing Paper.** Turn the panel up on edge, fold the two cut pieces slightly together, and slice through the paper backing to complete the

cut. This step is easier if someone else holds the drywall at the top.

4 **Make Any Necessary Cutouts.** Cut openings for plumbing and electrical protrusions with a keyhole saw. Start by drilling holes in the corners of the shapes or by making repeated passes with the utility knife.

5 **Position the Drywall on the Studs.** Positioning the panels is easier if you have a helper to hold the panel in place while you attach it. If you are installing the panels vertically, cut their lengths about ¾ inch shorter than the wall height. Place the panel against the wall and use a foot lever, as shown, to push the panel up snug to the ceiling structure. Don't worry about the gap at the floor. It will be covered by base molding.

6 Attach the Drywall to the Studs. Have a helper hold the panel against the wall (use your shoulder if you're working alone) as you use your foot to push the drywall snug against the framing and drive a few nails or screws to hold it in place. Drive nails or screws around the edge, spaced 6 inches or less, and into each stud, spaced 12 inches apart. Sink the fasteners to dimple—but not break—the facing paper.

Finishing Drywall

Drywall intended as a base for wall-covering or paint should be finished with drywall tape and joint compound. The compound should be sanded smooth because even the smallest dents and ridges show through paint, especially paint with a glossy sheen. For a top-notch job, plan on applying joint compound in three stages, sanding the surface after each application. Drywall meant to receive tile simply needs to be taped with one coat of compound.

Difficulty Level: 🔩🔩 to 🔩🔩🔩

Tools and Materials
☐ Utility knife
☐ 6-inch-wide drywall knife
☐ 12-inch-wide drywall knife
☐ 100-grit sandpaper
☐ Mud pan (or an old loaf pan from the kitchen)
☐ Tin snips (if you need to cut metal corner bead)
☐ Ready-mix joint compound
☐ Perforated paper tape or fiberglass mesh tape
☐ Metal corner bead (only if outside corners are present)
☐ Pole sander with swivel head and 100-grit sandpaper inserts (optional)

1 Fill the Mud Pan. Open the container of joint compound. If liquid has separated from the rest of the material, stir it in. Use your 6-inch-wide knife to put a working gob of compound into your mud pan.

2 Fill the Drywall Joint. Begin by applying compound to a joint with the 6-inch knife. Force the compound down into the tapered drywall joints to fill them level with the wall. At butt joints, where the nontapered ends of two

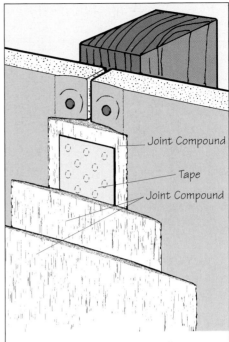

Finishing Drywall. A drywall joint contains paper or fiberglass mesh tape embedded into joint compound. Two or more coats of compound, sanded smooth, ensure a seamless appearance.

panels join, fill the crack and create a slight hump. This hump will be finished flat later.

3 Embed Tape into the Joint Compound. Cut a length of joint tape and, beginning at the top,

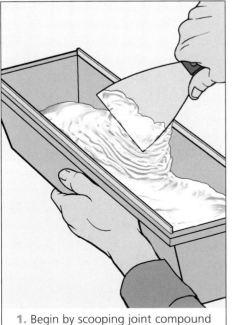

1. Begin by scooping joint compound out of the bucket and into a mud pan (or an old loaf pan).

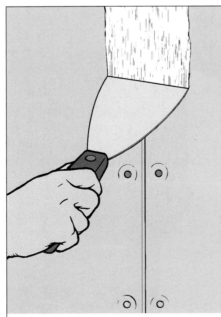

2. Fill the joint with compound to a thickness of about 1/8 inch.

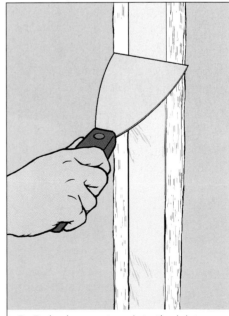

3. Embed paper tape into the joint with a 6-inch-wide knife, avoiding wrinkles. If using fiberglass tape, stick it to the joint before applying compound.

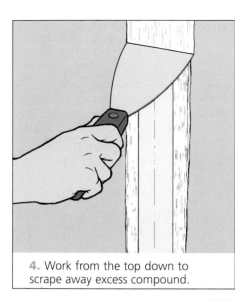

4. Work from the top down to scrape away excess compound.

place it over the compound-filled joint. Be sure to center the tape over the joint. Spread a thin layer (⅛ inch thick) of joint compound over the tape, holding the knife at a 45-degree angle.

NOTE: If you use self-adhering fiberglass mesh tape, apply the tape over the joint before you apply the first coat of compound. Fiberglass tape is stronger than paper tape and easier to apply. But because fiberglass won't give, the joints may work apart in time, enough to be noticeable. This is less likely with paper because it expands and

contracts along with the paper facing on the drywall.

4 **Remove the Excess Compound.** Go back over the joint with the drywall knife to scrape away any excess compound. Clean the knife against the edge of your mud pan.

5 **Tape the Inside Corners.** If you are using paper tape, start by filling both sides of the inside corner joints. Fold a length of paper tape along its center-line and place it over the joint. The tape is precreased for this purpose. Finally, spread a thin

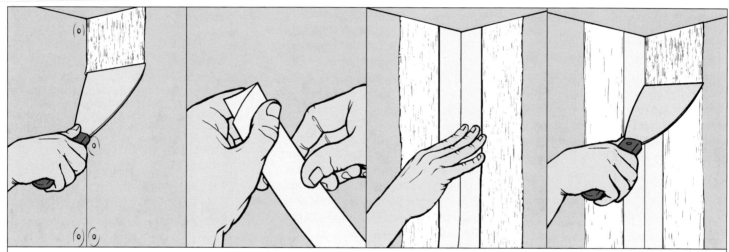

5. Start finishing inside corners by filling both sides with joint compound, to about ⅛ inch thick (left). If you're using fiberglass tape, put the tape on the joint before applying compound. Fold paper tape by creasing it along the prescored centerline (second from left). Press the folded tape into joint compound at the corner (second from right). Apply compound to both sides of the tape. Be sure to remove the excess compound (right).

6. Nail a metal corner bead over any outside corners (left). Fill the corner with joint compound, using the raised bead edge as a guide (right).

7. Fill all dimples and dents with joint compound.

layer of compound over the tape. If you are using mesh tape, apply it first then fill the joint. Remove the excess compound.

6 **Fix a Metal Bead to the Outside Corners.** If you have any outside corners, use tin snips to cut a length of metal corner bead to the wall height. Angle the cut ends inward a little to ensure a better fit. Nail the bead to the wall with dry-wall nails. Fill the edges with joint compound, using the bead to guide your knife.

7 **Fill in the Nail (or Screw) Dimples.** Fill all nail (and/or screw) holes and dimples with joint compound.

8. Sand the compound between applications. To make sanding easier, use a pole sander.

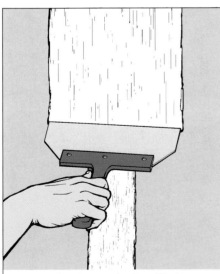

9. Finish joints and other filled areas with a wide-blade drywall knife.

8 **Sand the Joint Compound Smooth.** After 24 hours or when the compound is completely dry, sand all joints and dimples smooth. Fix a sheet of 100-grit sandpaper into your pole sander, if you have one. If you are hand sanding, use a sheet of sandpaper folded into quarters.

9 **Apply the Finish Coats of Compound.** Use a wide (12-inch) drywall knife to apply a second coat of compound to the joints and dimples. Sand again and repeat as necessary until you have a completely smooth surface.

Installing Roof Windows & Skylights

Installing a roof window or skylight is possible for most do-it yourselfers, but before deciding to go ahead, be sure you are up to the task. You may need to do some of the work inside a cramped attic and you'll do part of it crawling around on the roof. If you build a light shaft between the roof and ceiling, you're in for measuring and cutting framing and finish materials that have tricky angles.

When you have selected your sky-light or roof window, read and follow the manufacturer's instructions. The steps below cover some things not always included in the instructions.

Difficulty Level: 🔨 🔨 🔨

Tools and Materials
- ☐ Basic carpentry tools
- ☐ Electric drill
- ☐ Goggles
- ☐ Roofing compound
- ☐ White chalk
- ☐ Adjustable bevel gauge
- ☐ Framing lumber (as needed)
- ☐ Framing anchors
- ☐ 12d and 16d common nails
- ☐ Hard hat
- ☐ Circular saw with carbide-tipped blade
- ☐ Keyhole saw (or reciprocating saw)
- ☐ Aluminum step flashing (comes in bundles of 100)

Opening the Ceiling

1 **Make a Test Hole.** Use a key-hole saw to cut out a piece of the ceiling about 2 feet square near the center of where you think the shaft opening will be. Standing on a ladder and armed with a flashlight, go up through the test hole and inspect the roof and ceiling framing to determine the final opening location.

2 **Locate and Mark the Opening.** When you crawl through your test hole, be sure to explore the ceiling and roof framing. Locate the final ceiling

1. Begin by cutting an exploratory hole in the ceiling just large enough to crawl through.

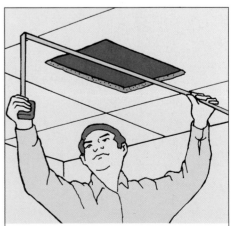

2. When you have determined the best position for the ceiling opening with respect to the framing, transfer the dimensions to the ceiling below.

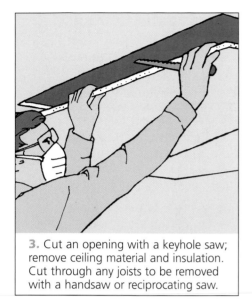

3. Cut an opening with a keyhole saw; remove ceiling material and insulation. Cut through any joists to be removed with a handsaw or reciprocating saw.

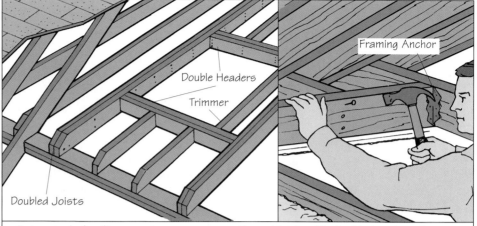

Double Headers

Trimmer

Doubled Joists

Framing Anchor

4. In a typical ceiling opening, span across the cut joists with double headers, then put in trimmers as necessary to achieve the desired width (left). Nail the headers to the ends of cut ceiling joists. Connect the headers to the sides of ceiling joists with framing anchors (right).

opening to minimize your rework of the framing.

3 **Make the Full Ceiling Opening.** Mark the final opening on the ceiling. Cut the outline with a keyhole saw, and remove the ceiling finish. Cut through joists with a handsaw or reciprocating saw. Wear protective head- and eye-wear while working overhead. Do not cut through roof trusses. Cut through other framing if you are sure you won't be damaging the roof structure. You may need to support cut joists temporarily while modifying the framing.

4 **Frame Out the Ceiling Opening.** If you remove joists, provide double joists at the sides to compensate. Install double header joists across the opening at both ends. Use two pieces of lumber the same width as the ceiling framing. Then install trimmer joists to close in the sides of the hole to the final dimensions. Use 12d common nails. To provide a better connection than toenailing, use L-shaped framing anchors— 4-inch anchors for 2x4s, 6-inch anchors for 2x6s, etc.

Cutting the Roof Opening

1 **Mark Out the Roof Opening.** Hang a plumb bob from the underside of the roof to each corner of the opening in the ceiling and mark the positions. These marks indicate the corners of the rough opening to be cut through the roof.

2 **Drive Pilot Nails.** Drive a pilot nail up through the roof sheathing at each corner of the opening. The corners should fall on the inside of the skylight curb framing, described in Step 3, page 91.

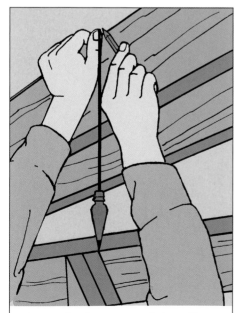

1. Transfer the corners of the ceiling opening to the underside of the roof with a plumb bob.

2. Drive a nail through each corner to locate the cutout on the top of the roof.

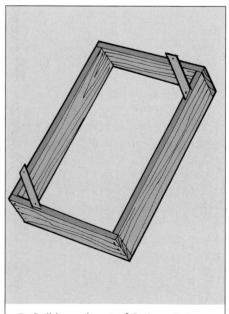

3. Build a curb out of 2x4s or 2x6s. Nail lumber scraps over two or more corners for temporary bracing.

4. After marking the outline of the skylight opening on the roof with chalk, cut asphalt shingles away with a utility knife.

5. Cut through shingles and roof sheathing with a circular saw fitted with a carbide-tipped blade. Use a board to guide your cut. Be sure to protect your eyes.

3 **Build the Curb.** Some prefabricated skylights and roof windows mount on top of wood curbs. Build a curb out of 2x4s or 2x6s to the size indicated in the manufacturer's instructions. Square and brace two opposite corners. Take the assembly up to the roof and center it over the nails poking through from below. Mark the outline of the curb on the roof with a piece of white chalk.

4 **Cut the Asphalt Shingles.** Cut asphalt shingles with a utility knife to bare the roof sheathing below.

5 **Cut Wood Shingles and/or the Sheathing.** Use a circular saw to cut the opening through the roof sheathing. When you cut through the shingles, place a board below the saw. This enables the saw to glide forward without bumping into the bottom of the shingles. Whenever you cut through shingles, you will probably hit nails, so be prepared to sacrifice the saw blade.

CAUTION: Wear protective goggles whenever you use a circular saw, especially when cutting through roofing.

Installing the Unit

1 **Frame the Roof Opening.** Reinforce the rafters at the sides of the openings and install double headers in the same way you framed the ceiling opening.

See Step 4, "Frame Out the Ceiling Opening," on page 90.

2 **Install the Skylight or Roof Window.** Follow the manufacturer's instructions for installing the window. Secure it in only one

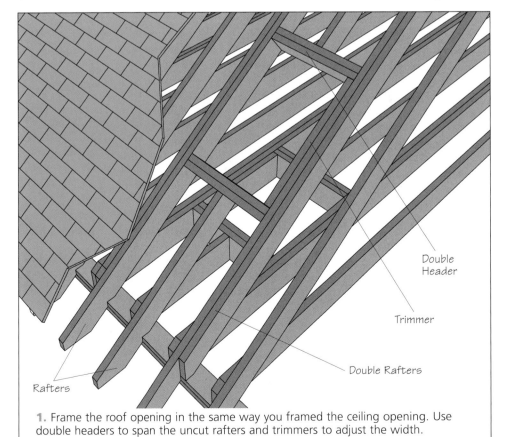

Double Header

Trimmer

Double Rafters

Rafters

1. Frame the roof opening in the same way you framed the ceiling opening. Use double headers to span the uncut rafters and trimmers to adjust the width.

2. Mount the skylight or roof window according to the manufacturer's instructions.

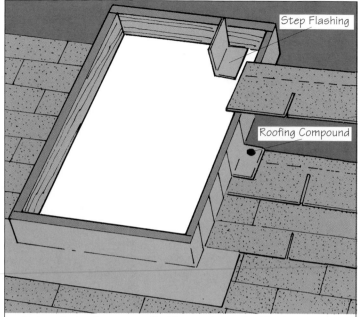

3. Install aluminum step flashing under each shingle as you go, applying a bed of roofing compound over each layer.

place until you have made sure that the window is properly aligned. If it is not straight, you'll likely notice it when you trim out the inside.

3 **Flash the Curb and Repair the Roofing.** Replace the shingles, installing lengths of aluminum step flashing as you go. Aluminum step flashing comes in packages of precut pieces. Interweave one flashing piece to overlap and under-lap each successive shingle, as shown. Apply roofing compound under flashing and shingles.

4 **Complete the Shaft.** Frame the sides of the shaft with 2x4s. Measure the angles with an adjustable bevel gauge. Cut the angles accurately. A circular saw makes this easier. Insulate the sides with fiberglass; carefully cut to fit between the framing. After insulating, staple a sheet of 6-mil polyethylene over the inside face of the studs for a vapor barrier. Use silicone caulk to seal the sheet to the existing ceiling barrier or backside of the ceiling drywall if there is no barrier. Finally, apply drywall as described in "Installing Drywall," page 85. Apply wood trim, if necessary, at the joint between the roof window and drywall.

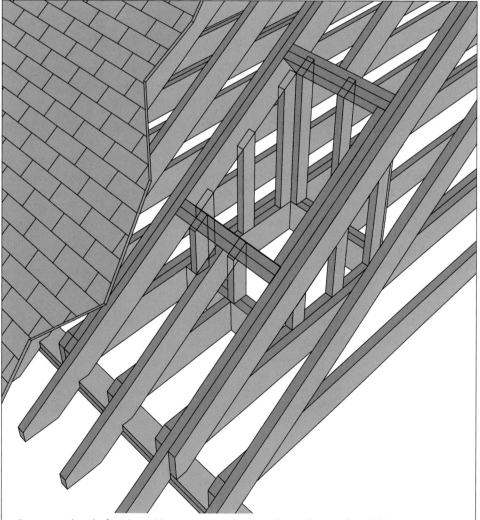

4. Frame the shaft sides with 2x4s, measuring angles with an adjustable bevel gauge. Insulate the sides with fiberglass, then staple a 6-mil poly sheet over inside face of studs.

Kitchen Plumbing Basics

Compared with the systems of pipes that carry water to and from a bathroom, a kitchen's plumbing needs are relatively simple: hot and cold water supply lines and a drainpipe where you plan to install the sink. If you'll be installing a gas range, the gas line routed to its location is also considered plumbing. All of your kitchen's other water users—waste disposer, dishwasher, water purifier, ice maker—tie into the same lines that serve the sink.

With luck, you already have supply and drain lines at or near the place where you'll put the sink. If not and you plan to move the sink more than a couple of feet, prepare for a sizable (and costly) plumbing project.

Explaining all the plumbing materials and skills needed to do your own plumbing work is beyond the scope of this book. However, an understanding of kitchen plumbing basics can help you deal knowledgeably with a plumbing contractor or indicate the plumbing procedures with which you'll need to become familiar.

Reviewing Kitchen Plumbing Anatomy

Hot and cold water come to a sink through a pair of supply lines made of copper, brass, plastic, or galvanized steel. If your kitchen was originally plumbed with steel, the pipes should be replaced. Galvanized steel hasn't been used in homes for about 45 years, and that's just about how long it lasts.

Because supply lines are small in diameter and the water flows under pressure, supply lines are easily rerouted. That's not so with drain lines, which depend on gravity. Water exits the sink through a curved trap, and a small amount retained in the trap forms an airtight seal that prevents sewer gases from leaking into the house.

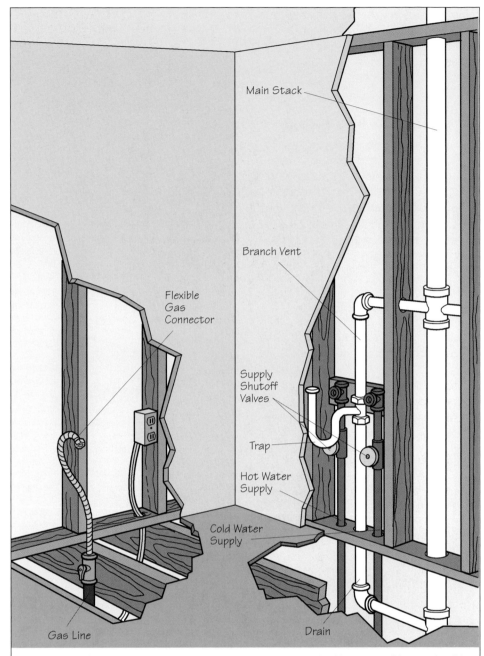

Reviewing Kitchen Plumbing Anatomy. Water is supplied by a set of hot and cold water pipes, each equipped with a shutoff valve. Appliances needing water, such as a dishwasher, are usually supplied by a branch from a sink line, but may have a separate line. Water leaves through a trap, which is connected to a vented drain line that empties into the main stack. The vent ensures that some water always fills the U portion of the trap, to block the backflow of sewer gas. A dishwasher and a waste disposer drain into the sink trap in most kitchens. The gas supply for a range usually comes up through the floor. A flexible connector provides some latitude in hooking up the range.

The trap in turn connects to a drainpipe. Waste water from the trap drops down the drain to a larger pipe called a stack, which probably also serves one or more of your home's bathrooms. An upper extension of the drain, known as a vent, also connects to the stack, which rises as a main vent through the roof to expel gases and prevent suction that could siphon water from the trap.

Plumbing codes restrict the distance a sink's trap can be located from its drain/vent line. The distance varies somewhat from one community to another, but don't plan on moving the sink more than about 36 inches without having to break into the wall and extend branch lines. You may even need to add an entirely new stack from basement to roof.

Bringing Gas to a Range

Compared with water piping, gas lines are simple and easy for even an amateur to work with. Gas travels through black iron pipes threaded together with couplers, elbows, and tees. Home centers sell lengths of pipe in a variety of sizes that you can juggle to take a gas line almost anywhere you'd like it to go. Consult a comprehensive plumbing how-to manual before undertaking a gas piping project. And remember always to test your installation after turning the gas back on by brushing all connections with soapy water; if the solution bubbles, tighten that connection. (To learn about hooking up a gas range, see "Range Installation" on page 187.)

Installing Shutoffs

Now, while your kitchen is devoid of cabinets, is the time to make sure all water and gas supply lines are equipped with shutoff valves. The valves enable you to hook up a sink and range without shutting down water and gas to the rest of your home.

Water shutoffs—sometimes called fixture stops—are made of plastic, copper, or chrome-plated brass. Gas shutoffs are made of iron or cast brass. The drawings on the right depict your water and gas shutoff options.

Complying with Codes

If you plan extensive plumbing changes, you'll probably have to apply for a building permit. In some communities a licensed plumber must sign off on any plumbing work, meaning he or she takes responsibility for it. In others, an inspector checks a job twice— once while the walls are still open and again after all fixtures have been hooked up.

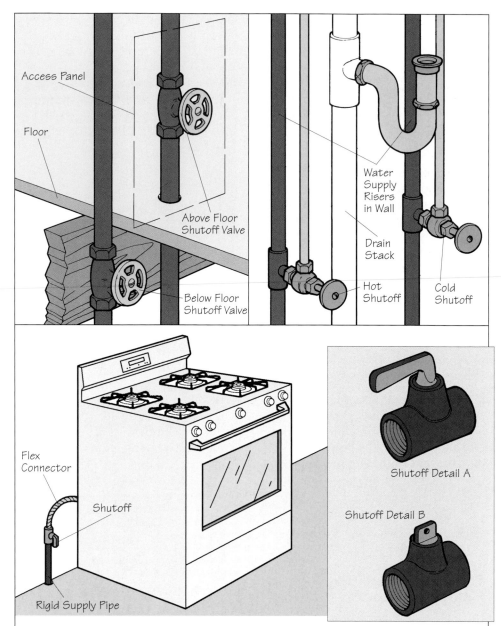

Installing Shutoffs. Straight-through water shutoff valves are best on pipes that come up through the floor. They may be hidden behind an access panel. Angled water shutoff valves are used when a tee or stub from a water supply line extends through a wall. With a lever-type gas shutoff (detail A), moving the lever 90 degrees, at a right angle to the pipe, stops gas flow. A key-style shutoff (detail B) must be operated with a wrench. The gas is off when the key is at a right angle to the pipe.

Wiring: Getting a Power Source

If your house is older than about 50 years, its electrical system is very likely outdated. Chances are that successive owners added bits and pieces over the years in no coherent fashion. Knowing this, you can choose to rewire the whole house or do it as you remodel various rooms. If you go room by room, at least make sure that the main electrical service is up to date and capable of carrying additional loads.

The main service consists of wires that come into the house from the outside and a main distribution center inside. If the system is up to current standards, the main service cable will contain three wires—two "hot," or "live," wires that carry 120 volts of electricity and one neutral wire. The cable is probably wrapped until it reaches the inside of the distribution center, or panel box. When you open the panel box, you can see that the cable separates into the three wires. The two hot wires feed a main breaker switch that shuts down power to the entire house, then goes on to supply power to branch circuits, each with its own cicuit breaker.

A short across any hot wire and a neutral or ground wire causes a sudden current overload. Unchecked, the overload would quickly burn off the wire's insulation and ignite any nearby combustible material. Circuit breakers or fuses protect against overloads by breaking the connection between the incoming electricity and the fault. Very old houses may be protected by a single fuse. When it blows, all power to the house shuts off. Even if your house has several fuses, consider replacing the fuse box with an updated panel and circuit breakers. It's much more convenient to flip the reset switch on a breaker than to replace a fuse.

Another item to consider for replacement is aluminum wiring. Aluminum may be used in the main service wires, but its use in branch circuits has been linked to an inordinate percentage of electrical fires, so if you spot it coming out of the panel, consider replacing it with copper. The National Electrical Code does not permit you to add new aluminum wiring.

Your kitchen lights and power outlets may be wired to a single circuit, protected by a 15- or 20-amp breaker in the panel. If you rewire or change around a few lighting fixtures or power outlets, you won't need to change the power source. If you add new devices, you may stand to overload the circuit, so get the advice of an electrician before proceeding.

Assuming the wiring is sound and you want to leave the wall finishes intact, you can replace a light fixture, switch, or outlet in the same location by simply removing the device and installing the new one. If you want to add an outlet or light, you can tap into the box of a previous fixture or come off a box containing an outlet. If you tap off an outlet box, you should replace the box with a larger one to contain the additional wiring.

New Wiring in Open Walls

Gutting floors, walls, or ceilings down to the framing gives you the opportunity to replace outdated wiring and to locate electrical fixtures just where you want them. The easiest kind of wiring to snake through the structure is plastic-sheathed, nonmetallic cable, called NM cable or sometimes by the brand name Romex. NM cable contains a black-sheathed (hot) wire, a white (neutral) wire, and a bare (ground) wire. Check with your electrical inspector to see which type and gauge of cable is acceptable for your project and by your local codes. As a rule of thumb, you will probably get by with 14-gauge cable for kitchen lights and outlets. Special equipment, such as disposers, dishwashers, and microwave ovens, will require 12-gauge or larger. Use the product literature as a guide.

Difficulty Level: 🔨

Tools and Materials
- ☐ Electric drill with ¾-inch bit
- ☐ Basic electrical tools
- ☐ Cable staples
- ☐ 5d nails
- ☐ Junction boxes, switch boxes
- ☐ Cable
- ☐ Metal stud plates (if needed)
- ☐ Hammer

Suiting the Box to the Task

Each switch, outlet, and light fixture must be installed into a metal or plastic box attached to the structure. Ask your building department which type of box is acceptable. Round or octagonal boxes are usually used for ceiling fixtures or junction boxes, boxes used to contain only wiring. Rectangular boxes usually contain switches or receptacles. You can choose among boxes that come with various types of fasteners, screws, nails, brackets, and clips suited for different conditions of new and existing construction.

The National Electrical Code limits how many wires you can install in any one box and does not permit any wire connections outside a box. A single switch or duplex (two-plug) outlet will fit into a 2½-inch wide box. More than one device in a box, or more wiring than needed just to serve the device, calls for a wider box. Use the chart below to determine the required box size.

Maximum Number of Wires Permitted Per Box

Type of Box (Size in Inches)	Wire Gauge		
	14	12	10
Round or Octagonal			
4x1½	7	6	6
4x2⅛	10	9	8
Square			
4x1½	10	9	8
4x2⅛	15	13	12
Rectangular Boxes			
3x2x2¼	5	4	4
3x2x2½	6	5	5
3x2x2¾	7	6	5
3x2x3½	9	8	7

1 **Install Boxes.** Before reworking any branch circuit, shut off the power to the circuit at the panel or fuse box. Begin your wiring by figuring out where you want the boxes to go and nailing them to the studs. Plastic boxes come with their own nails; use 5d nails for the flanges of metal boxes. Mount them so that the face of the box will be even with the finished wall surface. Switch boxes are usually mounted 48 inches above the floor, while outlets are mounted 12 to 18 inches above the floor. Mount boxes at any convenient height above a counter.

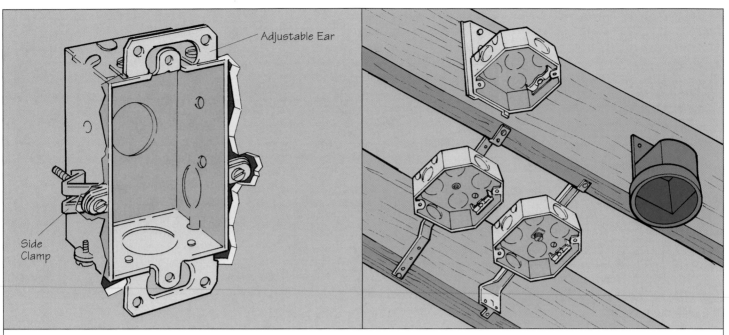

Suiting the Box to the Task. A metal box can be installed into an enclosed wall in one of two ways. First, a hole must be cut through the plaster or drywall and the box inserted. Then it can be secured by screws through the adjustable ears into the lath or by tightening screws at the sides (left). Ceiling boxes intended for fixtures and junction boxes are usually round or octagonal (group at right). Mounting methods include side clips (as with the metal and plastic boxes at the top) or offset hanger bars that can be adjusted to span between two joists (below).

2 **Drill Holes through the Studs.** Drill holes for the cable through the studs at least 1¼ inches back from the facing edge so they won't be punctured by nails or screws. If you can't drill, saw out notches of the same depth.

3 **Run the Cable through the Holes.** Starting from your power source (junction box) run the cable from outlet box to outlet box and run branches to the light fixture boxes. Leave 6 inches or so of cable ends poking out of the box to give you enough wire to connect the devices later. Where cable runs up studs, and just above or below each box, use a hammer to attach cable staples or clips to the studs. Use staples made for attaching electrical cable.

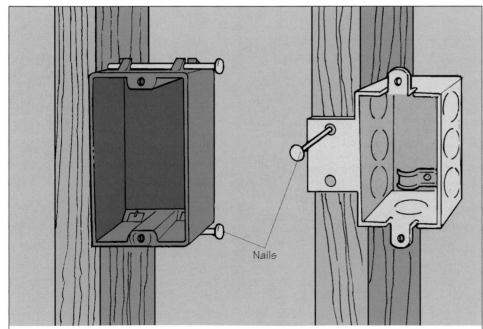

1. Boxes for switches and receptacles are made of plastic or galvanized steel, with various attachment options. Two 16d nails are driven through the side tabs of the plastic box (left) into the stud. These boxes come with nails inserted in them. The metal box (right) is nailed through a tab to the face of the stud.

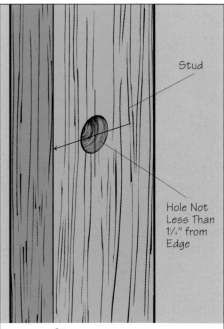

2. Drill ¾-inch holes (or saw notches, if necessary) at least 1¼ inches back from the stud face.

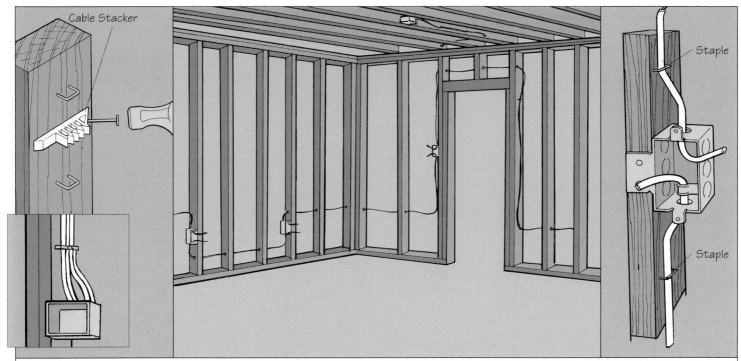

3. Plastic sheathed cable can be attached to studs by metal cable staples or a more recent development, cable stackers. Made of plastic, stackers allow you to install the fastener first (with a nail), then push the cable into the holding channels. The one shown is made to hold four cables (left). Run cables through the framing in a straight line, if possible, and secure the cable to the framing with a staple every 48 inches and within 8 inches of a box (right). Attach boxes to studs so that the face of the box is in line with the proposed wall finish. Boxes such as the one shown have tabs set back ½ inch. Staple the cable to the stud at each side of the box (right).

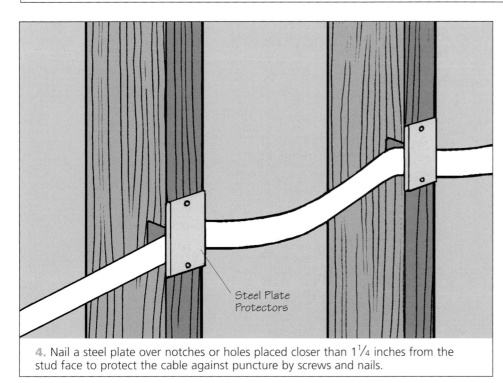

4. Nail a steel plate over notches or holes placed closer than 1¼ inches from the stud face to protect the cable against puncture by screws and nails.

Fishing Wiring through Enclosed Floors & Walls

4 **Add Plates over the Holes or Notches in the Studs.** Code requires that the cable be protected from punctures; that's why the holes must be 1¼ inches back from the face of the stud. If any cable ends up closer to the stud face, attach a metal plate over the stud at this location. You can get plates made for this purpose at your electrical supplier.

Snaking new wiring through floors, walls, and ceilings while leaving the surface finishes intact can be somewhat difficult, but it's possible to do. You'll still need to remove the wall finish at key spots. Fish tape is needed for this job. Flexible metallic wire wound in spools, fish tape bends over the end of electrical cable while you fish the other end through enclosed walls and floors. The cable and wire emerge some distance away through a hole that you have opened up in the wall. Then you simply pull the cable through. Make sure to turn off the power at the panel board before beginning. Here's how to run new wiring from a source in the basement to the kitchen upstairs.

Difficulty Level: 🔩 🔩 🔩

Tools and Materials

☐ Electric drill with ¾-inch bit
☐ Fish tape
☐ Basic electrical tools
☐ Keyhole saw
☐ Electrical boxes
☐ Metal plates for studs
☐ Electrical cable

1 **Drive a Pilot Nail and Drill a Hole.** If the first box you want to wire is on the first floor, begin by cutting a hole in the wall to fit the box. If you are bringing the wire to the second floor, start by making an access hole in the first-floor wall. Make the access hole near the floor and directly below where the receptacle will be. Drive a long nail through the floor close to the wall and directly below the first-floor receptacle or access hole. From the basement, drill a ¾-inch-diameter hole up through the ceiling into the wall cavity above, using the pilot nail as your guide.

2 **Insert the Fish Tape.** Take the roll of cable to the basement and bend the ends of the wires over to make a "U" shape. Feed the cable up through the hole in the floor. Have a helper stand upstairs and feed fish tape into the wall through the hole you drilled. Working together, move the cable and tape end around until they hook together, then have your helper pull on the tape to draw the cable up through the wall and out the opening.

3 **Pull the Cable Horizontally.** If you want to run the cable to another point on the wall, try to make the horizontal run in the open basement ceiling. If you can't run cable horizontally below the kitchen floor, as when wiring a second-story kitchen, you can run it through the kitchen walls by first cutting out access holes along the run, then pulling the cable and fish tape through, from one hole to the next. Begin by taping the cable end to the fish tape to prevent them from coming apart.

4 **Pull the Cable Vertically.** To pull the cable from somewhere inside the wall up to the ceiling, first remove part of the corner above the wall hole, where the wall meets the ceiling. Cut a notch in the framing to make a space for the cable to run. Then thread fish tape from the ceiling opening to the wall/ceiling joint opening then down the wall. Attach the cable to the tape and pull it back up through the structure and out the ceiling opening. Nail a metal protective plate over the cable in the corner notch before patching the opening. The procedure is similar if you are running cable to a second-floor receptacle. Use the notch to get into the second-floor wall, then use the cable to snag the tape through the receptacle hole upstairs. Allow at least 6 inches of cable protruding out of the box when you're finished.

5 **Install the Boxes.** Insert the cable into a box and place the box into the hole in the wall and secure it. How you attach the boxes to the studs depends on the finish of the walls and how much wall you want to remove. If you want to remove a portion of the wall to expose the stud face, you can nail the box directly to the stud. You can connect a box to a plaster wall by

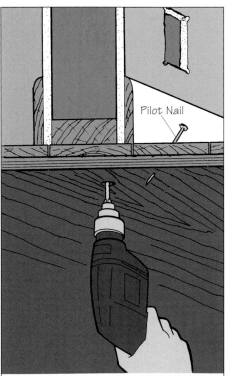

1. Drive a pilot nail through the floor below the new box, and use it to help find the wall from below.

2. Make a hook in the end of the cable and feed it through the hole while a helper tries to catch the cable with fish tape fed into the wall from above.

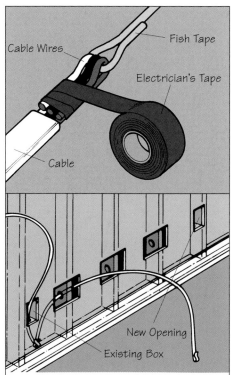

3. Attach the cable to fish tape (top). To route cable across a wall, cut an opening at each stud, drill holes, and fish the cable through (bottom).

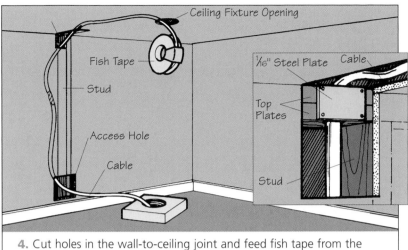

4. Cut holes in the wall-to-ceiling joint and feed fish tape from the ceiling box to the opening and through the wall below. Use the tape to snag the cable, then pull the cable up through. To pull cable through the ceiling as shown here, the joists have to be parallel to the direction of the cable. If they run the other direction, cut holes at each joist. Attach metal protection plates over the cable at the wall/ceiling joint before patching the wall.

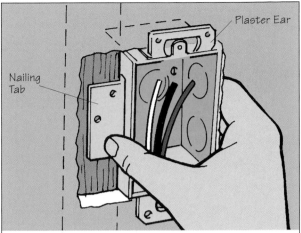

5. Attach an electrical box inside a finished wall by screwing the plaster ears to the lath, tightening the side clamps against the backside of the wall material, or cutting away the plaster or drywall at the stud and driving nails through the nailing tab into the stud face.

screwing through the plaster ears into the lath; by using a retrofit box and tightening the compression connectors to the backside of the lath; or by cutting away the plaster or drywall at the stud and nailing through the tab into the stud face.

Installing Receptacles

If you protect all outlets in the kitchen with a single GFCI circuit breaker (see "Putting in a GFCI Receptacle," page 104), you can install standard receptacles throughout the room. New receptacles accepted by the National Electrical Code contain three slots: two vertical slots of different lengths for the hot and neutral wires and a U-shaped slot for the ground wire. You can wire the outlets from the screws on the sides or by inserting the stripped end of a wire directly into the proper hole in the back of the receptacle. Some electricians don't consider the holes to be as reliable as screw attachments.

Receptacles are installed in the wall according to where they fall in the circuit, as described below.

Wiring Middle-of-the-Run Receptacles

Bring the incoming and outgoing cables into the box through the top or bottom holes. Connect the two hot (black) wires to the two brass-colored screws or insert the wires into the holes marked "black" on the backside. Attach the two

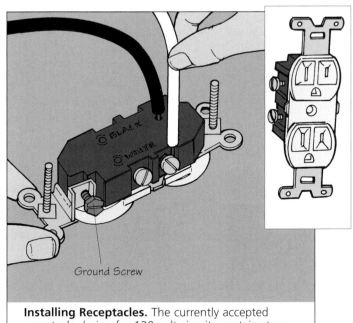

Installing Receptacles. The currently accepted receptacle design for 120-volt circuits contains two vertical slots of slightly different length for the hot and neutral wires and a U-shaped slot for the ground wire.

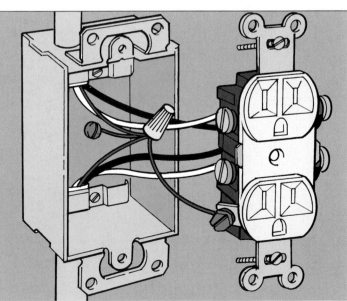

Wiring Middle-of-the-Run Receptacles. Connect the two black wires to the two brass-colored screws and attach the two white wires to the silver-colored terminals.

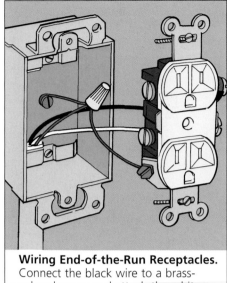

Wiring End-of-the-Run Receptacles. Connect the black wire to a brass-colored screw and attach the white wire to a silver-colored screw.

neutral (white) wires to the silver-colored screws or insert the wires into the holes marked "white." Connect the ground wires together and to the grounding screw in the box, if it's metal. Wrap electrical tape around the sides of the receptacle to protect the terminal screws from contact with ground wires.

Wiring End-of-the-Run Receptacles

Bring the incoming cable into the box through the top or bottom hole. Connect the hot (black) wire to a brass-colored screw or insert the wire into the hole marked "black" on the backside. Attach the

neutral (white) wire to the silver-colored terminal or insert it into the hole marked "white." Connect the ground wire to the grounding screw in the box, if it's metal. Wrap the sides of the receptacle with electrical tape.

Wiring Switches

Switches have only two active terminals and interrupt only the black hot wire. When the power goes from the switch to the light, attach the black wires to the terminals and connect the white wires together. If the power goes from the light to the switch, connect the white and black wires to the terminals and mark the white wire to show it's hot. Always make sure the ground wires are grounded.

120/240-Volt Receptacles

Electric ranges require a combination 120- and 240-volt electrical supply. The 120-volt circuit powers burners at lower settings, lights, timers, and a convenience outlet. The 240-volt line supplies power when burners are turned up or the oven is switched on.

Check your local electrical code before installing a receptacle for a range. Some require a direct connection to a junction box; others call for a plug-and-receptacle hookup.

CAUTION: Always turn off power to an existing circuit before starting work.

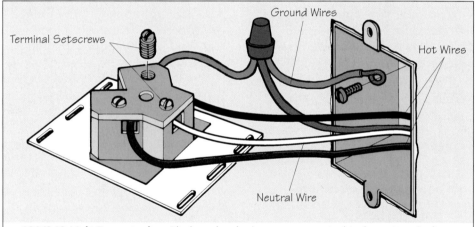

120/240-Volt Receptacles. Black and red wires are connected to brass terminals; the white wire goes to the terminal so marked. The ground goes to the box. Be sure to use No. 10 gauge wire.

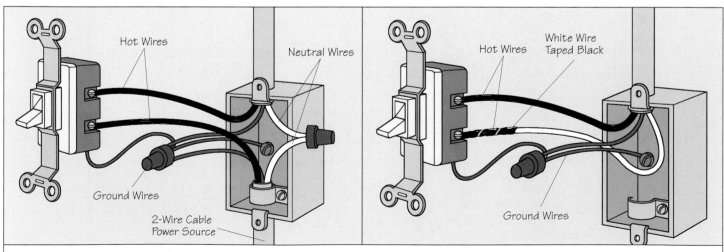

Wiring Switches. Switches have two terminals. When power passes through the switch to the fixture, attach only the black wires. Join the whites with a wire nut (left). If power comes to the light first, connect the black and white wires to the switch. Mark the white wire with black electrical tape to show it's hot (right).

Installing Wall Outlets

A wall receptacle for a 30-watt 120/240-volt circuit doesn't have a grounding device on it. The bare or green ground wire in the cable connects to the box.

Loosen the terminal setscrews, slide the white wire into the terminal marked "white" or "neutral," and tighten the screw. Connect the red and black wires to the other terminals; unless the terminals are labeled, it doesn't matter which wire goes to which terminal.

Installing Surface-Mounted Outlets

You can also bring 120/240-volt electrical service up through the floor to a surface-mounted receptacle. Remove the receptacle's cover to get at connections.

Connect the white (neutral) wire to the terminal so marked. Attach black and red power lines to the other two terminals. Wrap the green ground wire around a screw at the rear of the receptacle. Receptacles with the configuration of slots shown in the drawing provide 50 watts.

Dealing with No Neutral Wire

In some circuits the cable may enclose only a black and white wire (both are considered hot), and a ground wire. The black and white wires connect to the brass-colored terminals. Attach the ground wire to the outlet and the box with a pigtail.

Running New Circuits from the Panel

Appliances such as dishwashers and waste disposers often call for a separate circuit to power a pump and/or heater. Get the power requirements for any special equipment from the manufacturer's instructions. To get an additional circuit, you'll need to tap into the main panel. If the equipment must be

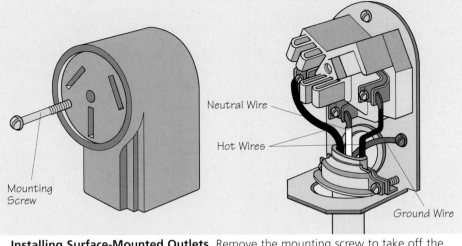

Installing Surface-Mounted Outlets. Remove the mounting screw to take off the outer housing of the outlet. Connect the white wire to the marked terminal and connect the black and red wires to the other terminals. Connect the green wire to the ground terminal on the back of the receptacle.

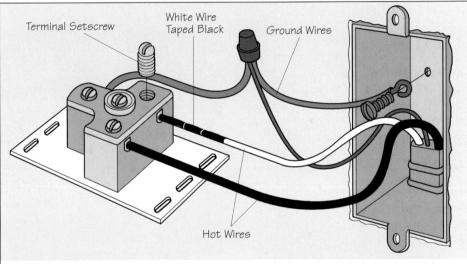

Dealing with No Neutral Wire. If the cable has only white and black wires with a ground, mark the white wire with black tape to show it's hot and attach both hot wires to the brass terminals. Connect and ground the ground wires.

connected to a dedicated circuit, follow the general steps below.

Working on a panel is dangerous, so take all safety measures. If your installation is special in any way or if you are not confident of completing the hookup correctly, have a licensed electrician do the work at the panel after you have done the room wiring. If you do work on your panel, it's a two-hand job so you'll need a helper or some kind of stand to hold your flashlight while you work with the house power off.

Begin by determining how many new circuits you need and the voltage each must carry. A 120-volt

circuit usually requires a single breaker of 15- or 20-amp capacity. A 220-volt circuit is wired to a special type of breaker.

Difficulty Level: ⫪⫪⫪

Tools and Materials
- Basic electrical tools
- Flashlight
- Cable (of type required by the manufacturer and code
- Circuit breakers of the required amperage and of the same make as your panel

1 Shut off the Main Breaker. Using your flashlight to see, turn off the power to the house

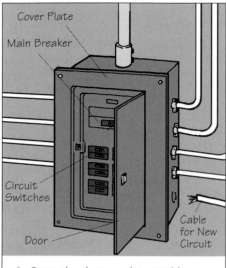

1. Open the door on the panel box, turn the main breaker to the off position, then unscrew the screws at the corners to remove the cover plate.

with the main breaker switch, which is usually mounted at the top of the service panel.

2 **Remove the Cover Plate.** Note the Breaker Arrangement. With the house power shut off, remove the panel's cover plate and note the breaker arrangement. Each breaker in use is connected to a circuit cable. A label on the cover plate should identify each circuit. Check to see whether there are any breakers not in use (spares) or spare slots for additional breakers. If there are no spare breakers but there are empty slots for breakers, you can add a new circuit. If all slots are in use, you may be able to add a double breaker, which is a device that puts two breakers in the

space of one. Or you may have to add a subpanel. In any case, if you don't see a spare breaker or slot, it's a good idea to get an electrician's advice.

3 **Bring the Cable into the Panel.** Here's how to connect a 120-volt circuit cable to a spare or new breaker. Use a screwdriver to pry out a perforated knockout from the side or top of the panel box.

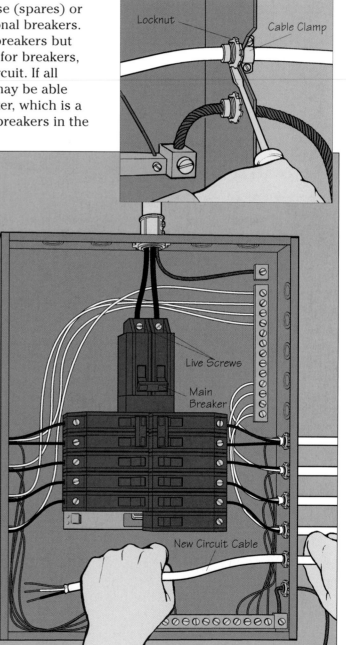

2. With the main breaker shut off, remove the cover plate and note the breaker arrangement. Check to see whether there are any breakers not in use (spares) or spare slots for additional breakers.

3. Pry out a perforated knockout from the side or top of the panel box with a screwdriver. Thread the cable through a cable connector, into the box, and through a locknut. Tighten the cable-connector screws and the locknut with a screwdriver.

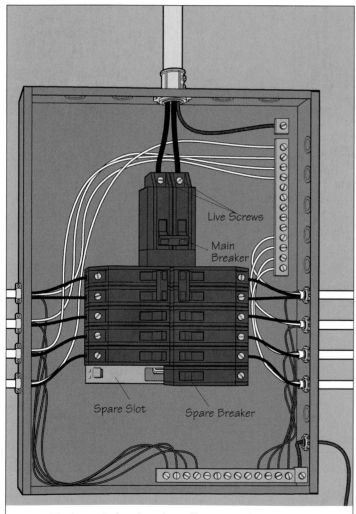

Attach a cable clamp and thread 12 or more inches of the cable through the connector, the hole in the box, and a locknut. Tighten the two screws against the cable with a screwdriver. Tighten the locknut with a screwdriver. Remove about 8 inches of the outer sleeve of the end of the cable and strip the wire ends.

4 **Connect the Neutral and Ground Wires.** Insert the ends of the white (neutral) wire and the bare ground wire into holes along the bus bars intended for these wires at the side or bottom of the panel and tighten the setscrews. Note how the other circuits are connected.

5 **Connect the Hot Wire and Snap the Breaker in the Panel.** If a spare breaker is not already in place, snap one into its slot on the panel board. Loosen the screw of the breaker and insert the black wire of the cable into the hole below. Then retighten the screw to secure the wire end.

6 **Replace the Panel Box Cover.** Screw the cover plate back onto the panel box and record the new circuit on the panel door. To prevent a power surge, turn off all the individual breakers, then turn on the main breaker. Now turn the individual breakers back on one by one.

If you need to add a breaker for a 240-volt circuit, such as might be needed for a wall oven or range, get a special breaker that occupies two slots in the panel box. The installation is similar to that just described, except the cable will have two hot wires—one black and one red. Insert one of the hot wires into each of the two holes in the double breaker.

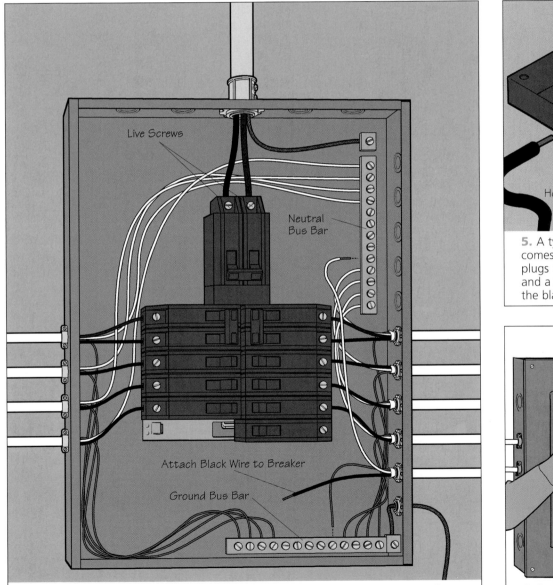

Live Screws

Neutral Bus Bar

Attach Black Wire to Breaker

Ground Bus Bar

4. Connect the end of the white wire to the neutral bus bar, where the other white wires are connected. Then connect the ground wire to the ground wire bus, usually near the bottom of the box.

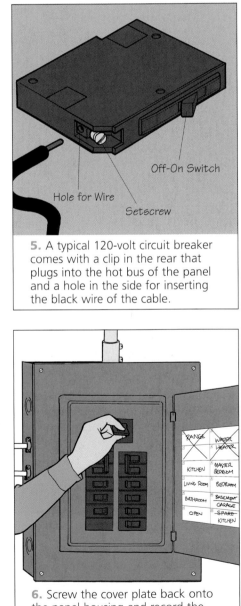

Off-On Switch

Hole for Wire

Setscrew

5. A typical 120-volt circuit breaker comes with a clip in the rear that plugs into the hot bus of the panel and a hole in the side for inserting the black wire of the cable.

6. Screw the cover plate back onto the panel housing and record the new circuit on the panel door. Turn the main breaker back on.

Putting in a GFCI Receptacle

Kitchens pose hazards not found in most other parts of the house because of the presence of two good conductors of electricity: water and metal pipes. If a person is in contact with the piping system while handling appliances or switches, the electrical current may pass through his or her body on its way to the ground. Ordinary receptacles, even when containing a grounding wire, don't completely protect you against the full brunt of an electrical shock. Ground-fault circuit interrupters (GFCIs) do. A GFCI senses an overload and cuts off the current in $\frac{1}{25}$ to $\frac{1}{30}$ of a second—25 to 30 times faster than a heartbeat.

Code requires that GFCIs be used in kitchen receptacles within 6 feet of a sink. You are required to install a GFCI in an older home any time you're replacing a receptacle in an area that is specified for a GFCI. In old circuits without a ground wire, this requires running a new three-wire cable from the panel. But beyond the code, GFCIs just make good safety sense in the kitchen.

There are three ways to protect circuits with a GFCI. The cheapest and easiest is a portable device that you simply plug into the outlet of the receptacle you want to protect. It protects only that outlet. At slightly more expense and effort, you can replace the receptacle with a GFCI receptacle, which offers the opportunity to protect receptacles downstream from the one you are replacing. Another way to protect all receptacles and devices connected to the kitchen is to wire them to a single circuit and install a GFCI breaker in the panel box (see "Running New Circuits from the Panel," page 101). This is also the most expensive way to achieve protection, as GFCI breakers cost about four times as much as an ordinary 120-volt breaker. The following steps describe how to install a GFCI receptacle. When you buy your GFCI receptacle, it may have four screws at the sides and one on the bottom. One pair of black and white lugs is marked "line," while the other pair is marked "load." The fifth—green—lug is the ground connection. Another type of GFCI has five color-coded wires instead of lugs.

Difficulty Level:

Tools and Materials
- ☐ Screwdriver
- ☐ Voltage tester
- ☐ Plastic wire connector
- ☐ GFCI receptacle(s)

1 Turn the Power Off. Go to the main panel box and trip the circuit breaker that controls the outlet receptacle. Make sure you have tripped the right breaker by plugging a voltage tester or lamp into the outlet.

2 Open the Outlet. Remove the cover plate and remove the screws that hold the receptacle in the box. Unscrew the hot (black) wires from the brass terminals and the neutral (white) wires from the silver terminals. Disconnect the ground wire and discard the receptacle.

3 Connect the GFCI. If there were two cables connected to the old receptacle, you need to use a voltage tester to determine which is feeding power into the box and which is taking power out of the box. Make sure all of the bare ends of the wires are safely away from the walls, well separated from each

Putting in a GFCI Receptacle. The cheapest and easiest way to protect a single receptacle is a portable GFCI that you simply plug into the outlet (left). To protect receptacles downstream, replace a standard one with a GFCI type (middle). The face contains a three-prong outlet at the top and bottom and test and reset buttons in the center. Install a GFCI breaker to protect an entire circuit just as you would any breaker, except that the white pigtail wire must be connected to the neutral bus board in the panel box (right).

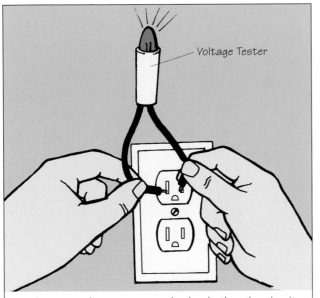

1. Insert a voltage tester to check whether the circuit has been shut down. If the indicator light comes on, the circuit is live.

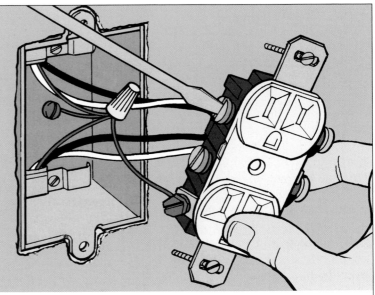

2. Disconnect and remove the standard outlet from the box.

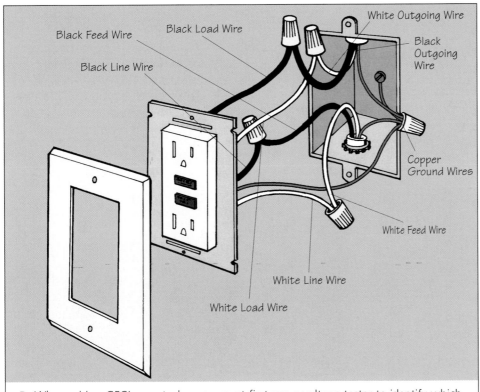

3. When wiring GFCI receptacles, you must first use a voltage tester to identify which cable is LOAD and which is LINE.

4. After securing the new receptacle into the box, replace the wall plate and restore the power.

5. Press the reset button to test the installation.

other. Then turn the power back on. Touch one probe of the voltage tester to a black wire, the other probe to a bare grounding wire. All of the bare wires should still be connected together. When the tester lights, that black wire is the feed. Turn off the power. Label the feed black and white wires. Connect the GFCI black and white leads labeled LINE to the feed wires of the same color. Connect the GFCI leads labeled LOAD to the outgoing wires in the box. If there are no outgoing wires, tape a wire cap onto each GFCI LOAD lead. Connect the green GFCI grounding wire to the other bare grounding wires in the box.

4 **Install the GFCI Receptacle into the Box.** Fold the wires neatly into the box, position the new receptacle inside the box, and secure it with the screws that came with it. Put on the wall plate and restore the power.

5 **Test the Device.** Make sure the button marked "reset" is pressed all the way in. Then press the button marked "test." The reset button should pop out. If it does, push it back into position. You are all set. But if the device does not work, turn off the power, open up the box, and check the connections.

Range Hood Installation

A range hood is one of the last items you'll install in your new kitchen, but if your hood requires ducting to the outside, now's the time to route ductwork for it. Here's what's involved:

Choosing the Hood

The size of the hood you need depends on the size of your range. It should overlap the cooking area by at least 3 inches on each side. Some ranges come with downdraft ventilation, in which cooking vapors are sucked through a central vent in the cooktop, and don't need a hood. For the fan, allow 40 to 50 cubic feet per minute (cfm) per foot of cooking area. For example, if your range is 36 inches wide, you'll need a 120- to 150-cfm fan. Downdraft ventilation requires a more powerful fan.

Planning the Ductwork

Ductwork comes in various sizes and shapes to accommodate different pathways. Elbow and offset fittings let you change directions as you route ducts through a wall, ceiling, soffit (dead space over cabinets or under eaves), and/or roof. Depending on the fan size you use, you'll be limited in the distance the ductwork can run. Elbows and other turns in ductwork further limit the length of your run. Fox example, every 90-degree angle takes up the equivalent of 10 linear feet of ductwork.

Wall and roof caps finish off the outside opening. Most ducting is made of sheet metal, but flexible ducting is also available. Rectangular-to-round converters connect ducts of different shapes.

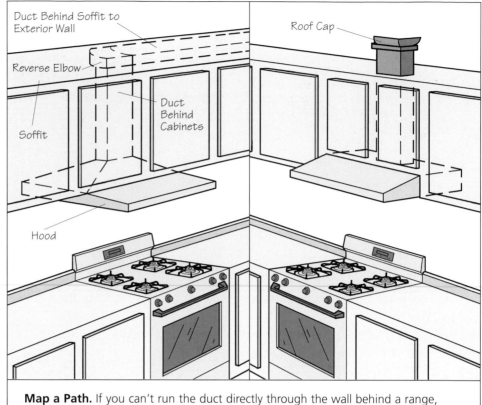

Map a Path. If you can't run the duct directly through the wall behind a range, route it through a soffit and out a wall (left). If there's dead attic space above your kitchen, the best way to go might be straight up through the roof (right).

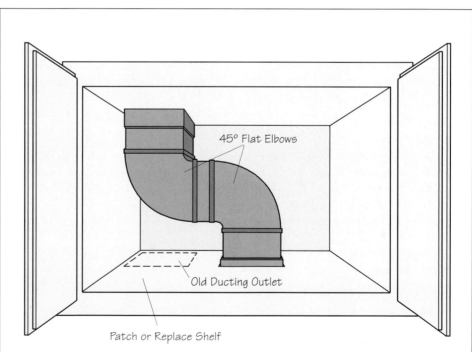

Connect Old Ducts. You may be able to connect a new hood to the old duct. A pair of elbows in the cabinet above the hood lets you adjust the location.

Map a Path. The pathway you choose will depend on how the house is built and the hood's location. If the range sits against an exterior wall, the shortest path is straight out the back of the hood. Most hoods can be adjusted to vent from either the top or rear. If the hood will be on an interior wall, avoid lengthy, twisted paths.

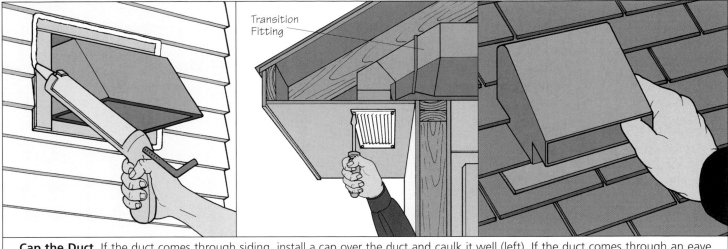

Cap the Duct. If the duct comes through siding, install a cap over the duct and caulk it well (left). If the duct comes through an eave soffit, embed the vent in caulking and screw it in place (middle). Make sure the damper in the cap or duct isn't binding. On the roof, let the duct extend over the shingles about ¾ inch (right). Cut the duct to match the roof pitch. Flashing goes under uphill shingles, over downhill shingles. Use plenty of roofing cement for a watertight seal.

Go straight up through wall space to the roof, if possible. If yours is a two-story house, pass ducting through a soffit over cabinets to an outside wall. Downdraft ventilators are often ducted through the floor, between floor joists.

Connect Old Ducts. If the new hood will be in the same place as the old one or nearby, connect the new hood to the old ductwork. Check the hood installation instructions to determine the required duct size. To make the connection you may need two elbows, as shown on page 106.

Connect New Ducts. Sometimes new ductwork is the best answer, especially if the old duct is grease-laden. If you reroute ductwork, you can either remove the old duct and patch the holes or screw down the damper in the exterior wall and caulk it closed, fill the duct with insulation, and repair only the interior opening.

Exit through the Wall or Roof. Cut the opening in the exterior of the house with a saber saw or keyhole saw. The opening should be slightly larger than the duct. If local codes require it, install casing strips around a wall opening in a wood-frame house.

Seal the Ductwork. Now it's time to make the final assembly of your duct run. Make sure all joints are tight and sealed with duct tape.

CAUTION: Wear work gloves when handling sheet metal.

Cap the Duct. How you cap the exterior of a range-hood duct depends on whether the ductwork exits through a wall, an eave soffit, or the roof. If the duct comes out through the side of the house, install a duct cap. If the duct goes through a soffit, you'll probably need a transition fitting, as shown above (middle). Embed the soffit vent in quality caulking compound. If the duct passes through the roof, it should extend at least ¾ inch above the high side of the roof.

Using asphalt roofing cement, completely seal the opening between the duct and the roof. Install the roof cap by inserting its high-side edge under the shingles and cementing them down.

Installing the Hood

The hood assembly simply fastens with screws to filler strips under the cabinet above. Some models must also be screwed to the wall. The steps for installing a range hood vary with the manufacturer. Specific instructions, like the ones shown below, come with the unit.

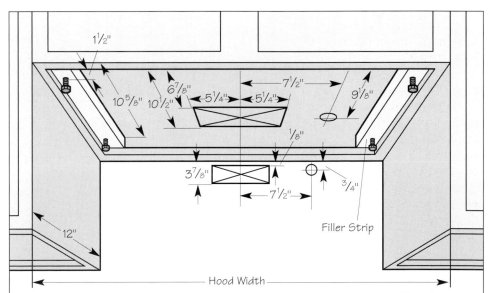

Installing the Hood. The instructions for installing a particular model of hood will include a diagram like this. Dimensions are given to locate the required openings for duct and power connections in both the rear wall and overhead, to accommodate any situation.

6

Projects:
Finishing Walls
& Ceilings

Now that you've done all the preliminary construction work for your kitchen, you need to dress up the bare plasterboard on the walls and ceilings. Spackling dry-wall and painting ceilings and walls are messy jobs, so it's good to get them out of the way before you finish the flooring and install the cabinets and appliances.

You'll find all you need to know in this chapter to end up with handsome walls and ceilings. We start with the basics of repairing walls and spackling, and take you through painting, hanging wallcoverings, installing ceiling beams, and wiring finished lighting fixtures.

Repairing & Painting

Before you can start painting, you must make sure the walls and ceiling are free from blemishes and irregularities. That's where scrupulous preparation comes in: careful scraping, spackling, and sanding.

The easiest and most economical finish for kitchen walls, ceilings, and wood trim, paint is also the easiest to apply. Unlike more demanding finishes, paint is forgiving, allowing you to make corrections and change the color easily. With all these pluses, paint can also provide a durable finish, if you prepare the substrate properly and take measures to deal with the heavy amount of moisture and grease that kitchens generate.

Choose paint with a high sheen. Gloss and semigloss paints resist moisture and are easier to clean than more porous flat or eggshell paints. Because oil-based paints are being phased out by anti-pollution legislation, the following steps apply to water-based latex paints.

You can paint intricate surfaces, such as wood trim or cabinets, and small wall areas with a brush only. If the project extends to larger walls or ceilings, you'll save time and effort by using a roller.

Difficulty Level:

Tools and Materials

Tools for Preparation
- ☐ Masking tape
- ☐ Putty knife
- ☐ 4-inch-wide drywall knife
- ☐ Hammer
- ☐ Nail punch
- ☐ Screwdriver
- ☐ Spackling compound
- ☐ Crack and hole filler
- ☐ 100-grit sandpaper
- ☐ Caulking gun
- ☐ Phosphate-free trisodium
- ☐ White shellac
- ☐ Fine- and medium-grit sandpaper
- ☐ Denatured alcohol (solvent for shellac)
- ☐ Caulk (match type to task)
- ☐ Fiberglass joint tape and drywall joint compound (for large plaster cracks)

Tools for Painting by Brush
- ☐ 1½- or 2-inch sash brush
- ☐ 4-inch paintbrush
- ☐ Pail
- ☐ Dropcloth
- ☐ Paint shield
- ☐ Razor blades

Tools for Painting by Brush and Roller
- ☐ 1½- or 2-inch sash brush
- ☐ Roller pan
- ☐ Roller with ¼-inch nap cover
- ☐ Paint shield
- ☐ Razor blade
- ☐ Dropcloth
- ☐ Roller handle extension (optional)

Preparing the Surface

The key to a successful paint job is what lies below the paint. Paints with a gloss or semigloss sheen reveal imperfections more than flat-sheen paints, so begin with a good substrate. Seal cracks between wood trim and walls with acrylic latex caulk. To seal cracks between a finished floor and wood baseboard, protect the floor with masking tape, then caulk the joint. If the baseboard doesn't have any shoe molding, you can add it to hide any gaps.

Wash previously painted surfaces with phosphate-free trisodium and water. If stains or marks remain after washing, brush white shellac over them.

To remove any adhesive that clings after stripping off an old wallcovering, brush on wallpaper remover solvent diluted with water according to the instructions.

Preparing Drywall

Finish new drywall by taping all joints and sanding the surface completely smooth (see "Finishing Drywall," page 87). Prepare old drywall as described below:

1 **Fix Popped Nails.** Drive new nails or drywall screws 1 or 2 inches above and below any popped nails, then remove the popped nails.

2 **Fill Any Voids.** Fill holes above reset nails with spackling com-

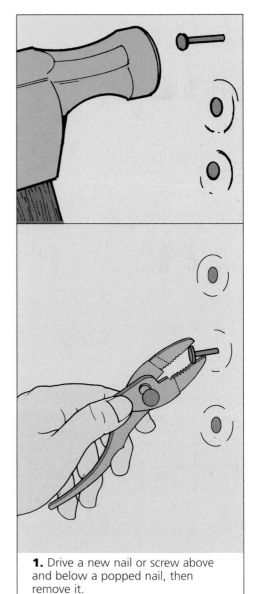

1. Drive a new nail or screw above and below a popped nail, then remove it.

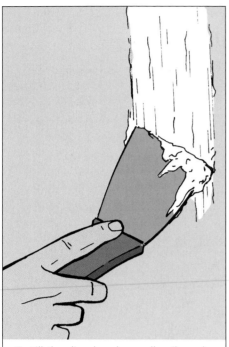

2. Fill the dimples above all nails and screws with spackling compound.

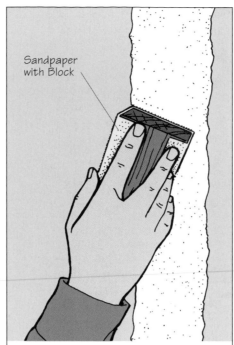

3. Sand spackling compound until smooth.

4. Spot-prime all filled areas and unpainted surfaces.

pound. Fill any cracks, dents, or other surface irregularities.

3 **Sand the Spackling Compound Smooth.** After the spackling compound has dried completely, sand all filled areas completely smooth with 100- or 150-grit paper.

4 **Spot-Prime the Walls.** Spot-prime all filled areas and unpainted surfaces. Use a latex-based primer if the topcoats will be medium to dark colored. To ensure an even color for very light topcoats, use a white shellac primer.

Preparing Old Plaster

Before repainting old plaster, take a hard look at its overall condition. If it has too many defects, such as being loose in spots and crumbling in others, you may be better off applying new drywall over the top or ripping it off and applying a new finish (see "Gutting a Wall or Ceiling," page 81). If the plaster is basically sound, use the following steps to repair the imperfections:

1 **Widen Hairline Cracks.** Use a pointed tool such as a utility knife or can opener to enlarge hairline plaster cracks and provide a toothed base for the filler. Clean the joint with a dampened brush and let it dry.

2 **Fill the Cracks and Sand Them Smooth.** Fill widened cracks with joint compound and sand them smooth, using 100- or 150-grit paper.

3 **Repair Large Cracks.** Larger plaster cracks are likely to reopen. To prevent this, gouge out the crack with a pointed tool, fill it with spackling compound, and let it dry. Then apply fiberglass mesh joint tape over the crack and finish it with joint compound. Sand the

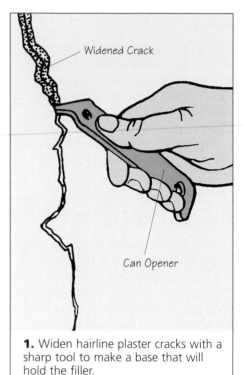

1. Widen hairline plaster cracks with a sharp tool to make a base that will hold the filler.

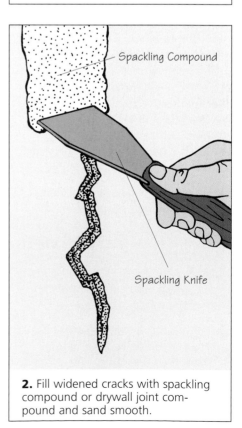

2. Fill widened cracks with spackling compound or drywall joint compound and sand smooth.

3. Fill deep or wide cracks with spackling compound and let it dry. Apply fiberglass mesh tape (top). Cover the tape with joint compound, sand it smooth, and recoat it (bottom).

dried joint compound smooth, recoat, and sand it again. Spot-prime all filled spots.

Preparing Woodwork

How you prepare wood, particleboard, or plywood depends on its present condition and what you want to end up with. You can repaint previously painted woodwork after repairing surface defects. To apply a natural finish, you need to start with raw wood or strip off any previous coating with a chemical stripper.

1 **Set the Nails.** Use a hammer and nail punch to set nailheads slightly below the wood surface.

2 **Fill Holes and Sand Smooth.** Fill all holes and cracks with

the appropriate filler and sand it smooth. If the wood is to be painted or repainted, use a powder-base or premixed wood filler. For natural finished woodwork, you will want the filled spots to match the color of the wood when finished. Doing this is more art than science, and may take a few tries. Select the closest premixed wood filler color to the species of wood and fill a hole in a scrap of the same color. When the filler is dry, apply the

1. Use a hammer and nail punch to set nails on new woodwork and drive any popped nails back into the surface.

3. Caulk the joints between the wood trim and walls with a high-grade flexible caulk.

natural finish and evaluate the color. Try a darker or lighter filler as necessary to get a close match.

3 **Caulk the Joints.** Caulk joints between wood trim and walls with a high-grade flexible caulk, such as acrylic latex (polyurethane is good but messier to work with).

4 **Prime the Surface.** Prime the woodwork to achieve the desired finish. Some of the options are listed on the next page:

2. Fill all holes and cracks with the appropriate filler and sand it smooth.

4. Prime woodwork with the appropriate first coat for a natural or paint finish.

Wood/Finish	Prime Coat(s)
Bare wood, penetrating oil	Penetrating oil; one or more coats
Bare wood, surface finish	Stain (if desired); two coats clear surface finish
Bare wood, paint finish	Two coats latex wood primer or white shellac
Prepainted wood, paint finish	Spot-prime filled areas with latex wood primer or white shellac

Painting Walls & Ceilings

To get the best finish on new surfaces, figure on one coat of primer and two coats of semigloss or gloss enamel. Most paint covers about 400 square feet per gallon, so estimate the amount you will need by first determining the square footage of walls and ceilings, multiplying by the number of coats, and allowing for waste. Before beginning, protect fixtures and floor surfaces with dropcloths. The usual sequence is to do the large surfaces first and wood trim later. But if all surfaces are to be painted with the same color and type of paint, it will be simpler to begin with the brushwork—wood trim, adjacent walls, and inside corners—and do the large surfaces with a roller.

1 **Remove Cover Plates and Trim.** It's tempting to try to paint around switch plates and fixture trim strips, but removing these items is usually easy, and you'll get a much better job for your efforts. When you remove the cover plates, you also risk electrical shock or short circuit if you happen to jab a finger or wet brush into a bared receptacle, so it's a good idea to shut off the power to the circuit before painting.

2 **Cut-in the Ceiling.** Use a sash brush to cut-in (trim) around the walls and edges around fixture openings. Overlap the joint where the ceiling meets the wall.

3 **Paint the Ceiling Field.** Use a wide brush or roller to finish off the large surface (field) of the ceiling, beginning at one wall and working across the ceiling to the opposite wall. If the ceiling area is extensive, consider adding an extension handle to the roller. This will allow you to paint the ceiling from a standing position on the floor. After dipping the roller in the pan, roll paint onto the surface in a zigzag pattern about two roller-widths wide and 36 inches long. Finish off by rolling the spots between with smooth, vertical strokes.

4 **Cut-in the Walls.** Paint the corners and edges around open

1. For a neater job, remove all cover plates and trim strips before painting. Shut off electrical power before painting around electrical boxes.

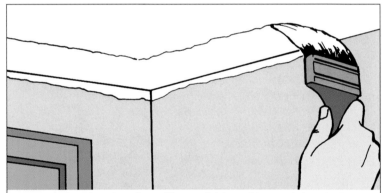

2. Begin by trimming the ceiling-wall joint with a sash brush. Don't worry about overlapping the wall—it's easier to cut a finish trim line on the wall than the ceiling.

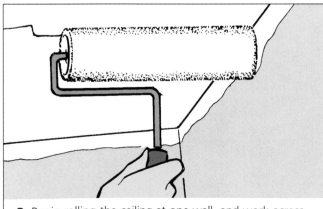

3. Begin rolling the ceiling at one wall, and work across to the opposite wall.

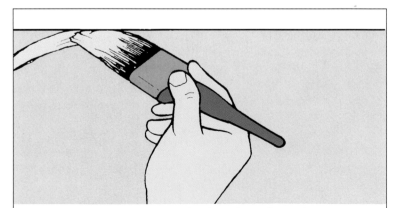

4. If the ceiling is a different color than the wall, cut the trim line on the wall with a sash brush, working the paint up against the ceiling line as shown.

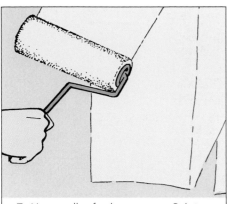

5. Use a roller for large areas. Paint each section in a zigzag pattern, then finish off with up and down strokes until all spots are covered equally.

wall surfaces with a sash brush. If the wall color differs from the ceiling, let the ceiling dry completely, then cut the wall-ceiling joint carefully.

5 **Paint the Wall Field.** Use a roller to paint the wall field. Start at one corner and work across the wall, applying the paint to rectangular sections as described in Step 3, page 112.

Painting Woodwork

Remove any knobs from doors and cabinets before painting to get a clean job. Unless you need to paint large surfaces, use a small sash brush (1½ to 2 inches wide) to paint all wood. Paint the edges of doors first, ending with the larger surfaces. Use a paint shield to protect the floor while painting baseboards.

When painting window sash, cut the trim as close as practical to the glass, but don't worry about paint that slops over onto the glass.

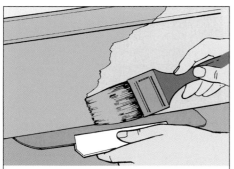

Painting Woodwork. A paint shield may help you protect adjacent surfaces when painting against materials such as tile and wood.

Go back when the paint dries and scrape any spills off the glass with a razor blade. You can't remove paint quite so easily from tile, so if you are not confident of cutting a clean edge on wood trim next to tile, protect the tile with masking tape.

Wallcovering Basics

Wallcovering covers a wide range of products, from traditional paper to treated fabrics and fabric-backed vinyl, paper-backed grass cloths, and even more exotic variations.

Choosing Wallcovering

Several factors go into the choice of a wallcovering. Does the area to be covered get a lot of abuse? If it does, look for a covering that withstands scuffs and cleans easily. In most kitchens this means solid vinyl, though vinyl-coated paper might be suitable for an eating area.

Most wallcoverings now come prepasted but some types, including solid vinyl, still must be pasted strip by strip as they go up. However it's pasted, a wallcovering must be applied to a clean, smooth surface. No matter how attractive the covering, any blemish in the wall beneath will show through and spoil the effect.

Preparing for a Project

If your kitchen's walls are already papered and the covering is still sound, you can probably scuff the surface with sandpaper to promote adhesion and apply a new wall-covering right over it. Check this with your dealer before making a decision. It's frequently necessary to strip an old covering.

Planning the Job

Wallcovering is sold in rolls of various widths. Because patterned coverings must be matched side to side along the edges of the strips, there may be a fair amount of waste in trimming to keep the pattern repeating properly. To estimate

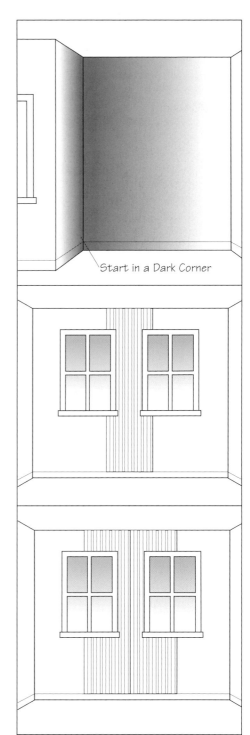

Start in a Dark Corner

Planning the Job. If you're putting wallcovering all the way around a room, the pattern won't line up perfectly where the first and last sheets abut. Plan the project so this mismatch will occur in the least conspicuous place, such as in a corner (top). On walls with windows, use a roll of wallcovering as a measuring stick to divide the wall into increments as wide as the roll. If the strips at either corner will be less than half a roll wide, start with a strip centered on the middle of the room, as shown in the middle; otherwise, start as shown at the bottom.

material needs, as a general rule determine the number of square feet in the area to be covered (less openings like windows, doors, and fireplaces) then divide by 30—a number derived by subtracting the likely wastage from the standard 36 square feet in a roll. Round up to the nearest whole number for ordering standard rolls. If you're buying other than standard 36-square-foot rolls, consult your dealer about how many you need.

The repeating pattern in wallcovering also requires careful planning of where the covering job should start and end. The drawing on the previous page illustrates your options. Windows require advance planning, too, as illustrated in the drawing.

Difficulty Level:

Tools and Materials

- ☐ Wallcovering
- ☐ Long table
- ☐ Bucket and brush (for unpasted paper)
- ☐ Bucket of water
- ☐ Water tray (for prepasted wallcovering)
- ☐ 48-inch level
- ☐ Measuring tape
- ☐ Pencil
- ☐ Long straight-edge scissors
- ☐ Mat knife
- ☐ 6-inch broad knife
- ☐ Smoothing brush
- ☐ Sponge
- ☐ Seam roller
- ☐ Seam adhesive

Cutting Wallcovering

1 **Cut for Height.** Because wallcovering comes in rolls, it must always be cut to fit the height of the wall. Also, because full widths don't always fit exactly across a wall, wallcovering often has to be cut narrower along its length. To cut a piece of wallcovering to length, allow about 2 inches of overlap at the top and bottom. You'll trim this waste after the paper is on the wall. The extra length lets you adjust a sheet up or down a little to match the pattern properly.

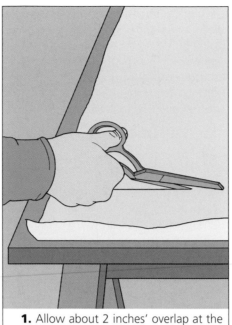

1. Allow about 2 inches' overlap at the top and bottom of each strip. Unroll the paper, then mark and cut it.

2 **Cut for Width.** Long cuts on wallcovering should be marked at both ends, measuring from the edge that will meet the piece already on the wall. Long cuts are usually made to fit the covering into corners. Measure at the top and bottom of the wall, because corners are rarely plumb.

Pasting Wallcovering

1 **Mix Paste.** Wallcovering paste is available both premixed in liquid form and dry for mixing with

1. To mix your own paste, work powder into the water until it has a smooth, viscous consistency.

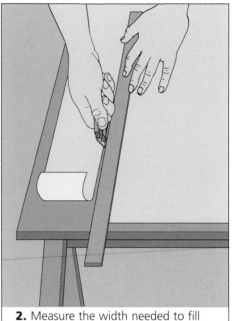

2. Measure the width needed to fill an odd space and mark the strip. Make the cut with a razor knife.

water at home. If you're mixing your own, make it up about 30 minutes before you start.

2 **Apply Paste.** Lay a piece of covering that has been cut to length on your pasting table with one edge flush with a long edge. Apply paste with a paste brush, from the table edge to the middle and about half the sheet's length. Shift the covering across the table so that the other edge lines up along the other edge of the table, and paste the rest of that side. Lining up

2. Spread paste with a pasting brush. To keep paste off the table, align the strip with the table's edge.

with the table edges prevents paste from getting on the tabletop.

3 **Complete the Pasting.** Fold the strip over on itself as shown and pull the remainder up on the table to apply paste. With prepasted paper, soak each roll in a water tray, then proceed as depicted in Step 4.

4 **Book the Strip.** When the entire sheet is pasted, fold it, paste side to paste side, into a manageable package that will be easy to carry to the wall. This folding procedure is called booking. The booked packets can be set aside a few minutes to allow the paste to soften the backing.

3. Fold the pasted section of a strip over on itself (called booking) and paste the remaining section.

4. When the strip is completely pasted, book it as shown so you can easily carry it to the wall.

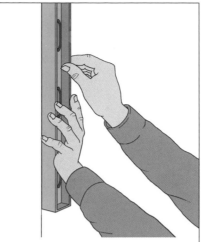

1. Mark a plumb line at the beginning point of your wall as a reference where you will hang the first strip.

Hanging Wallcovering

1 **Establish a Plumb Line.** Decide at what point in the room you'll start hanging the covering and, using a level, mark a vertical line at that point on the wall, as shown. This guideline will establish the positions of subsequent sheets. Don't assume that corners and window or door frames are perfectly plumb.

2 **Carry the Strip to the Wall.** Carry a booked piece of wallcovering to the wall, holding it as shown with the top corners between the thumb and forefinger, and the rest of your hand supporting the rest of the sheet. This method enables you to position the wallcovering at the top and let the rest fall into place.

3 **Position the Strip.** Put the top of the wallcovering against the ceiling, leaving about 2 inches of overlap, and shift it into position along the vertical guideline. This first piece must be placed precisely. Pull the strip free and adjust it if necessary.

4 **Brush the Wallcovering.** Once the strip is in position and laid reasonably flat by hand, use a wallpaper brush to smooth out any wrinkles. Brush from the midline of the sheet toward the edges and corners. Use the brush to tuck the covering into corners and along

2. Hold the strip between your thumb and forefinger and let it fall from the top when you hang it

3. Put the top of the strip in place along the guideline and let the rest drop down the wall.

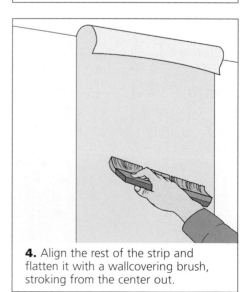

4. Align the rest of the strip and flatten it with a wallcovering brush, stroking from the center out.

the ceiling and baseboard. Finish the surface by wiping it with a damp sponge.

Trimming to Fit

When you've hung and brushed out the wallcovering strip, trim it with a razor trimmer. Hold a minimum 6-inch broad spackling knife where the wallpaper meets the ceiling, floor, or corner to act as a guide for the razor trimmer. Cut along the width of the knife. Hold the trimmer in position, then drag the knife to the new position in front of the trimmer and continue cutting the wallcovering. At windows, hang a sheet over the window around which the covering must be cut. Notch the corners back to the edge of the window casing, then trim the covering as described above.

Hanging Tight Seams

1 **Butt Sheets.** Position a second strip along the edge of the first so the pattern lines up and

1. Hang the second sheet so that the pattern matches up; the strips should be tightly butted, not overlapped.

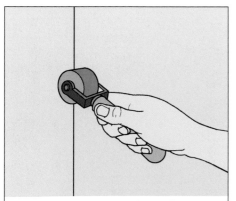

2. Finish the seam with a wallcovering roller. Don't go over the seam repeatedly or you'll a leave a track.

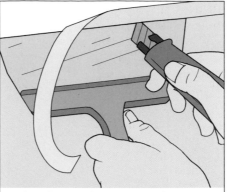

Trimming to Fit. Get a straight, accurate cut by firmly pressing a wide spackle knife into the corner to form a crease. Then cut along the knife with a razor trimmer. To be sure the trimmer is sharp, change razor blades often.

the edges of the sheets are butted together tightly—not overlapped or pulled apart—with a slight ridge at the junction. This will flatten out when the wallcovering dries.

2 **Roll the Seams.** After the paste has started to dry and the edges have shrunk back to the wall, use a seam roller to flatten the seam and press the edges of the sheets firmly into the paste. Roll once up and down. Don't roll over the seam repeatedly. You could create an indentation or a shiny track on the wallcovering.

Turning Inside Corners

1 **Measure for the Strip.** Corners are rarely straight in any but a brand-new house, so wallcovering usually must be cut and fitted to maintain the pattern through the corner. When you come to a corner, measure from the edge of the last full sheet into the corner at the top, middle, and bottom of the wall.

2 **Hang the First Strip.** Add ⅛ inch to largest of these measurements, transfer it to a sheet, and cut the wallcovering lengthwise. Hang the sheet against the edge of the previous sheet, letting the other edge turn the corner. Brush the sheet out and tuck it into the corner.

3 **Mark the Reference Line.** Measure the width of the

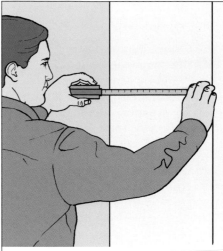

1. Measure from the edge of the last full sheet into the corner in three places: top, middle, and bottom.

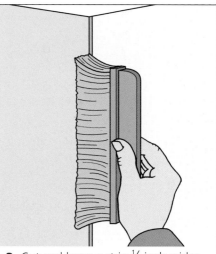

2. Cut and hang a strip ⅛ inch wider than the distance from the last sheet to the corner. It may turn the corner a bit.

3. Mark a plumb line a distance from the corner equal to the width of the remainder of the first strip.

4. Use the vertical guideline to position the remainder strip. Brush the overlap into the corner.

remaining section of the covering. Transfer this measurement to the uncovered wall at the corner by drawing a line that's absolutely plumb. Mark this vertical line carefully to guide hanging the next piece.

4 Hang the Remainder Strip. Hang this second, remainder strip against the plumb line and brush the wallcovering out as usual. Use the brush to smooth the edge that meets the corner. Run a bead of wallcovering seam adhesive along the corner to be sure you secure any overlap that occurs.

Ceiling-Beam Installation

Ceiling beams can change the appearance of a kitchen, giving it a warm country look. If you've removed a bearing wall and added a structural beam, disguise its presence by flanking it with fakes.

False beams come prefabricated in wood that's been assembled into U-shapes with distress marks and gouges on the outside that look like hand-adze marks. Beams are also available in molded foam that attaches to the ceiling with adhesive, but these are often too obviously fake.

Instead of buying manufactured beams, you can make your own by nailing together three-sided boxes of one-by lumber.

Building Your Own Beams

Difficulty Level: 🔩🔩

Tools and Materials
- ☐ Basic carpentry tools
- ☐ One-by lumber
- ☐ Wood glue
- ☐ 6d finishing nails
- ☐ Nail set
- ☐ Rasp, sandpaper, or plane
- ☐ Wood putty
- ☐ Stain or paint
- ☐ Two-by blocking
- ☐ 16d common nails

1 Make the Beams. Measure the ceiling and decide on a plan, spacing the beams evenly. Mark guidelines on facing walls. Make the beams of 1x4s or 1x6s glued and nailed with either butt or miter joints. Set all the nails.

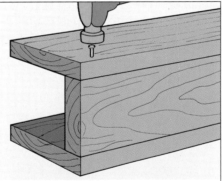

1. Cut three pieces of one-by lumber to length and build a box with butt joints as shown, or with miter joints as in the next drawing

2 Finish the Beams. There are a great many ways to finish a false beam. You can paint it, stain it to look like any of several woods, or give it a modern look with a clear finish. If you want a rough-hewn look on a homemade beam, abrade the surface with a rasp before staining. Smooth the corners with sandpaper, a plane, or a rasp, depending on the effect you want. If you're painting, fill cracks and nailholes with wood putty first; if you're staining, fill afterward with putty that matches the stain.

3 Attach the Blocking. Find the joists and use 16d nails to attach lengths of 2x4s or 2x6s (the interior width of your false beam) on the ceiling as a track. Nail across or along the joists, depending on your plan.

4 Install the Beams. Slip the milled or homemade beam onto the blocking and attach it with nails through the sides of the false

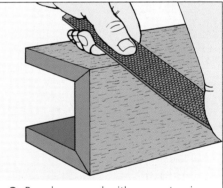

2. Roughen wood with a rasp to give it a rustic appearance; fill any cracks and sand the surface smooth for a modern look.

3. With a helper, attach blocking to the ceiling by nailing into the joists above. Use a single-width piece or two narrow strips spaced to the inside width of the beam.

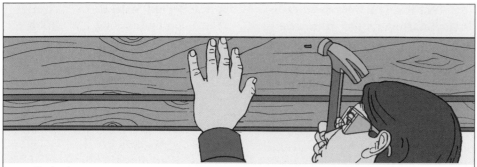

4. Lift the beams into position and nail through the sides of beams into the wood blocking. Use 6d finishing nails; set them with a nail set and fill the nailhole with wood putty.

beam. Set and fill these nails and touch up as necessary.

Ceiling-Mounted Light Fixtures

In just a few minutes you can replace an old ceiling fixture with a new one. The main thing you need to do is determine which mounting devices are needed for the project. Different-weight fixtures require different devices, as illustrated below.

CAUTION: Always turn off power at the circuit-breaker panel before replacing a fixture. Turning off the switch that controls a fixture does not necessarily de-energize it.

Changing a Light Fixture

Difficulty Level: 🔧

Tools and Materials
☐ Basic electrical tools
☐ Coat hanger

1 **Drop the Old Fixture.** Depending on the style of the fixture, remove its globe or light diffuser and bulbs. The canopy, escutcheon, or fixture base is held to the ceiling electrical box with a locknut or fixture bolts. Remove the fastener and cover to expose the ceiling box.

2 **Disconnect the Wiring.** Have a helper hold the fixture while you disconnect the black and white wires leading to it. Wires are usually connected by screw-on

wire connectors. If a helper isn't handy, hang the fixture from a hook support fashioned from a bent coat hanger. If there are more than two wires in the box, diagram the connections. The other wires could be switch and grounding wires. If the fixture is held by a hickey or nut and a stud, unscrew these connectors, releasing the fixture.

3 **Install the New Fixture.** Have a helper hold up the new fixture or support it with a coat hanger while you connect the fixture wires

1. Support the fixture and unscrew the fastener(s) to remove the fixture base.

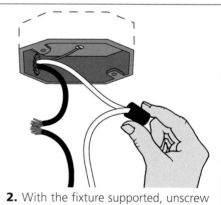

2. With the fixture supported, unscrew the wire connectors.

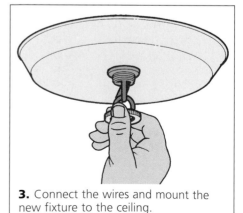

3. Connect the wires and mount the new fixture to the ceiling.

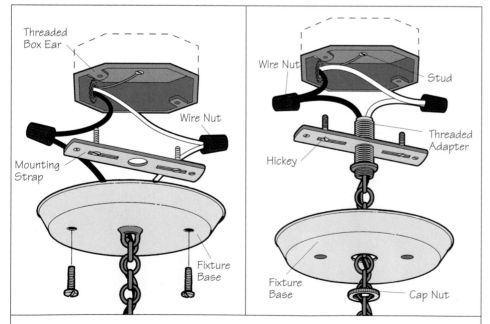

Ceiling-Mounted Light Fixtures. A strap across the ceiling box holds the fixture (left). Screws secure the strap to the box and the base to the strap. Use a stud, hickey, and/or threaded adapter for a heavy fixture (right). The parts usually come with the fixture.

to the circuit wires. Remove approximately ¾ inch of insulation from the wires for the connections. Twist the black wire of the fixture together with the black wire of the circuit cable; do the same with the white wires and ground wires, if any. Use wire connectors and wrap each connection with electrical tape. Secure the mounting devices as shown to complete installation of the new fixture.

Track Lighting

If you're fortunate enough to have a switch-controlled ceiling box in the right place, dramatizing your kitchen with track lighting isn't much more difficult than changing a single fixture. You simply start at the existing box and run the track from it in a single direction, or in opposite directions with the box in the center. Otherwise, fish wires to a new box as explained in "Fishing Wiring through Enclosed Floors & Walls," page 97, then put up the track.

CAUTION: Always turn off power to the box where you'll be working—from the circuit-breaker panel, not at a wall switch. Run an extension cord from another circuit for a work light if necessary.

Installing Track Lights

Difficulty Level: 🔨

Tools and Materials
- [ ] Basic electrical tools
- [ ] Pencil
- [ ] Straightedge
- [ ] Drywall fasteners or screws

1 **Mount the Connector Plate.** A special adapter plate covers the junction box and holds the track connector and the electrical housing. Assemble these pieces. Splice like-colored wires together with wire connectors to attach the track wires to the cable wires. Then fasten the adapter assembly to the junction-box ears with the screws provided.

2 **Plot the Track Run.** Working from the mounting slot of the track connector, draw a line along the ceiling where the track will run.

3 **Install the Track Clips.** Some tracks are held in position by special clips spaced evenly along the track. Hold the clips in place on your line and mark pilot-hole locations for them on the ceiling. Other tracks are fastened directly to the ceiling. With these, hold the tracks in position and mark their screw locations.

4 **Put Up the Track.** Drill holes and attach the clips or tracks, using drywall fasteners in a hollow ceiling or screwing them directly to joists. Plug the tracks into each other and the adapter's connector before tightening the fasteners. To complete the installation, install the

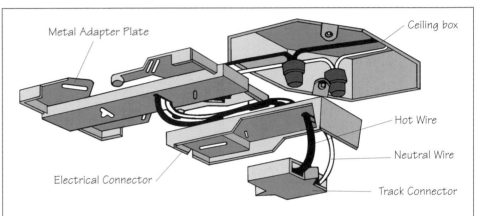

1. Connect the track wiring to the house wiring, using the metal adapter plate. Screw wire connectors on the splices and wrap them with plastic electrical tape. Fasten the assembly to the ceiling box.

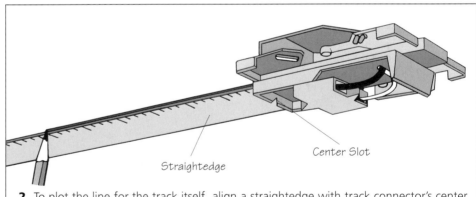

2. To plot the line for the track itself, align a straightedge with track connector's center slot. Draw a line on the ceiling to the point where you want the track run to end.

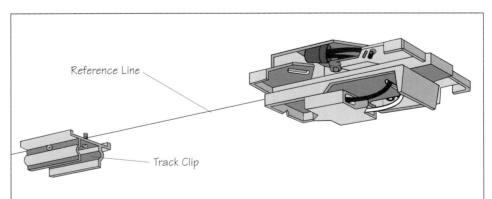

3. Some tracks are held to the ceiling by plastic clips. Center the clip on the reference line and mark the screwhole.

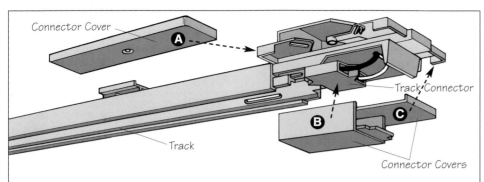

4. Once you've attached the track to the ceiling, complete the installation by snapping on the connector covers A, B, and C as shown in the drawing. Then you can attach lights anywhere you like along the track.

adapter's cover and attach track lights anywhere you wish.

Built-in Lighting Basics

Fixtures and track lights aren't the only ways to shed effective light in a kitchen. Although it calls for some simple carpentry work, built-in lighting can also provide excellent general, task, and accent lighting. In addition to individual fixtures—called high hats—recessed into the ceiling, there are four major types of built-in lighting. Here's a survey of the options:

Lighting with a Valance

A valance attaches to a wall, cabinet, or ceiling to deflect and concentrate light downward, upward, and sometimes both. The valance also conceals the fluorescent or incandescent light source. For best results, plan dimensions that approximate those given in the drawing.

Lighting with a Cove

Coves direct light upward for soft, even illumination that bathes the upper wall and ceiling in a warm glow. Locate a cove's base not less than 12 inches from the ceiling, parallel to it and perpendicular to the wall. Mount fluorescent or incandescent fixtures to the wall just above the cove base. Attach a second board at least 5 inches wide to the cove base at a 45-degree angle. The angle deflects light upward and out, away from the wall and into the room.

Lighting between Beams

If you're installing ceiling beams, consider building a light box

between them. On a flat ceiling without beams, recess special lighting fixtures flush with the ceiling, between joists. The bottom drawings (left) show a typical between-beam setup.

Lighting Up a Beam

You can also include strip lighting in beams themselves. Construct and install beams as explained in "Ceiling-Beam Installation" on page 117, substituting a plastic diffuser for the beam's bottom surface, as shown in the bottom drawing at right. Use easily removed trim (with screws) so you can change burned-out tubes.

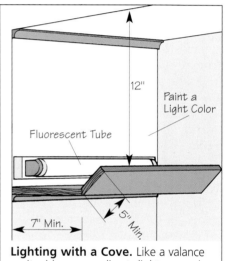

Lighting with a Valance. A board hung from the ceiling with angle irons directs light downward. Paint inside surfaces white for maximum reflectivity.

Lighting with a Cove. Like a valance on its side, a cove directs light upward and across the ceiling. Build the unit first; install it with angle irons.

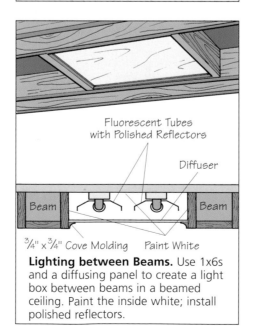

Lighting between Beams. Use 1x6s and a diffusing panel to create a light box between beams in a beamed ceiling. Paint the inside white; install polished reflectors.

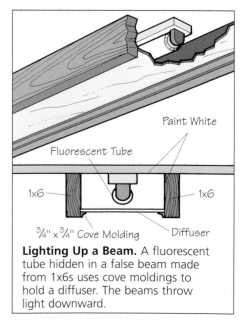

Lighting Up a Beam. A fluorescent tube hidden in a false beam made from 1x6s uses cove moldings to hold a diffuser. The beams throw light downward.

7

Projects:
Laying New Flooring

A beautiful new floor can be the crowning touch for a remodeled kitchen. Installing a finished floor is usually the last construction aspect of the project. Once all the messy work is done, it's easier to keep the floor in pristine shape.

If you already have a wood floor, you may be able to repair and refinish it to look like new. If not, you'll have to prepare the subfloor and install any under-layment necessary to get the floor ready for a new surface. Then you can install your pre-ferred floor: resilient vinyl, ceramic tile, or wood.

Insulating Crawl Spaces

If your kitchen sits above a crawl space, you can prevent cold feet by making sure there is enough insulation in either the floor or the surrounding foundation. If you insulate the floor itself, you'll need to enclose any water piping on the warm side of the insulation to prevent it from freezing. For this reason, many builders prefer to insulate the foundation wall.

Another must for a crawl space is a continuous plastic vapor barrier placed over the earth, to keep moisture from wicking up through the soil and condensing on the wood structure above. Installing these items is relatively easy to do from above when the subfloor is removed, but more difficult with the floor intact. Working from below in a tight space among spiderwebs and who knows what else is no fun. Equip yourself with a good source of light and protect yourself with a dust mask, goggles, hard hat, full-length trousers, and a long-sleeved shirt. Working from above, you probably don't need the hard hat.

Insulating a Floor above a Crawl Space

Difficulty Level: 🔨🔨

Tools and Materials

☐ Long scissors (or knife)
☐ Staple gun
☐ Staples
　¼ inch if installing insulation to top of joists
　½ inch if installing insulation to the foundation
☐ Fiberglass insulation
☐ Duct tape
☐ 4- or 6-mil polyethylene sheet
☐ 48-inch-wide housewrap
☐ 2x4s or bricks

1 **Place Insulation between the Joists.** Cut lengths of insulation with long scissors or a sharp knife, using a piece of 1x4 as a guide and a piece of wood below as a cutting surface. Fit a piece of insulation between each pair of joists.

If you are working from above the floor, use kraft paper-faced insulation and pull the paper tabs out and over the tops of the floor joists. Staple the tabs at 8-inch intervals. Cut the strips of insulation short enough to manage easily, 4 feet or so. Fit each one up in a joist space. Staple sheets of housewrap to the bottom of the joists to keep the insulation from dropping down. If you are working from below, use unfaced fiberglass friction-fitted into place.

2 **Insulate around Pipes and Ducts.** Wrap insulation around each heating duct and water pipe. Use duct tape to make the insulation continuous.

3 **Put a Vapor Barrier over the Ground.** Place strips of 4- or 6-mil poly sheet over the soil, over-lapping the joints at least 12 inches. Run the sheet up the wall and staple it to the sill plate.

Insulating the Sides of a Crawl Space

Insulating between the joists is often harder than insulating the sides of the foundation and keeping

1. Install unfaced blanket insulation between the floor joists from below by fitting pieces into the spaces. Staple a sheet of housewrap below the insulation to hold it in place.

2. Wrap all heating ducts and water pipes below an insulated floor. Seal the joints with duct tape.

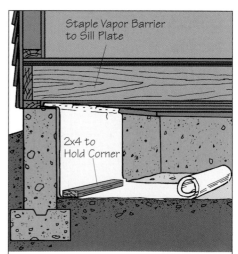

3. Attach polyethylene sheeting to the sill plate. Completely cover exposed soil, overlapping the poly sheets by at least 12 inches. Weigh down the edges and corners with bricks or 2x4s.

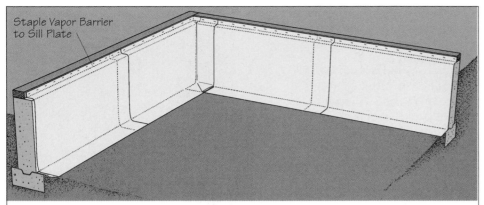

1. Staple strips of polyethylene sheeting to the sill plate. Run the strips down the inside of the foundation wall and let them extend about 12 inches over the ground soil. Overlap the sheets by at least 12 inches.

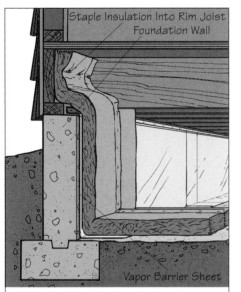

2. To insulate the foundation, hang strips of kraft-faced insulation from the rim joist. Run the strips out over the soil 36 inches.

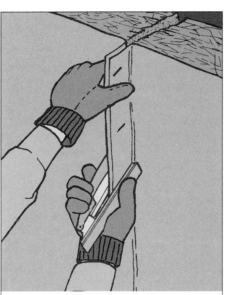

3. Hold the tabs of adjoining pieces of insulation and staple them together about every 8 inches.

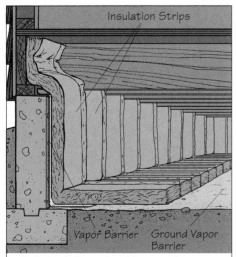

4. Polyethylene should cover the exposed ground, overlapping the joints by at least 12 inches on the sides.

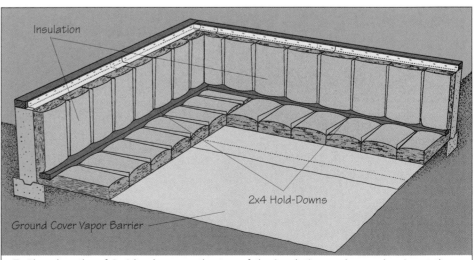

5. Place lengths of 2x4 lumber over the top of the insulation and vapor barrier at the joint between the wall and ground.

the crawl space heated. The latter approach also does away with the need to wrap pipes and ducts to keep them from freezing. If you choose this method, be sure to close off any foundation vents to the outside. The tools and materials you'll need are the same as for insulating a wood floor, except you'll also need some 2x4s.

1 **Hang a Vapor Barrier over the Wall.** Staple strips of 4- or 6-mil poly sheet to the sill plate. Run the strips down the inside of the foundation wall and 12 inches over the soil, overlapping the joints at least 12 inches.

2 **Measure, Cut, and Hang the Strips of Insulation.** Measure the vertical distance between the top of the rim joist and the ground and add 36 inches. Cut strips of insulation to this length. Place one end of each piece of insulation between two floor joists with the paper facing toward the crawl space and staple the ends to the rim joist. Drape the insulation strips down the inside of the foundation and out over the ground.

3 **Connect the Tabs.** Connect the strips of insulation by stapling the tabs of adjoining pieces together at 8-inch intervals.

4 **Install a Vapor Barrier on the Ground.** Insert strips of 4- or 6-mil poly sheet under the portion of insulation that extends over the soil. The poly should cover all exposed soil. Be sure to overlap the sheets by at least 12 inches.

5 **Use 2x4s to Hold Down the Corners.** Place lengths of 2x4 lumber over the top of the insulation and vapor barrier at the joint between the wall and the ground. This will help hold the bottom edges of insulation in place.

Selecting the Right Underlayment

The proper underlayment will ensure that your new floor covering will lie flat and level, and resist water for several years. Selecting the right thickness will help you match the new floor level to that of an adjacent floor, or at least minimize the difference. It's important to match the floor covering to a compatible underlayment. Always avoid particleboard, especially in the kitchen; it swells when wet, causing floor coverings to separate or bubble.

Underlayment-grade plywood made from fir or pine is available in 48x96-inch sheets in thicknesses of ¼, ⅜, ½, ⅝, and ¾ inch.

Because it can expand when damp, plywood is not as good a choice for ceramic tiles as cement board.

Lauan plywood, a species of mahogany, is often used under resilient flooring. It is available in 48x96-inch sheets. The usual thickness for underlayment is ¼ inch.

Cement board is also called tile backer board. It is made of a sand-and-cement matrix reinforced with fiberglass mesh. It is usually available in 36x60-inch sheets in a thickness of ½ inch. This is the preferred base for ceramic tile and stone floors in wet areas.

Resilient floor coverings (vinyl, rubber, and linoleum sheet and tiles) and wood parquet can be laid over an existing layer of similar material if the original is in good condition. The existing covering should be tightly adhered and have no cupped edges or evidence of water damage. If the old flooring is not in good condition, remove it and smooth down the old underlayment before installing the new floor covering. If you can't remove the old floor covering, just apply the new underlayment over it.

Ceramic and stone tile can be applied over existing ceramic tile if the original flooring is tightly adhered and in good condition.

The tiles can also be applied directly over a concrete slab floor. Tile is usually set onto the underlayment via a troweled-on adhesive. When installed on wood floors, the underlayment of choice for ceramic and stone tile is underlayment-grade plywood.

Installing Plywood & Hardboard Underlayment

Difficulty Level: 🔨

Tools and Materials
- [ ] Basic carpentry tools
- [ ] Putty knife
- [ ] 1-inch ring-shank nails
- [ ] Wood filler
- [ ] Circular saw with plywood blade

The following steps assume a separate underlayment is applied over the subfloor:

1 **Measure and Cut.** To prevent nails from popping out, let the underlayment acclimate to the room for a few days before installation. Measure and cut each section of underlayment into lengths that will allow the joints to be staggered. Place the boards over the subfloor so that the joints are offset from the joints in the subfloor or existing underlayment. Leave a gap of

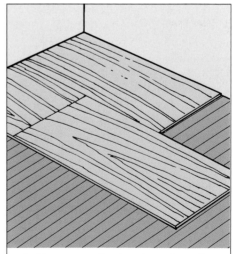

1. Measure and cut each section of underlayment into lengths that will allow the joints to be staggered. Place the material over the subfloor so that the joints are offset from the subfloor joints. Leave a gap of ¹⁄₁₆ inch between the sheets and ⅛ inch at the wall.

Underlayment Options

Floor Covering	Acceptable Underlayments
Resilient floor coverings	Old vinyl or linoleum floor in sound condition
	Underlayment-grade plywood
	Lauan plywood
Wood parquet flooring	Old vinyl or linoleum floor in sound condition
	Underlayment-grade plywood
	Lauan plywood
	Hardboard
Ceramic tile and stone	Old ceramic tiles, if sound
	Concrete slab
	Cement board
	Underlayment-grade plywood

2. Use ring-shank nails to secure the underlayment to the subfloor. Place nails at 4-inch intervals and ½ inch from the edges of the boards.

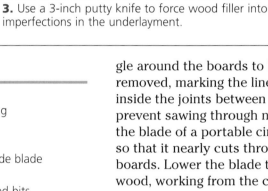

3. Use a 3-inch putty knife to force wood filler into imperfections in the underlayment.

⅟₁₆ inch between sheets and ⅛ inch at the walls. Place full sheets first, then cut pieces to finish up the floor. Cut the underlayment with a circular saw equipped with a plywood blade. Use a saber saw or keyhole saw to cut openings for drainpipes.

2 **Nail the Underlayment to the Subfloor.** Begin at one corner of the room. Nail the underlayment to the subfloor with ring-shank nails. For ¼-inch-thick material, use 2d nails; for ⅜-inch material, use 3d nails. Space nails in rows no more than 4 inches apart and ½ inch in from the edges.

3 **Fill in Holes, Dents, and Cracks.** Fill any holes or imperfections in the boards with a plastic-type wood filler. Sand the filler smooth after it sets.

Damaged Floorboard Replacement

There are two ways to replace floorboards. The easier way is to remove a rectangular area encompassing the damaged boards and nail new boards in place. This method leaves a noticeable patch. The second way is to remove individual boards in a staggered pattern. Although the staggered method takes more time, it results in a patch that's virtually invisible.

Difficulty Level: 🔩🔩

Tools and Materials

- ☐ Floorboards for patching
- ☐ Basic carpentry tools
- ☐ Framing square
- ☐ Circular saw with carbide blade
- ☐ Nail set
- ☐ Electric drill and assorted bits
- ☐ 8d finishing nails
- ☐ 1-inch wood chisel
- ☐ Wood putty
- ☐ Sandpaper
- ☐ Floor finish to match existing floor

Using a Rectangular Patch

1 **Make the Cut.** With a square and pencil, measure a rectan-

gle around the boards to be removed, marking the lines ¾ inch inside the joints between boards to prevent sawing through nails. Adjust the blade of a portable circular saw so that it nearly cuts through the boards. Lower the blade to the wood, working from the center of a line outward. With a hammer and chisel, finish the cut, keeping the beveled side of the chisel facing into the damaged area. Then, beginning at the midpoint of a cut side, lift the board out with a pry bar. Use a small block of wood under the bar for leverage, being careful not to mar good boards in the area.

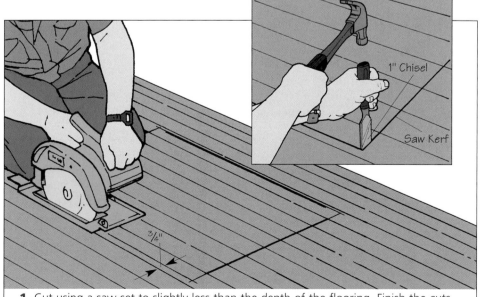

1" Chisel

Saw Kerf

¾"

1. Cut using a saw set to slightly less than the depth of the flooring. Finish the cuts with a chisel.

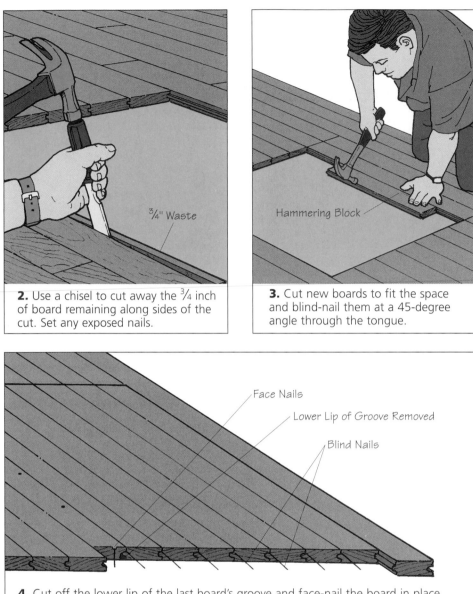

2. Use a chisel to cut away the ¾ inch of board remaining along sides of the cut. Set any exposed nails.

3. Cut new boards to fit the space and blind-nail them at a 45-degree angle through the tongue.

Face Nails

Lower Lip of Groove Removed

Blind Nails

4. Cut off the lower lip of the last board's groove and face-nail the board in place.

holes. Set the nails and fill the holes with wood putty. Then sand and seal the new boards, staining them to match the surrounding boards.

Using a Staggered Patch

1 **Start the Cut.** Mark the boards to be removed, then score them with a hammer and 1-inch chisel. Stagger the marks so you cut each board a different length. Next, face the beveled side of the chisel toward the damaged area at a 30-degree angle and chisel completely through the boards. Leave sharp, clean edges at the ends of sections to be removed.

2 **Finish the Cut.** Split the damaged area by making an incision with a chisel along the face of each board, parallel with the wood grain. Move the chisel along the board and keep striking until the board splits. Split the board again, using the same chiseling technique. Insert a pry bar in the incision and pry out the middle section. Be careful not to damage any good boards. Next pry out the strip on the groove side of the board, then pry out the strip on the tongue side. Begin the removal of each strip in the center of the section and work out to the ends. Remove the remaining damaged

2 **Finish the Cut.** Use a hammer and chisel to cut away the ¾ inch remaining behind the saw cuts. Cut carefully and slowly so as not to ruin the edges of adjacent boards. When the ¾ inch is removed, set any exposed nailheads in the boards that border the cut area.

3 **Nail New Boards.** Measure, cut, and install the new boards one at a time. Cut one end square, butt it against the old board, mark the other end even with the board beneath, and cut the new board. Keep the saw blade on the waste side of the mark so the kerf won't shorten the board. Use a hammer and a block of flooring to tap the

new board into place, locking its groove over the tongue of the old board. Drill pilot holes through the tongue at a 45-degree angle, and nail the new board with 8d finish nails. Cut and install the remaining boards until you reach the last one.

4 **Install the Last Board.** To lay the final board, remove the lower lip of the groove with a chisel and sand the rough edge. Insert the final board's tongue into the existing flooring groove and tap the board into place, using a hammer and a block of wood. Drill 45-degree pilot holes about ¾ inch from the board's groove edge, spaced every 12 inches. Face-nail the board with 8d finishing nails driven into these

1. Mark off the damaged area, score the cuts with a chisel, then chisel toward the marks at an angle.

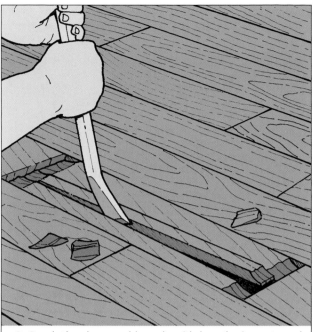

2. Break the damaged boards with lengthwise cuts and pry out the pieces, starting with the middle piece.

Hammering Block

3. Slip a board, cut to fit, against the tongue edge of the old floor and tap it into place with a block.

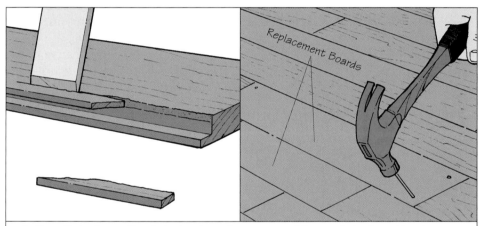

Replacement Boards

4. Cut off the lower lip of the last board's groove and face-nail the board in place with 8d finish nails.

boards by cutting the ends and splitting them out. Set any exposed nails you come across.

3 **Replace the Boards.** Use a scrap of flooring as a hammering block and tap a cut-to-size replacement board into place sideways so that the groove side goes over the tongue of the old board. Drill pilot holes, then drive 8d finishing nails through the tongue of the new board and set them.

4 **Set the Last Board.** You can't slide the last board in place. Instead remove the lower lip of its groove with a chisel and tap the piece into place, securing it with 8d

finishing nails driven into predrilled holes. Set the nails and fill holes with matching wood putty.

Laying Resilient Floor Tiles

Installing resilient floor tiles is fairly simple and requires only a few tools. For a professional effect, though, you'll need to plan the layout and prepare the substrate properly. Try to complete the installation all at one time when you won't be interrupted. Most resilient floor tiles now come in 12-inch squares. Trim

strips in various accent colors are available in ¼- to 6-inch widths. When ordering, figure the areas in square feet to be covered (length times width) and add 5 to 10 percent for waste.

Start with the Right Base

When you pick out a resilient flooring material, check the manufacturer's instructions for acceptable substrates. This will guide you as to the type of underlayment to put down and the corresponding adhesive. Here are some commonly acceptable substrates for resilient tile and sheet flooring and what to watch out for:

Old resilient tile, sheet flooring, and linoleum. Clean, free of wax, tightly adhered with no curled edges or bubbles.

Ceramic tile. Clean and free of wax. If the surface is porous, make sure it is completely dry. Joints should be grouted full and leveled.

Concrete. Smooth and dry. Fill cracks and dimples with a latex underlayment compound.

Wood flooring. Strip flooring will serve as an underlayment only if it is completely smooth, dry, free of wax, and has all joints filled. Even then, the wood strips can shrink and swell, so a better bet is to put down an underlayment of ½-inch underlayment-grade plywood or ¼-inch lauan plywood.

Plywood. Fir or pine plywood that bears the stamp "Underlayment Grade" (as rated by the American Plywood Association) provides the best underlayment for resilient flooring. Use only material of ¼-inch or greater thickness. Lauan, a tropical hardwood, is also used, but make sure you get Type 1, with exterior-grade glue. All plywood should be firmly attached, with surface cracks and holes filled and sanded smooth. Nail ¼-inch-thick plywood at 4-inch intervals around the edges and at 6-inch intervals inside the panel.

Unacceptable Substrates

Particleboard. Never use particleboard for resilient flooring, due to its tendency to swell when moist.

If you have particleboard on the floor now, remove it or top it with underlayment-grade plywood or ¼-inch lauan plywood.

Hardboard. Though often used as a substrate, hardboard is specifically rejected by some manufacturers.

A Solid Color or Pattern?

Unlike sheet flooring, resilient tile flooring gives you the opportunity to mix squares of different colors to create a custom pattern. If this intrigues you, measure the floor and draw it to scale on a sheet of graph paper. Use colored pencils or markers to explore a few patterns. Your options are greatest if the room is large. Too much pattern on the floor can make the room feel cluttered. Muted colors are safest to use—save bright colors for accents.

Tools and Materials

- ☐ Framing square
- ☐ Chalkline
- ☐ Measuring tape
- ☐ Scribing or utility knife
- ☐ Rolling pin
- ☐ Resilient tiles
- ☐ Adhesive
- ☐ Solvent
- ☐ Notched trowel (notch size as specified by adhesive manufacturer)

Preparing the Layout

1 **Mark the Floor.** Measure the room to find the center point of the walls. Have a helper hold one end of a chalkline at the center of one wall, while you hold the line at the other and snap a line on the floor. Then do the same for the two adjoining walls. Use a framing square to make sure the intersection of the lines is square. If not,

1. Find the center points of the surrounding walls and, with a helper to hold one end of the chalkline, snap lines on the floor between the points to make work lines. For diagonal patterns, measure the shorter dimension (x) of the two intersecting work lines and mark it on the long walls. Then run a chalk line diagonally between the marks on opposite walls to create diagonal work lines on the floor (inset).

2. Lay the tiles out on the work lines. If the fit isn't right, adjust the lines. Place a row of tiles along each of the chalk lines to check your layout. If the last tile will have to be cut down too much, move the appropriate work line (inset left). Test a diagonal pattern by first laying tiles down, point to point, along the perpendicular lines, then laying two rows along the diagonal line (inset right).

change one chalk line, which will mean cutting the tiles along one wall at a slight angle.

For a diagonal pattern, you'll run diagonal lines through the center of the intersecting perpendicular lines. In a rectangular room, measure the shorter chalk line from the intersection to the long wall. Mark that measurement twice on each long wall, measuring from the midpoint of the wall and going in both directions along the wall. Run a chalkline diagonally from one of the points you just marked across to the corresponding point on the opposite wall, and snap the line. Do the same with the other diagonally opposite points.

2 **Make a Dry Run.** Place a row of tiles along each of the chalk lines to check your layout. If the last tile will have to be cut down to the size of a skinny strip, move the appropriate chalk line up or down on the floor a few inches.

Test a diagonal pattern by first laying tiles down, point to point, along the perpendicular lines, then laying two rows along the diagonal line.

Setting the Tiles

1 **Spread the Adhesive.** Once you're satisfied with your layout, begin at the intersection of the perpendicular chalk lines and spread adhesive along one line with the smooth side of a notched trowel. Then distribute the adhesive into even grooves by holding the trowel notched side down at an angle of about 45 degrees. Leave part of the line exposed for reference. Set a row of tiles into place; drop, rather than slide, the tiles into position. Starting at the center, set an intersecting row of tiles, then fill tiles in the spaces between the two guide rows.

Begin a diagonal pattern at the intersection of the diagonal lines and lay a row along one diagonal. This row will serve as the baseline for the rest of the pattern.

2 **Roll the Tiles.** Use a rolling pin to apply pressure to each row of tiles as you set them.

3 **Trim the Edges.** Place a dry tile exactly above the last set tile from the wall. Then put a third tile over these two tiles, pushed to the wall. Using the edge of the

1. Spread adhesive in a relatively small area, so that you can lay the tiles before it starts to dry.

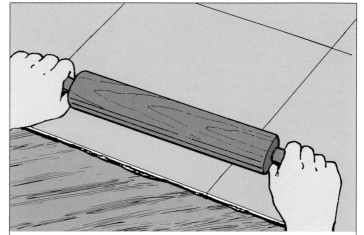

2. Embed the tiles into the adhesive with a rolling pin.

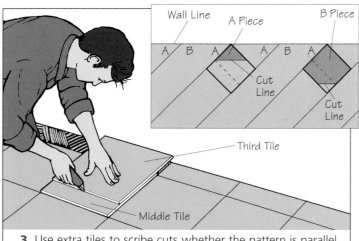

3. Use extra tiles to scribe cuts whether the pattern is parallel to the wall or diagonal (inset).

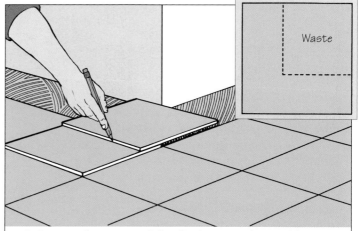

4. Set two tiles on top of the tile closest to the outside corner. Mark one cutout dimension, then shift the two tiles to the other side of the corner to mark the other dimension.

topmost tile as a guide, scribe the middle tile with a utility knife and snap it in two to make a trim piece.

A diagonal pattern requires two different shapes of edge tiles: a small triangle (A) and a larger 5-sided piece (B), unless the wall line happens to fall exactly on a tile diagonal. Place a tile over the laid tiles with one point touching the wall. Mark off a line where the left side of the tile intersects the first joint line and cut to make an A piece. Place another tile similarly, but mark where the right side of the tile intersects the joint. Cut this tile to give you a B piece.

4 **Trim the Outside Corners.** Put a tile directly above the last set tile at the left side of a corner. Place a third tile over these two and position it ⅛ inch from the wall. Mark the edge with a pencil, then without turning it, align it on the last set tile to the right of the corner. Mark it in a similar fashion. Cut the marked tile with a knife to remove the corner section. Fit the remaining part around the corner. When all tiles are laid, use the solvent recommended by the adhesive manufacturer to clean any adhesive from the top of the tiles.

Laying Sheet Flooring

Unlike setting tiles, putting down sheet flooring will require you to manipulate a roll of material inside a small room—a challenge for anyone. So think twice about doing it yourself.

If you do decide you are up to the challenge, begin with a scale drawing of the room on graph paper, showing the exact outline of the flooring. Bring the roll into the kitchen and let it acclimate to the room's temperature and humidity for at least 24 hours. Some resilient sheet flooring requires no adhesive, some requires adhesive around the outer edge, and some is stuck down with double-sided tape. The tried-and-true method described here is for adhesive-applied flooring. In any case, begin on a good base (see "Start with

the Right Base," page 127). Remove any edge trim, such as the base shoe, before you start.

Difficulty Level: 🔩 🔩 🔩

Tools and Materials

- ☐ Linoleum roller (rent one from your flooring supplier)
- ☐ 6- or 12-foot-wide roll of resilient flooring
- ☐ Notched trowel (notch size as specified by adhesive manufacturer)
- ☐ Framing square
- ☐ Chalkline
- ☐ Measuring tape
- ☐ Utility knife
- ☐ Straightedge
- ☐ 24-inch-long 2x4
- ☐ Handsaw
- ☐ Seam roller
- ☐ Rolling pin
- ☐ Adhesive
- ☐ Solvent

Cutting & Fitting

1 **Make the Rough Cuts.** Unroll the flooring in a room big enough to lay out the whole sheet. With a marker, draw the kitchen's edges on the flooring; add an extra 3 inches on all sides. Cut the flooring to the marks with a straightedge and a utility knife. Roll up the cut piece and take it into the kitchen, then lay the longest edge against the longest wall. Position the piece so that about 3 inches of excess goes up every wall.

2 **Lay the Second Piece (if Necessary).** Sometimes it isn't possible or practical to cover the floor with a single sheet. A deep jog in the wall may require seaming a second piece to the main piece. With the first piece in position, measure and cut the second piece

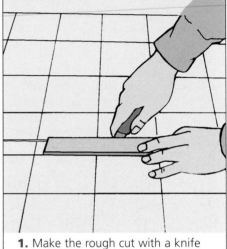

1. Make the rough cut with a knife and straightedge in an area where you can lay out the entire piece of flooring.

2. If you can't make the installation without a seam, roll out a second piece and pull it over the first piece until the patterns match. Cut it to the approximate size.

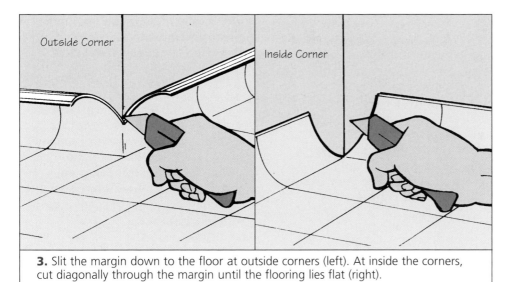

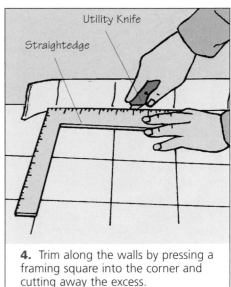

3. Slit the margin down to the floor at outside corners (left). At inside the corners, cut diagonally through the margin until the flooring lies flat (right).

4. Trim along the walls by pressing a framing square into the corner and cutting away the excess.

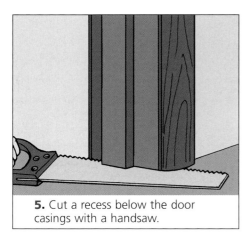

5. Cut a recess below the door casings with a handsaw.

as you did with the first one, leaving a 3-inch overlap at the seam.

3 **Trim the Corners.** At the outside corners, cut a slit straight down through the margin to the floor. Trim the inside corners by cutting the margin away with increasingly lower diagonal cuts on each side of the corner. Eventually you will have made a split wide enough to allow the flooring to lie flat.

4 **Trim the Flooring at the Walls.** Crease the flooring into the joint at the wall with a 24-inch-long piece of 2x4. Then place a framing square in the crease and cut along the wall with a utility knife, leaving a gap of ⅛ inch between the wall and the flooring.

5 **Trim the Flooring at the Door Casing.** Use a handsaw to cut a recess in the wood door casing just above the underlayment and wide enough to slide the flooring beneath. Trim the flooring to match the angles and corners of the door casing; allow about ½ inch of the flooring to slip under the casing.

Completing the Operation

1 **Apply the Adhesive.** Roll back the flooring to the center and apply adhesive to the floor with the smooth edge of a notched trowel, following the manufacturer's directions. Comb out with the notched edge. Push the flooring immediately into the adhesive. Repeat for the other half of the flooring.

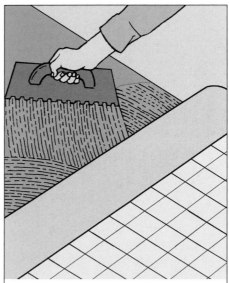

1. Roll the floor covering back to the center of the room, apply adhesive, roll the covering back down. Repeat for the other half of the flooring.

2 **Making a Seam (if Necessary).** If a second or third sheet of flooring must join the first, stop the adhesive short of the edge to be seamed by 2 inches or so. Spread adhesive on the floor to receive the second piece, stopping about 2 inches from the first sheet. Position and align the second piece carefully. With a straightedge and sharp utility knife, cut through both sheets along the seam line. Remove the waste. Peel back both edges, and apply adhesive. Press the flooring into place, Clean the seam and use the seam sealer recommended for your flooring.

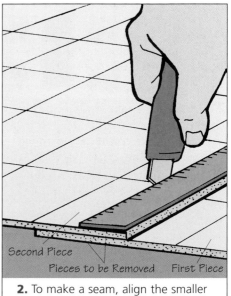

2. To make a seam, align the smaller piece with the first piece, matching the pattern. The two pieces should overlap by about 3 inches.

3. Use a rented seam roller to force out any ridges and air bubbles in the flooring; roll from the center to the edges.

3 **Clean Up and Roll Down.** Clean excess adhesive off the surface with the solvent recommended by the manufacturer. Then roll the flooring firmly into the adhesive with a roller, working from the center outward. Finally, replace the baseboard and shoe molding. When replacing the shoe, nail it into the wall rather than the floor covering to allow the floor covering to expand and contract.

Thin-Setting Tiles on Kitchen Floors

Ceramic and stone tiles can be set into adhesive (thin set) over a ply-wood or cement board underlayment or over smooth concrete using the guidelines that follow.

Tile is an expensive finish that lasts for years, so choose your material carefully and install it with patience and care. Sizes range from 1 to 12 inches square. There are many shapes to choose from, so you can create your own interesting patterns. Keep in mind, though, that trimming out nonrectangular tiles can be challenging.

Difficulty Level: 🔩 🔩 🔩

Tools and Materials

- ☐ Hammer
- ☐ Rubber float
- ☐ Pail
- ☐ Sponge
- ☐ Soft cloth
- ☐ Tiles
- ☐ Tile spacers
- ☐ Grout
- ☐ Jointing tool or toothbrush
- ☐ 1x2 or 1x4 battens
- ☐ Notched trowel (notch size as recommended for the tile and adhesive you want to use)
- ☐ Tile cutter (rent from supplier)
- ☐ Tile nippers (rent from supplier)
- ☐ 12-inch piece of 2x4 wrapped with carpet
- ☐ Adhesive (type and quantity as recommended by supplier)
- ☐ Solvent (as recommended for the adhesive)

1 **Mark the Floor and Attach the Guides.** You can lay tiles from one corner or from the center of the floor, using chalk lines as described in Step 1 under "Preparing the Layout," page 128. If the floor is small and the tiles are larger than 4x4 inches, one way to lay out the design is to use the tiles as templates and mark each tile's position on the floor. In any case, it is usually easier to have something other than the chalk line itself to work from.

Some tiles have nubs on the edges that space the tiles apart for grout lines. Plastic spacers are available for tiles without nubs.

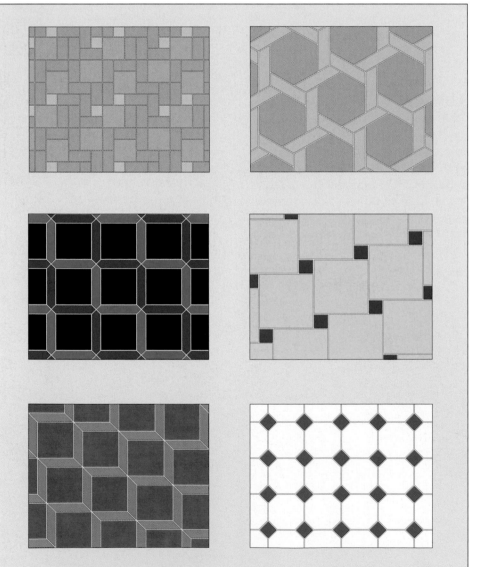

Thin-Setting Tiles on Kitchen Floors. *It is possible to make many patterns with ceramic floor tiles, but nonrectangular tiles can be challenging to cut at the edges of the floor.*

To lay out the pattern from one corner of the room, make guide strips by temporarily nailing 1x2 or 1x4 battens to the underlayment. If your tiling to concrete, weigh down the ends of the guides with heavy weights, such as a few stacked bricks. Place a strip parallel to each of two adjacent walls, with their leading edges positioned on the first joint line. To make sure the strips are at right angles, measure 3 units (36 inches, if the room is big enough) from the corner along the guide line (or strip) and mark the spot. Measure out 4 units (48 inches) along the long guide line, and mark the spot. Now measure the diagonal between the two points. If the diagonal measures 5 units (60 inches), the two guides are at right angles. Adjust the lines (or strips) as necessary.

2 **Make a Dry Run.** Check the layout with a dry run. Use tile spacers to indicate the width of the grout joint; if using mesh-backed tile sheets, you don't have to worry about joint spacing. Try to lay out the tiles to avoid narrow pieces of tile (less than 1 inch) abutting a wall. If this happens, adjust the layout.

3 **Spread the Adhesive.** Remove the tiles from the floor. Spread adhesive over about a 16-inch-square area of the substrate with the smooth side of a notched trowel, following the manufacturer's directions. Comb out with the notched edge.

Note that you may have only a limited time to work before the adhesive sets up. If you are not using wood strips as guides, take care not to cover the chalk lines with adhesive.

4 **Set the Tiles into the Adhesive.** Press each tile or sheet of tiles into the adhesive. Set mosaic tiles by rolling each sheet up loosely, then setting one edge and rolling the rest of the sheet out. Insert a spacer (except with mosaics) and lay up the next tile or sheet. If you notice that the tiles are getting progressively out of line with each other, wiggle them into position instead of lifting them out of the adhesive. Make frequent checks for alignment—every two

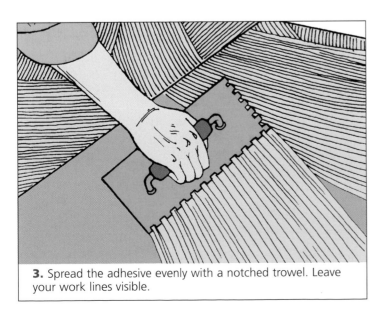

1. Check that your guide lines or guide strips are at right angles.

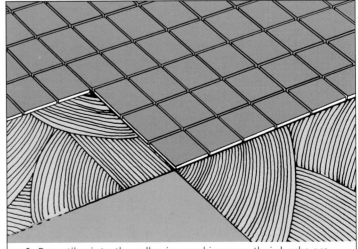

2. Lay out the tiles dry to check their position. Avoid skinny pieces of tile next to the walls.

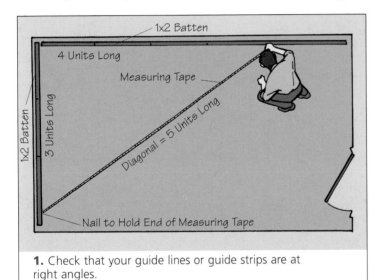

3. Spread the adhesive evenly with a notched trowel. Leave your work lines visible.

4. Press tiles into the adhesive, making sure their backs are completely covered.

Bedding Block

5. Embed the tiles into the adhesive by moving a padded board, or bedding block, over the surface and tapping the block with a hammer.

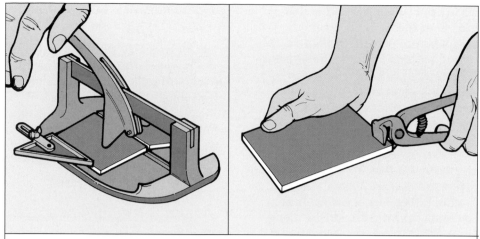

6. Cut whole tiles with a tile cutter. Moving the lever across the tile scores the cut line. Pressing down then snaps the tile apart (left). Make minor or irregular cuts by biting off small pieces of the tile with a pair of tile nippers. Keep jaws parallel to get an even cut (right).

sheets with mosaic tiles, every row with individual tiles. Before adhesive dries, wipe off any excess from the surface of the tiles.

5 **Embed the Tiles.** After laying several rows of tile, embed them into the adhesive with a carpet-wrapped 2x4. As you move the board around, tap it firmly with a hammer. Use a framing square to make sure the surface is level, row to row.

6 **Cut the Edge Tiles.** Use a tile cutter to make long straight cuts and a nipper to make irregular cuts.

Laying a Saddle (Threshold)

The transition from the tiled kitchen floor to an adjacent floor of a different material and, possibly, height is made with a saddle, or threshold. Choose among trim pieces of tile

that come with a molded edge, a solid-surface saddle (cultured marble), or hardwood. A hardwood threshold offers the chance to cut and shape the piece to blend floors of two different heights. Apply adhesive to the floor and bottom of the saddle. Allow space between the saddle and tile for a grout joint.

Grouting the Joints

Allow the adhesive to dry for the length of time recommended by the manufacturer before filling in the joints with grout. Premixed grout is ready to apply. If you buy the grout as powder, mix it as directed. Grout

may be white or colored to match or complement the tile color. Ask your tile dealer to show you the range of color available.

1 **Apply the Grout.** Spread the grout over the tiles and press it into the joints with a rubber float held at a slight angle. Work diagonally over the tiles, taking care to fill all joints.

2 **Remove the Excess Grout.** After the surface is well covered, remove any excess grout with the rubber float. To avoid removing too much grout, work across the tiles diagonally.

Laying a Saddle. Set the saddle in place before laying the last row of tiles.

1. Force grout into the joints with a rubber float.

2. Remove the excess grout by working the rubber float diagonally across the joints.

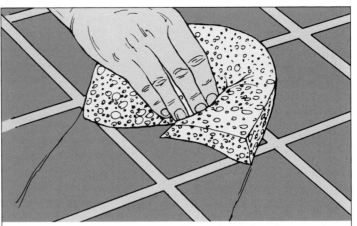

3. Wipe the remaining grout off the tiles with a dampened sponge.

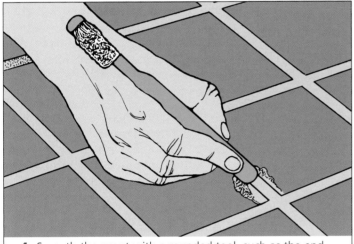

4. Smooth the grout with a rounded tool, such as the end of a toothbrush, making a slight depression.

5. Seal unglazed tile and grout with a sealant made for that purpose.

3 **Wipe Off Any Remaining Grout.** Wipe the surface with a wet sponge, squeezed out frequently in a pail of water. Get as much of the grout off the surface of the tiles as you can without eroding the joints. Then wait 30 minutes or so until the residue dries to a thin haze. Wipe this off with a soft cloth.

4 **Tool the Joints.** For large tiles, you may want the joints to be smoother than they appear after the grouting and cleaning steps. Tool the joints with a jointing tool you can obtain from your tile supplier or use the end of a toothbrush.

5 **Seal the Surface.** To prevent moisture from penetrating the grouted joints and any unglazed tiles, seal the surface with a sealant recommended by your supplier.

Some sealants are applied with a roller; others come in a spray can. Allow two weeks for the grout to dry thoroughly, then apply one coat of sealant. Apply another coat after the tiles have been down about two years.

Wood Floor Renewal

Refinishing a floor may seem like a difficult and time-consuming process as you consider it, but the work is largely done by machine. A floor sander can strip an old finish from a floor and create a completely smooth, fresh surface in a matter of two or three hours. You'll use two size sanders: The large sander has a vacuum bag and should control much of the dust; the small sander may not have this feature.

After the floor has been stripped, you may want to stain the flooring, which means you'll need to fill the pores of the wood and, after staining, apply a clear sealer that protects the stain and the wood's surface. Another alternative is to forgo the stain and apply the final finish directly over the freshly sanded wood. The usual choices for a final finish on wood flooring are urethane varnish and water-borne polyurethane.

Removing the Old Floor Finish

Considerable dust is created when sanding, so wear a dust mask. The masks are sold in paint and hardware stores. You also should wear goggles or safety glasses, especially if you wear contact lenses.

Difficulty Level: 🔩🔩 *to* 🔩🔩🔩

Tools and Materials

- ☐ Scraper and putty knife
- ☐ Wood putty if necessary
- ☐ Pry bar
- ☐ Floor sander (rented)
- ☐ Random-orbit hand sander
- ☐ Broom
- ☐ Shop vacuum
- ☐ Duct tape
- ☐ 6-mil plastic sheets
- ☐ Tarps
- ☐ Tack cloth

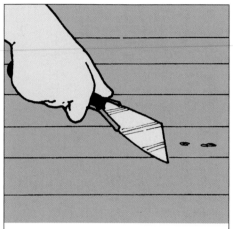

1. Before sanding the floor, check for exposed nailheads and clean up any sticky material.

1 Clean the Floor. Before beginning to refinish the floor, check the entire surface for exposed nailheads or raised corners of boards. Either of these can rip to shreds a rapidly moving sandpaper belt. Clean the floor of sticky material, which will clog your sandpaper quickly. If the floor has holes, nicks, or dents, fill these with appropriately colored wood putty.

2 Obtain Proper Equipment. Floor-sanding equipment is usually rented, and you should not have any difficulty obtaining a unit at your local rental store. You will be supplied with a drum sander, which has rollers that revolve the sandpaper at high speed. You will also need a disc or orbital hand sander for working on the perimeter of the room. All the sandpaper you will require for the job should be part of the rental price—the sandpaper will include coarse, medium, and fine grades.

You will also require a hand scraper for removing the finish in the deepest corners and a vacuum for taking up sanding dust that the sander's vacuum bag misses.

3 Clear the Room. Before beginning the sanding process, seal all electrical outlets and switches and all heating ducts and cold air returns. Use duct tape and heavy plastic sheets to cover the openings. Any dust that gets into the electrical or heating system can ignite explosively.

As an additional safety precaution, hang heavy drop sheets on either side of any door leading into the area in which you will be sanding. This will help retain the dust within that area.

Remove everything, including curtains and window shades, from the room in which you will work. Remove anything that hangs on the walls or is stored on countertops or open shelves.

Not only will it be easier to work in a completely empty room, but anything left in the room would be exposed to damage from the dust and grit produced during the sanding.

As you work, you will have to remove the dust between sandings and scrupulously clean all surfaces before refinishing. Extraneous

2. A power sander will come with a large dust bag that will control most, but not all, dust. This equipment will make the job much easier.

3. For safety reasons, seal all electrical outlets, switches, and heating and air ducts before starting the refinishing job. Hang plastic sheets over doors to keep dust from migrating into adjoining rooms.

objects in the room will merely collect dust that must be removed. If you leave fabric-covered objects like upholstered furniture or drapes in a room, the dust that the sanding produces will get into and between the fibers.

4 **Prepare to Sand.** Your rental dealer should provide you with full instructions on how to install the sanding belts and how to operate the machine. If he does not, be sure to ask him for full instructions; they will vary from machine to machine. The sander is a big, heavy machine with small metal rollers on which to wheel it when not in use. The sand-

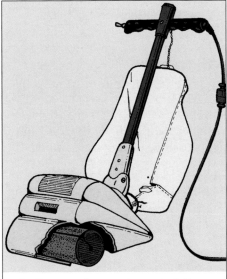

4. Floor sanders can be rented. Be sure to ask for operating instructions, as models vary.

ing belt is one piece and slips over the rollers from one side. The belt is held in place by the pressure of the rollers. In use, the machine is pushed in one direction rather like a lawnmower. There is an on-off switch in the handle.

5 **Do Rough, Medium, and Fine Sanding.** Start in one corner of the room and work diagonally so that you push the sander at a 45-degree angle to the length of the flooring. This will eliminate any irregularities on the edges or joints of the floor planks. Tilt the machine on the roller wheels so the sandpaper belt is NOT in contact with the floor, and turn on the machine. Push the machine forward, gradually lowering the machine so that the sandpaper belt makes contact with the floor.

CAUTION: Some homes may not have sufficient current to run a sander. If a fuse blows or a circuit breaker trips, unplug the machine before replacing the fuse or switching the breaker. Never start the machine with the sandpaper belt touching the floor. Never stop moving the machine when the sandpaper belt is in contact with the floor. Otherwise, you will gouge the floor.

Push the machine until you are opposite your starting point. As

you reach the other side of the room, tilt the machine and lift the sandpaper off the floor.

Move the machine as close to the wall opposite your starting place as you can without touching the wall. Tilt the handle of the machine down to lift the belt off the floor and pull the sander back to your starting point. Resand the same strip until all the finish has been removed. If there is only a single coat of finish on the floor, you may have to go over the strip only once. If there are many layers, you may have to resand two or three times. When the strip is free of finish, roll the machine to an adjacent area and position it so the belt will overlap the first strip by approximately 3 inches.

Repeat this procedure until you have sanded the entire floor and have taken off all the finish. Remember to move the machine slowly but steadily and never stop when the sanding belt is in contact with the floor.

When you have finished with this first rough machine sanding, you will still have a perimeter of un-sanded area. Use the hand-held disk sander to remove the finish in this area. Move the hand sander back and forth from left to right. You will have to hold this unit

5. If you run the sander diagonally across the floor during the first rough sanding, the unevenness will smooth out (left). A small but powerful sander allows you to sand off the finish in all but the very corners and edges of the floor (middle). You will need a hand scraper for removing the finish from the extreme corners and edges (right).

tightly because it will seem to want to "run away." For this first sanding, use coarse sandpaper, just as you did with the drum sander.

You will be able to do the border of the room with the disk sander, except for the absolute corners. To clear the corners, use the hand scraper to scrape the finish off. A small block of wood with a strip of sandpaper wrapped around it is also useful for working in corners. These two tools will also help you remove the floor finish in areas under radiators or other places where the disc sander cannot reach.

It should take approximately one-half hour to rough-sand a typical 12x15-foot room.

When the first, rough, sanding has been completed, use a broom and vacuum to clean up as much of the sanding dust as possible. Any dust left will clog the next grade of paper as you work, and grit may scratch the floor surface. It is a good idea to wear soft cotton socks on your feet as you sweep so there is no chance of grinding any of the dust into the floor with your shoes.

Continue with the medium sanding. Load the machine with medium sandpaper and repeat the procedure in exactly the same manner as before, however this time sand from one end of the room to the other. When the main area of the floor has been sanded, use the disk sander, loaded with medium paper, to do the borders of the room. Use the scraper and block of wood wrapped in sandpaper to do corners and other places the machines cannot reach, as you did the first time.

When you have finished the medium sanding, sweep and vacuum up all the dust again. Be sure to wipe away dust that has settled on the tops of window and door frames and on window sills and the top edges of molding. The room should be as dust-free as possible when you plan to apply the final finish. Any dust

that settles on the wet coat of finish will cause problems.

Finish sanding with fine sandpaper. The medium sanding should have made the floor very smooth; fine sanding will produce a surface that is nearly silky smooth and absolutely even. Follow the same sanding procedures used for the rough and medium sanding. Sand in overlapping strips, following the direction of the boards and always keeping the machine moving. Sand the main area first, then the borders and the corners. Sweep and vacuum up the dust. Wipe down the walls and ceiling, and complete the job by wiping with a tack rag, especially in corners and under obstructions such as radiators.

Filling, Staining & Finishing Wood Floors

While a clear finish is suitable for most wood floors, many people use colored stains to bring out the natural beauty of wood.

Some open-pore woods, such as oak, walnut, and mahogany, require filling before any stain and final finish are applied. Otherwise the finish can seep inti pores and create a rough appearance. If your floor is oak, you may want to fill the newly sanded surface for a glasslike final finish. Floors made of maple, a close-grain wood, do not need filling.

Applying the Filler

Obtain paste filler and thin it as needed with the recommended solvent, following the directions on the label. One of the most effective methods is to apply filler with burlap. Rub against the grain to force the filler into the pores of the wood. Both neutral and colored fillers are available. Color can be added to a filler if you wish to match your floor.

Rub the filler on the floor and apply the compound to as much of the floor as you can at one time. After

it has set for one-half hour, rub it in so the filler is forced into the pores. Before the filler dries, remove the excess with a rag moistened with turpentine. If you do not remove the excess, you will be left with a rough surface.

Choosing & Testing the Stain

Stain should be applied immediately after completion of the fine sanding and after all the dust has been removed with a vacuum, a broom, and a tack rag. One can choose among various types for a floor, but it is important to select a stain that is compatible with the final finish material. Check the label before making your selection. Consider the effect of the stain on the wood as well. For example, stain is a pigmented material that wipes on and colors the wood. While this is easy to apply, some stain tends to be opaque and may hide the grain pattern of the wood. Test the stain on an inconspicuous area before applying to the entire floor. The ideal test area is the floor of a closet. The next best choice for a test area is a spot on the floor that will be covered by a rug or hidden by furniture.

Applying the Stain

Apply stain to your test area and let it set. Then wipe off the stain with a clean, dry cloth. Repeat the procedure at increasing intervals so you can judge how long it should stand on the floor. Once you have determined a setting time for the stain, use a brush, paint pad, or clean cloth to apply the stain, keeping the overlapping strokes to a minimum. Let the stain seep into the wood. Wipe away the excess with clean, dry cloths. Plan the application of the stain so that you are always working in a dry area. The worker who paints or stains himself or herself into a corner is more common than you may think.

Allow the stain to dry for at least 24 hours before applying filler or finish.

Applying the Filler. Steel wool or burlap will force filler into pores of wood. Rub across grain to force filler in; rub with grain to remove any excess.

Applying the Floor Finish. Use a wide (4- to 6-inch) brush or a roller to apply the floor finish. Follow manufacturer's instructions.

Reversing Direction

If you intend to lay boards in hallways or closets that open off the room, you will have to butt two boards, groove end to groove end, at the transition point. To reverse tongue direction, place a slip tongue (available from flooring dealers) into the grooves of the last course of boards nailed down and slip over it the grooves of the boards that will reverse the tongue direction. Then nail the reversed boards into place, driving the nails through the tongues, and proceed as usual.

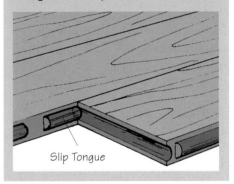

Slip Tongue

Applying the Floor Finish

When all the dust has been wiped from the entire surface of the room, including the walls and ceiling, the final finish can be applied. The most common finishes are polyurethane and water-borne polyurethane.

Polyurethane. The urethane added to this varnish increases the durability of the surface. In general, the higher the urethane content, the more durable the finish. Application may be made with either a brush or a roller.

This type of varnish is more forgiving than regular varnish when it comes to application. One of the greatest advantages of this type of varnish is that it can be applied to floors with a roller, which simplifies the job considerably. However, no roller can complete the perimeter of the floor without touching the wall, so you first must use a brush to cover the floor around the room perimeter.

Water-Borne Polyurethane. This can also be applied with a roller. It goes on milky white but dries clear. Most so-called clear finishes give a yellow or orange cast to wood, especially as they age, but water-borne finishes dry clear and remain clear. Water-borne finishes tend to raise the grain of wood floors, though, so they must be sanded well, especially after the first coat. Apply at least three coats.

New Hardwood Floors

Assuming the substructures are sound and sturdy, the subfloor must be adequately prepared to receive the new flooring. A wood floor will make a good subfloor if there are no seriously damaged boards. Drive down all nails until they are flush, correct any flaws, and replace badly warped or split boards. With a resilient tile floor, be sure the tiles are all fixed tightly; replace or recement any loose ones. If a wood or tile floor is badly damaged, lay a new subfloor.

Concrete makes a good subfloor if it is dry. A moisture barrier—a thin sheet of polyethylene sandwiched between sleepers made of 2x4s—will keep out dampness that could rot the floor.

When ordering boards, judge the quality by standards set by the National Oak Flooring Manufacturers Association. In order of decreasing quality they are: clear, select, No. 1 common, and No. 2 common. The standards are determined by color, grain, and imperfections such as streaks and knots. When ordering $\frac{3}{4}$x$2\frac{1}{4}$-inch boards, multiply the number of square feet in the room by 1.383 to determine the amount of board feet you will need in judging wastage. For other-size boards, ask your dealer how to compute the quantity.

Installing Wood Strip Flooring

Difficulty Level: 🔩 🔩

Tools and Materials
- ☐ 15-lb. Felt building paper
- ☐ Chalkline
- ☐ Basic carpentry tools
- ☐ Wood flooring
- ☐ Electric drill with assorted bits
- ☐ Cut nails
- ☐ Nail set
- ☐ Pry bar
- ☐ Rented nailing machine
- ☐ Circular saw or handsaw

1 Lay Building Paper. Remove the baseboard and shoe moldings and tack down any loose boards in the subfloor, setting all exposed nailheads. Lay a covering of 15-pound asphalt-saturated felt building paper over the subfloor. Lap the seams slightly and cut the edges flush with the walls. Nail around the edges of each sheet. When it is in place, you will use chalk to mark the joist positions.

2 Lay Work Lines. After you have laid asphalt-felt building paper, it is important to lay work lines based on either a wall that is square or on the center of the room. First mark the joist lines on the building paper with chalk. Next find the midpoints of the two walls that are parallel to the joists and snap a chalk line between them. From this line, measure equal distances to within about ½ inch of the end wall where you will begin laying strips. Snap a chalk line between these two points and let this be your work line for the first course of flooring, regardless of how uneven the wall behind it may be. Any gap between the first course and the wall can be filled with strips trimmed to fit or covered with the baseboard and shoe molding. If the room is square, cork expansion stripping can be added before replacing base trim, or the strips can be started against the wall.

3 Align a Starter Course. Along the work line that is drawn ½ inch from the wall, lay out the

1. Cut building paper to fit closely around obstructions, tack down, and mark joist locations.

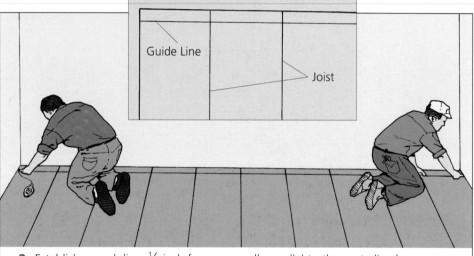

Guide Line

Joist

2. Establish a work line, ½ inch from one wall, parallel to the centerline by measuring from both sides of the centerline.

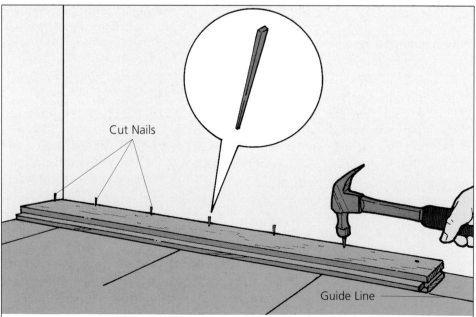

Cut Nails

Guide Line

3. Using the work lines as a guide, position the first course of boards and predrill; face-nail in position and set nails.

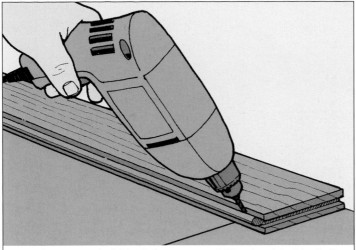

4. The tongue is fairly delicate so predrilling is advisable. Drill nailholes at the places marked for joists.

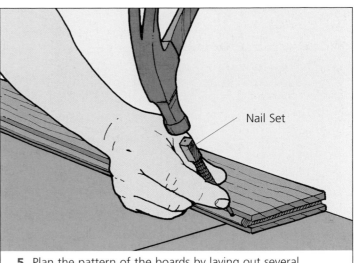

Nail Set

5. Plan the pattern of the boards by laying out several courses. Seat strips against one another, angling them into position. Put the nail into a drilled hole and drive it in most of the way; finish with a nail set.

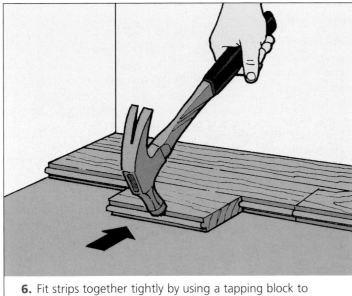

6. Fit strips together tightly by using a tapping block to protect the tongue of the board.

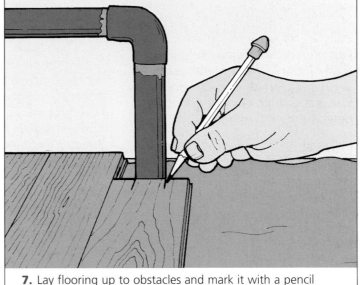

7. Lay flooring up to obstacles and mark it with a pencil where it needs to be cut to fit.

starter course (the first row of strips) the full length of the wall. Drill holes along the back edges of the strips and over the joists, slightly smaller than the nails. Then face-nail.

4 **Nail Through the Tongue.** Predrill holes through the tongue of the first course of strips into the joists. Then drive finishing nails and set them. The first few rows of strips will be too close to the wall to use a power nailer.

5 **Lay a Field.** Lay out several courses of strips the way they will be installed. Plan as much as

six or seven rows ahead. Stagger the end joints so that each joint is more than 6 inches from the joints in the adjoining rows. You may have to cut pieces to fit at the end of each row. Try to fit the pattern so that no end piece is shorter than 8 inches. Leave ½ inch between the end of each row and the wall. When you have laid out a field of rows, begin to fit and nail.

6 **Fit and Nail.** As you lay each row, use a scrap of flooring as a tapping block. Do not hit the block too hard or you may damage the tongue. To keep from marring the

strip with the hammer when you nail, do not hammer nails flush into the tongue. Instead leave the nail-head exposed, place the nail set on the nailhead, and drive the nail home by hammering the nail set. Use the tip of the nail set to countersink the nail into the board.

7 **Cut Around Obstacles.** When you come to an obstacle such as a radiator or a corner, trial-fit the boards and measure carefully, making a cardboard template if necessary to transfer the cut onto the board. Decide whether you should save the tongue or groove.

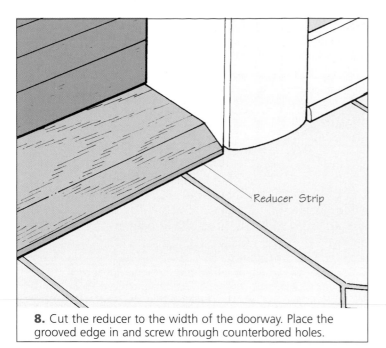

8. Cut the reducer to the width of the doorway. Place the grooved edge in and screw through counterbored holes.

Pry Bar

9. Use a pry bar between the wall and the last course to wedge it into position.

Clamp the board to a workbench and cut it to fit with a handsaw.

8 **Finish Doorways.** To finish a doorway where the new floor will meet a floor that is lower, install a clamshell reducer strip by screwing or face-nailing it. The name comes from its rounded top, which resembles half of a clamshell. The reducer strip is made so that one side will fit over the tongue of the adjoining piece of flooring. The strip also can be butted to meet flooring that runs perpendicular to the doorway.

9 **Install the Final Piece.** For gaps of more than ½ inch between the final strip and the wall, remove the tongue sides of as many strips as you need, cut them to width, and wedge them into place with a pry bar. Hold them tightly with the pry bar by placing your foot on the bar while its hooked end pulls the filler piece up tightly against the last strip. Face-nail these last boards, then replace the base trim and shoe moldings.

Laminated Wood Floors

In addition to solid-wood strips and planks, wood flooring comes in an easy-to-install prefinished laminated version. As its name suggests, prefinished laminated wood flooring comes with a factory-applied finished topcoat and is manufactured by cross-laminating layers of wood veneer. The ½-inch-thick flooring comes in strips 2 to 4 inches wide or in planks that run more than 4 inches wide. The planks are often made of a number of narrow strips assembled together to resemble strip flooring when installed. In both forms, strip and plank, the flooring locks together with tongue-and-groove edges.

Installing a Floating Floor

Because it's made from layers of wood plies, laminated flooring is more stable than solid wood and can be installed where ordinary wood flooring might have problems, say below grade and over concrete. This stability also enables the flooring to be installed as a floating floor system over a ⅛-inch thick layer of high-density foam underlayment. The tongue-and-groove joints are glued; no nails are used in the installation. Laminated flooring

Using a Nailing Machine

When you reach the fourth row or so of flooring strips, you will have enough room to use a rented nailing machine. Begin about 2 inches from the wall and slip the nailing machine onto the tongue of the last strip laid. Strike the plunger with a heavy rubber-headed mallet, hard enough to drive a nail through the tongue and into the floor. Drive a nail into each joist and into the subfloor halfway between joists. Be careful when using this machine to keep it from marring the new floorboards.

may be laid over any smooth, dry, level subfloor.

Difficulty Level:

Tools and Materials

- ☐ 6-mil-thick plastic as a vapor barrier when installing over concrete
- ☐ Foam underlayment
- ☐ Duct tape
- ☐ Laminated flooring
- ☐ White glue
- ☐ Hammer
- ☐ Measuring tape
- ☐ Pencil
- ☐ Handsaw or circular saw

1 Prepare the Floor. Roll out the foam underlayment and cut it to fit the room. Butt the joints and seal them with duct tape. If you're installing the floor over concrete, first lay a vapor barrier of polyethylene sheeting at least 6 mil thick. Overlap the vapor barrier joints by at least 6 inches and tape them with duct tape.

2 Lay the Planks. Leave a ½-inch expansion gap around the perime-ter of the room. Start the installation on the longest wall of the kitchen, with the panel's groove facing the wall.

3 Join the Planks. Try to work in room-length runs. Join the planks by running a bead of white glue in the bottom edge of the groove as you install each succeeding section.

4 Finish the Job. Tap the sections together tightly with a hammer and a scrap piece of flooring as a hammering block. Mark, cut, and install planks in irregular areas just as you would a normal wood floor.

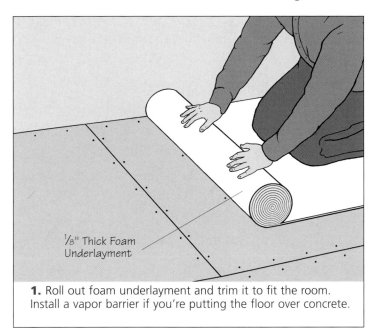

1. Roll out foam underlayment and trim it to fit the room. Install a vapor barrier if you're putting the floor over concrete.

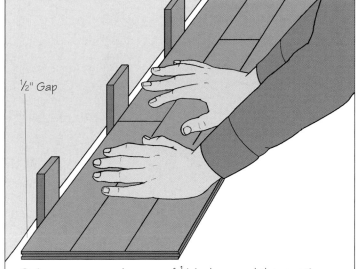

2. Leave an expansion gap of ½ inch around the room's perimeter and begin laying the planking with the groove side against the wall.

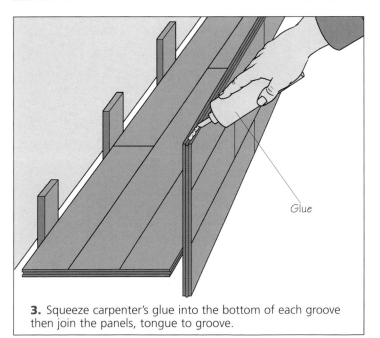

3. Squeeze carpenter's glue into the bottom of each groove then join the panels, tongue to groove.

4. Tap the joint tight along the entire run of planking with a hammer and block made from scrap flooring.

8

Projects:
Putting It All Together

This stage of the project is when everything finally comes together. You've finished the walls the ceilings. You've finished the floor. Now's the time to assemble your cabinetry and appliances and reclaim the kitchen for your family.

If you're particularly ambitious, you might want to build your own base, wall, and/or pantry cabinets rather than order them ready-made. You'll find complete instructions here to do just that. If your cabinets are in good shape but just need to be dressed up a bit, you can reface them. We also show you how to install and trim the cabinets, make and install a new countertop, and install built-in appliances like waste disposers, dishwashers, and ranges.

Building Your Own Base Cabinets

This simple but handsome base cabinet is designed to go with the wall cabinet featured on page 151. The Materials List provided is for a cabinet that's 18 inches wide, a standard cabinet width. You'll probably want to gang several cabinets together for the counter length you need. Standard commercially avail-

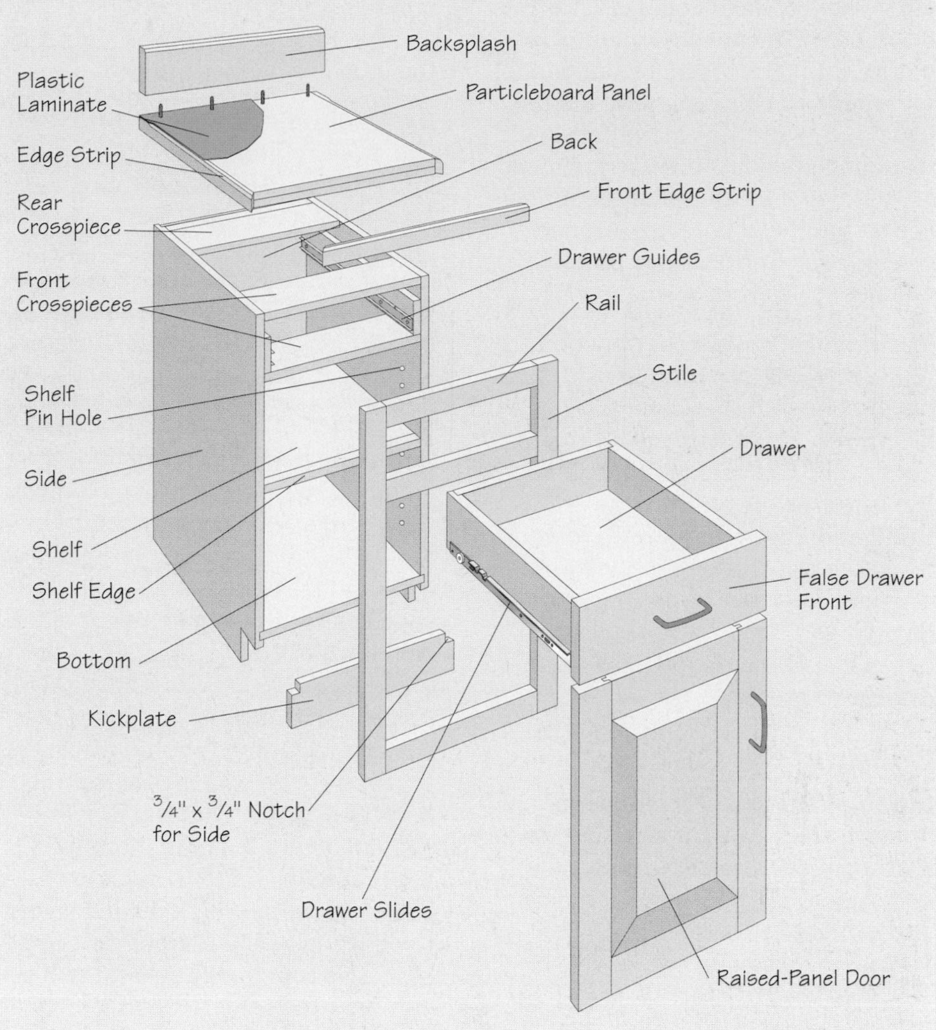

Building Your Own Base Cabinets. The cabinets are made primarily from plywood. You can make the face frames from hardwood for staining or from pine for painting.

Difficulty Level:

Materials List

Quantity	Part	Dimensions
Carcase and face frame		
2	Plywood sides	$3/4$" x $23\,1/4$" x $35\,1/4$"
1	Plywood bottom	$3/4$" x $22\,7/8$" x 17"
1	Plywood back	$1/4$" x $17\,1/4$" x $35\,1/4$"
1	Plywood shelf	$3/4$" x $21\,1/4$" x 16"
1	Kickplate	$3/4$" x 5" x 18"
1	Nailing cleat	$3/4$" x $1\,1/2$" x $16\,1/2$"
3	Plywood crosspieces	$3/4$" x 5" x $16\,1/2$"
2	Solid-wood slide hangers	$3/4$" x $3\,1/4$" x $22\,7/8$"
1	Solid-wood shelf edge	$3/4$" x $3/4$" x 16"
2	Solid-wood stiles	$3/4$" x $1\,1/2$" x 31"
3	Solid-wood rails	$3/4$" x $1\,1/2$" x 15"
Door (with $3/8$" overlay)		
1	Solid-wood panel	$3/4$" x $12\,1/2$" x 20"
2	Solid-wood stiles	$3/4$" x 2" x $23\,1/4$"
2	Solid-wood rails	$3/4$" x 2" x $12\,1/2$"

Quantity	Part	Dimensions
Drawer		
2	Plywood sides	$1/2$" x 3" x $23\,1/2$"
1	Front	$3/4$" x 3" x $13\,1/2$"
1	Back	$3/4$" x $2\,1/2$" x $13\,1/2$"
1	Plywood bottom	$1/4$" x $13\,1/2$" x $23\,1/8$"
1	False front	$3/4$" x $4\,3/4$" x $15\,3/4$"
Hardware		
	3d, 4d & 6d Finishing nails	
	$3/4$ & $7/8$-inch Brads	
4	Adjustable shelf pins	
1 pair	Side-mounted drawer slides	
1 pair	Overlay hinges	
2	Door/drawer pulls	
	#6 x 2-inch Flathead wood screws	
	#6 x $1\,1/4$-inch Flathead wood screws	

able base cabinets come in widths from 9 to 36 inches in 3-inch increments, and 36 to 48 inches in 6-inch increments. With commercial cabinets, exact width is made by site-trimming standard filler strips. One advantage of custom-built cabinets is that you need not waste space with filler strips. You can build cabinets to fit your space exactly.

Make the cabinets from plywood. Use hardwood plywood for side panels that will show and AC-grade fir plywood for side panels that abut other cabinets or walls. Make the face frames, doors, drawer front, and edge trim from hardwood to match the hardwood plywood. The kickplate can be solid wood or plywood. The drawer sides and backs can be matching hardwood or clear pine.

Building the Carcase

Cut the Plywood. Cut the sides, bottom, shelf, crosspieces, and back to the dimensions in the Materials List. Adjust the dimensions for the size cabinet or cabinets you'll be

building. Cut a notch for the kickplate in each side panel as shown in the drawing.

Drill Holes for the Shelf Pins. Drill holes in the inside faces of both side panels as shown for the adjustable shelf pins. Shelf pins come in a variety of styles. Some include brass insets that you tap into the holes, dressing them up a bit and making them more durable. Most shelf pins require a ¼-inch-diameter hole, but this varies.

To ensure perfect horizontal alignment, make a simple drilling template from a scrap of ¼-inch-thick plywood. Rip the scrap to about 5 or 6 inches wide and make it about 5 inches shorter than the inside height of the cabinet. Mark one long edge of the template as the "register edge." On this template, lay out the hole spacing you want. A good spacing is to make the holes 2 inches from the register edge. Lay out the first hole about 8 inches from the bottom of the template and then lay out a hole about every 1½ inches from the bottom of the template. Stop about 3 inches from the top of the template.

To drill the holes, use a stop collar or a piece of tape on the drill bit to mark the depth you want to drill. Align the register edge of the template to the front edge of the cabinet. Make sure the bottom of the template rests on the bottom of the cabinet. Clamp the template in place and drill the holes. Now flip the template over so you will be drilling through the other side. Push the register edge against the back of the cabinet. Drill the holes. Repeat this process for the holes in the opposing panel.

Dado and Rabbet the Sides. Dado and rabbet the side panels as shown in the drawing at left. Use a dado blade in your table saw for the dadoes, grooves, and

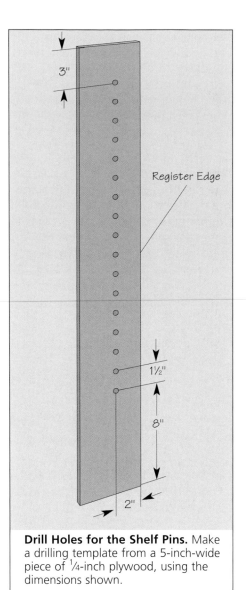

Drill Holes for the Shelf Pins. Make a drilling template from a 5-inch-wide piece of ¼-inch plywood, using the dimensions shown.

rabbets. If you don't have a dado blade, make multiple passes on the saw with a regular blade. The rabbet for the back is ⅛ inch deeper than the plywood to create a fitting allowance for a less-than-perfect wall. Note that the drawing shows one cabinet side. Don't forget to make the other side in a mirror image.

Assemble the Carcase. Use glue and 6d finishing nails to join the sides to the bottom shelf. Cut the nailing cleat to the dimensions in the Materials List. Glue and nail the nailing cleat to the sides. Glue the rear crosspiece to the nailing cleat and nail it to the sides. Install the remaining crosspieces as shown in the drawing on page 145. Note that the lower crosspiece is 4¾ inches

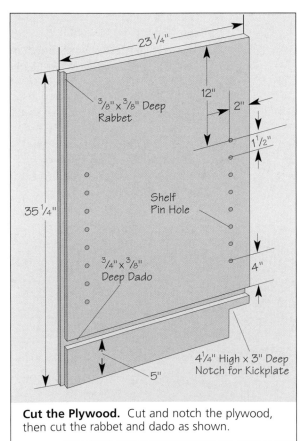

Cut the Plywood. Cut and notch the plywood, then cut the rabbet and dado as shown.

below the top crosspiece. This will give you a 4-inch-high drawer opening. Notch the kickplate and install it at the bottom front of the carcase with glue and 4d finishing nails.

Install the Drawer Slide Hangers. Cut the drawer slide hangers to the dimensions in the Materials List. The top of the hangers will fit under the nailing cleat while the bottom of the hangers will rest on the lower front crosspiece. Glue and screw the hangers to the cabinet sides. Use #6x1¼-inch flathead wood screws.

Install the Back. Use a framing square to make sure the sides are square with the upper crosspiece. Apply glue to the rabbets in the side panels, lay the back in place, and secure it with ⅞-inch brads.

Make the Shelf. Cut the shelf edge to the dimensions in the Materials List. Glue and clamp it to the front edge of the shelf.

Cut and Attach the Stiles and Rails. The rail dimensions in the Materials List will make the stiles flush to the sides of the cabinet. This looks best for a freestanding cabinet. If you're building a run of cabinets, you may want to add ¼ inch to the rail lengths. This way the stiles will extend ⅛ inch past each side of the cabinet. This will allow for warped cabinet sides or irregular walls. If you do this, you'll need to adjust the door widths accordingly. Cut the stiles and fasten them with glue and 6d finishing nails. Then cut the rails to fit between and fasten them the same way.

Building the Frame-and-Panel Doors

Cut the Rails and Stiles. The door dimensions in the Materials List are for a door that overlays the face frame by ⅜ inch on all sides. Cut the stiles to door height. Cut the rails to door width plus the length of the two tenons, less the width of the two stiles. For example, if the door is 20 inches wide with 2-inch-wide stiles and you want ⅜-inch tenons, you

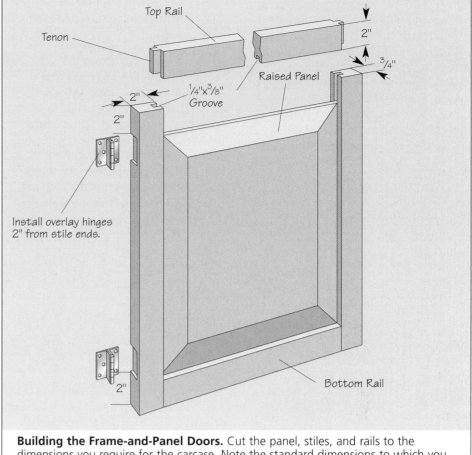

Building the Frame-and-Panel Doors. Cut the panel, stiles, and rails to the dimensions you require for the carcase. Note the standard dimensions to which you must work.

would cut the rails 16¾ inches long (20 + ¾ - 4 =16¾). Do this work with the miter gauge on the table saw.

Groove the Stiles and Rails. Adjust the dado cutter in your saw to a width that matches the thickness of your door panels. Measure the panel to be sure. Position your rip fence to guide the frame member sides when milling the panel grooves. It's important that the grooves are centered on the frame edges. To test your fence position, turn on the saw and guide a scrap cutoff against the fence and through the cut. Now turn the piece around and, with the groove facing down, guide its opposite side against the fence to make a second pass. If your fence is set correctly, the width of the groove shouldn't increase with the second pass.

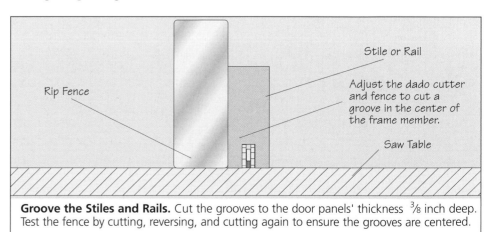

Groove the Stiles and Rails. Cut the grooves to the door panels' thickness ⅜ inch deep. Test the fence by cutting, reversing, and cutting again to ensure the grooves are centered.

Cut the Tenons. Each rail tenon is as thick as the door panel and is ⅜ inch long. Lay out a sample tenon on a piece of rail stock. Adjust the dado cutter's height to ¼ inch. Screw a piece of stock to your table saw's miter gauge so it will support stock close to the blade. Clamp a stop block to the rip fence ahead of the blade. Adjust the fence and stop block so that it positions the shoulder layout to the blade. Hold or clamp the rail securely to the miter gauge and slide it past the stop block and over the dado cutter. This way there is no danger of pinching the work between the cutter and the rip fence. Flip the rail over and cut the other side of the tenon. Before cutting the actual rails, cut some scrap wood stock to check the tenon's fit in the groove.

Then adjust the stop block or cutter height until you get a perfect fit. Cut the tenons on both ends of each of the rails.

Cut the Panel. The panel in a frame-and-panel door should be ⅛ inch shorter and narrower than the groove measurements of the frame. The easiest way to determine this is to test-fit the stiles and rails and to measure the opening where the panel is to fit. This will also give you a chance to see how the frame fits together. Square up the frame, then measure the height and width of each opening. Add ⅝ inch to each measurement to get the finished dimensions of each panel for a door that has ⅜-inch grooves. Cut the panel to size, then raise it.

Raise the Panel. You'll need an auxiliary fence tall enough to support the wide panel. Make the fence from a piece of ¾-inch plywood or a straight 1x6 or wider board and bolt it onto your saw's fence according to your saw's instructions. Raise the saw blade to about 2 inches. Tilt the blade away from the fence 15 degrees from vertical. Set the fence ¼ inch from the blade's near teeth. Back the panel against the auxiliary fence. Select a scrap of 1x3 or 1x4 that is a little longer than the panel. Place this scrap guide board on top of the auxiliary fence and clamp it to the panel as shown in the drawing. Press firmly on the guide board as you run the panel through the saw. Cut the two bevels that go across the grain first. That way, any tear-out will be eliminated when you cut the bevels that run with the grain.

***NOTE:** On most table saws the blade tilts to the right of the operator's side. In this case, you will have to place the fence to the left of the blade.*

Build the Door. Glue the tenons and assemble the door frame around the panel. Be careful not to glue the panel into the grooves accidently. The idea is to give the panel freedom to expand and con-

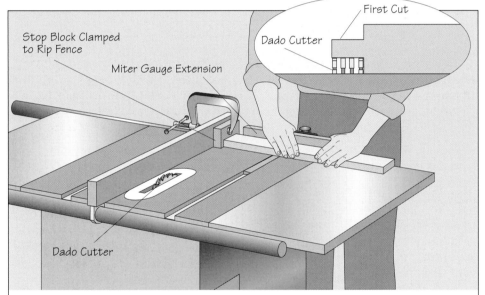

Cut the Tenons. Use a miter gauge extension and a stop block on the rip fence to cut ⅜-inch-long tenons in the rails. Make the tenons the same thickness as the panel.

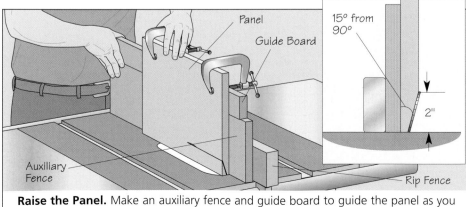

Raise the Panel. Make an auxiliary fence and guide board to guide the panel as you bevel it. Adjust the saw blade, then cut the bevels going across the grain first.

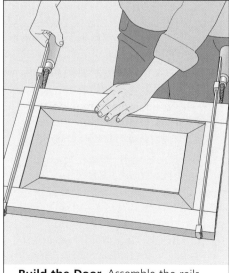

Build the Door. Assemble the rails and stiles. Glue the tenons but don't glue the panel into the grooves.

tract with changes in humidity without pushing the frame apart. Draw the stiles against the rails with bar or pipe clamps and let the door stand overnight.

Installing the Overlay Doors

Install the Hinges on the Doors. You'll find overlay hinges available in a variety of styles and finishes. Mark the hinge locations and drill pilot holes for the hinge screws. Install the hinges on the doors.

Install the Hinges on the Cabinet. After the cabinet or cabinets have been installed, set the door or doors in place with the hinges already attached. With the doors correctly positioned, mark the face frame for the hinge-screw pilot holes. Drill the holes in the face frame, hang the door, then attach the door pulls.

Building the Drawers

The instructions and drawings here assume your drawers will overlay the face frame.

Cut the Parts. The drawer shown is a simple box with a false front that overlays the drawer opening by ⅜ inch on all sides. Cut the parts according to the dimensions in the Materials List.

> You might find it difficult to square up a drawer after the bottom is installed. Some cabinet-makers recommend making the drawer bottom ¹⁄₃₂ inch shorter in length and width to allow some room for adjustment.
>
> Test-fit the bottom before permanently installing it. Clamp the panel in place and check for square. If you find that you cannot coax the drawer square, plane or sand the edges off the bottom panel to provide a little more leeway.

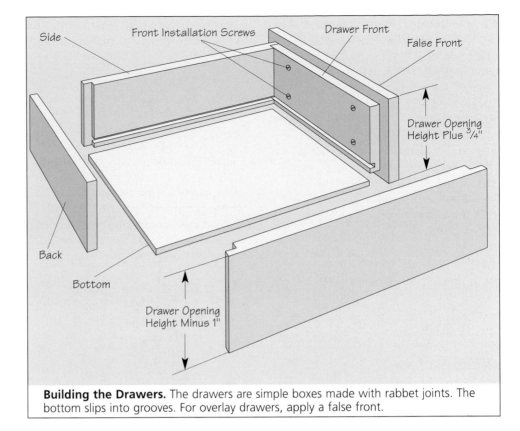

Building the Drawers. The drawers are simple boxes made with rabbet joints. The bottom slips into grooves. For overlay drawers, apply a false front.

Groove the Side and Front Panels. Set the table saw blade ¼ inch above the table and ⅝ inch away from the fence. Run the front panel and each side panel over the blade to create a ⅛-inch-wide by ¼-inch-deep groove in each panel. Move the fence ⅛ inch closer to the blade, and run each piece through again to widen the groove to ¼ inch. Leave the fence set as it is for the next step.

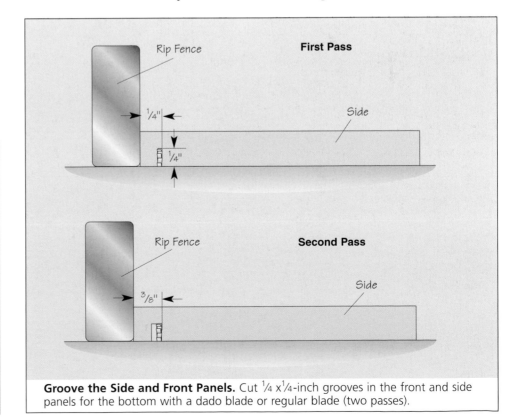

Groove the Side and Front Panels. Cut ¼ x¼-inch grooves in the front and side panels for the bottom with a dado blade or regular blade (two passes).

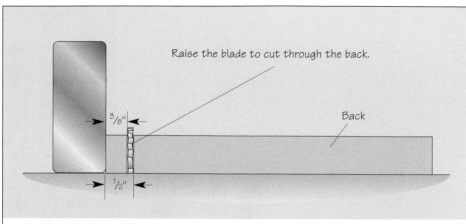

Raise the blade to cut through the back.

3/8"

1/2"

Back

Trim the Rear Panel. Leaving the rip fence set up as shown for cutting the grooves, cut through the drawer back panel so it will sit on top of the drawer bottom.

Trim the Rear Panel. Don't move the rip fence, but raise the blade about ½ inch. Rip ⅝ inch from the rear panel. Be sure to use a push stick, not your hand, to move this narrow piece between the fence and blade. Now the rear panel will be precisely the right height and width to fit above the drawer bottom grooves.

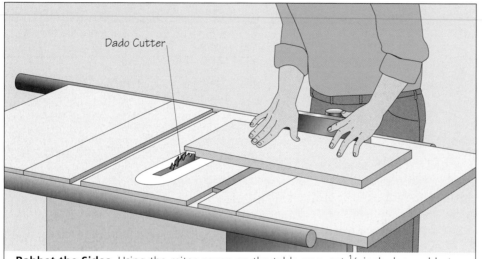

Dado Cutter

Rabbet the Sides. Using the miter gauge on the table saw, cut ¼-inch-deep rabbets in the drawer sides. Cut with a dado cutter or make multiple passes.

Rabbet the Sides. Set the dado cutter for a width that matches the thickness of your wood. Raise the cutter to ¼ inch above the table saw. Remove the fence from the saw. Use the miter gauge to mill a ¼-inch-deep rabbet that has a width that matches your wood. Rabbet each end of each side panel. In the absence of a dado cutter, make each rabbet with multiple passes over the saw blade.

Assemble the Drawer. Apply glue to the front rabbets in the side panels and the ends of the front panel, and attach the side panels to the front panel with three 3d finishing nails on each side. Slide the bottom panel into position, all the way forward. Apply glue to the rear rabbets in the side panels and to the ends and bottom edge of the rear panel. Put the rear panel in

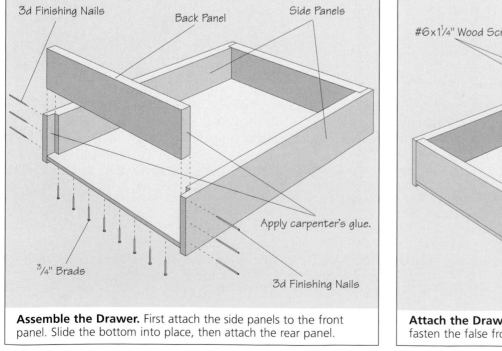

3d Finishing Nails

Back Panel

Side Panels

Apply carpenter's glue.

¾" Brads

3d Finishing Nails

Assemble the Drawer. First attach the side panels to the front panel. Slide the bottom into place, then attach the rear panel.

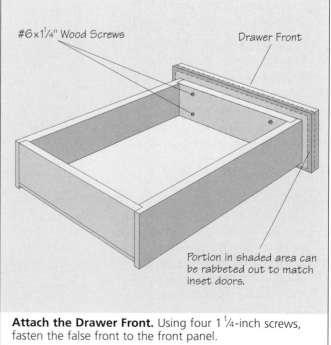

#6 x 1¼" Wood Screws

Drawer Front

Portion in shaded area can be rabbeted out to match inset doors.

Attach the Drawer Front. Using four 1¼-inch screws, fasten the false front to the front panel.

place, flush with the top of the side panels and nail on the sides. Check the drawer for square; then secure the bottom to the rear panels with ¾-inch brads.

Attach the Drawer Front. Attach the false front to the front-end panel with four #6x1¼-inch wood screws driven through countersunk pilot holes near each front inside corner of the drawer.

Finish the Cabinet or Cabinets. Apply stains and/or clear finish to the cabinets. Polyurethane is a good, durable choice for kitchen cabinets as a final finish. Install the drawer pulls with the screws provided and install the shelf on the adjustable shelf pins in the lower portion of the cabinet.

Installing Drawer Slide Hardware

Install the Drawer Slides. Use screws supplied to attach the drawer slides to the bottoms of the sides, locating the rollers at the rear of the drawer. The non-roller end should touch the back of the drawer front.

Install the Drawer Guides. Align the drawer guide perpendicular to the cabinet front, resting on the bottom of the cabinet drawer opening with the wheel at the front of the opening. Most guides have both oblong and round holes for mounting screws. If you first mount the guides to the sides of the cabinet using the oblong holes, you can make fine adjustments before permanently installing the guides using the round holes.

Building Your Own Wall Cabinets

Base cabinets are the foundation of a kitchen remodel, but well-designed wall cabinets make the first impression. Because they're at eye level, they are often the first thing people see in a kitchen, as well as the first place people reach

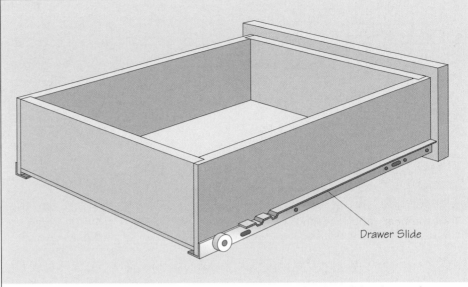

Install the Drawer Slides. Align the slides with the back edge of the drawer front as shown. Orient the slides so the roller sits at the rear of the drawer.

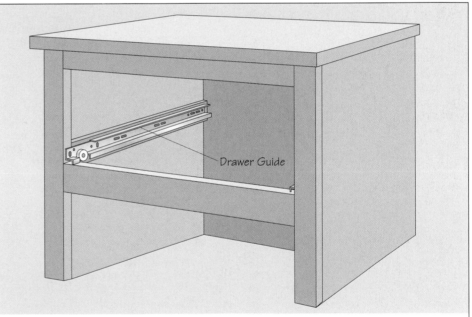

Install the Drawer Guides. Rest the guides on the bottom of the drawer opening and install them so they are level, with the roller at the front of the opening.

for kitchen supplies. The wall cabinet on the next page is designed to go with the base kitchen cabinet that's featured on page 145.

Like the base cabinet it matches, the wall cabinet is 18 inches wide, a standard cabinet width, and the Materials List reflects this. However, you can modify the dimensions to suit your needs. For example, a common modification of upper cabinets is to re-size them to fit around a range hood or over a re-frigerator. Because the basic wall

cabinet has no fixed shelves, it's particularly easy to modify for height; simply shorten or lengthen the sides, face frame, and door by the same amount.

Similarly, if you have a wider expanse to cover, you may want to widen the cabinets. A good solution is to make the cabinet twice as wide and install double doors. If you make such a modification, you'll need to add a center stile to the face frame. Make the center stile twice as wide as the side stiles.

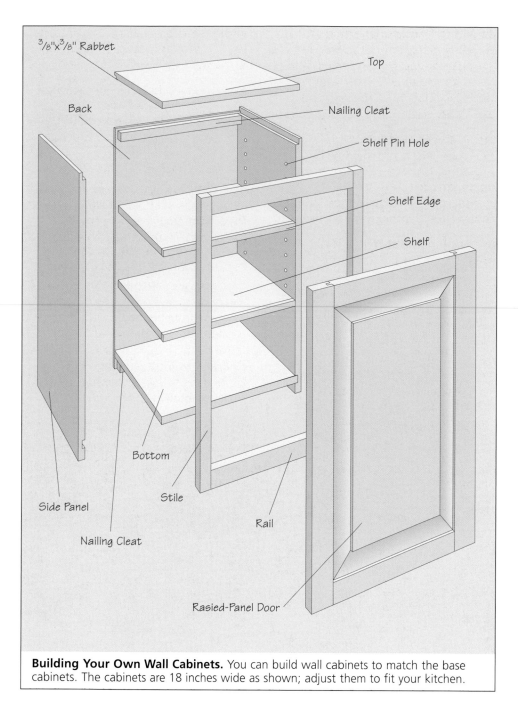

3/8"x3/8" Rabbet

Top

Back

Nailing Cleat

Shelf Pin Hole

Shelf Edge

Shelf

Side Panel

Bottom

Nailing Cleat

Stile

Rail

Rasied-Panel Door

Building Your Own Wall Cabinets. You can build wall cabinets to match the base cabinets. The cabinets are 18 inches wide as shown; adjust them to fit your kitchen.

To make the basic wall cabinet, use hardwood plywood for the side panels that will show and AC-grade fir plywood for the side panels that abut other cabinets or walls. Face frames, doors, and edge trim should all be hardwood to match the hardwood plywood you use.

Building the Carcase

Cut the Plywood. Cut the sides, bottom, shelves, and back to the dimensions in the Materials List. Adjust the dimensions for the size cabinets you want to build.

Predrill for the Shelf Pins. Drill holes in the inside faces of both side panels for the adjustable shelf pins as shown in the drawing on the next page.

To ensure perfect horizontal alignment, make a simple drilling template from a scrap of ¼-inch-thick plywood as shown on page 146. Rip the scrap to about 5 or 6 inches wide and make it about 5 inches shorter than the inside height of the cabinet. Mark one long edge of the template as the "register edge." On this template, lay out the hole spacing you want. A good spacing is to make the holes two inches from the register edge. Lay out the first hole about 8 inches from the bottom of the template and then lay out a hole about every 1½ inches from the bottom of the template. Stop about 3 inches from the top of the template.

Difficulty Level: 🔩 🔩

Materials List

Quantity	Part	Dimensions
Carcase and face frame		
1	Plywood top	¾" x 11¼" x 17¼"
2	Plywood sides	¾" x 11¼" x 30"
1	Plywood bottom	¾" x 11" x 17¼"
2	Plywood shelves	¾" x 10¼" x 16¼"
1	Plywood back	¼" x 17¼" x 29⅝"
2	Nailing cleats	¾" x 1½" x 16½"
2	Solid-wood shelf edges	¾" x ¾" x 16¼"
2	Solid-wood stiles	¾" x 1½" x 30"
2	Solid-wood rails	¾" x 2¼" x 15"

Quantity	Part	Dimensions
Door (with ⅜" overlay)		
1	Solid-wood panel	¾" x 12½" x 23"
2	Solid-wood stiles	¾" x 2" x 26¼"
2	Solid-wood rails	¾" x 2" x 12½"
Hardware		
12	Adjustable shelf pins	
	6d Finishing nails	
	⅞-inch Brads	
1 pair	Overlay hinges	
1	Door pull	
	3-inch Drywall screws	

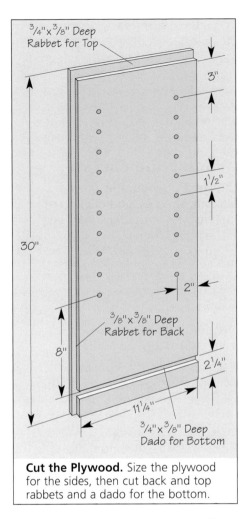

Cut the Plywood. Size the plywood for the sides, then cut back and top rabbets and a dado for the bottom.

To drill the holes, use a stop collar or a piece of tape on the drill bit to mark the depth you want to drill. Align the register edge of the template to the front edge of the cabinet. Make sure the bottom of the template rests on the bottom of the cabinet. Clamp the template in place and drill the holes. Now flip the template over so you will be drilling through the other side. Push the register edge against the back of the cabinet. Drill the holes. Repeat this process for the holes in the opposing panel.

Cut Side and Top Dadoes and Rabbets. Dado and rabbet the side panels as shown in the drawing above. The rabbets for the back in the sides and top are ⅛ inch deeper than the thickness of the back to create a fitting allowance for less-than-perfect walls. Note that the drawing shows one cabinet side. Make the other side in a mirror image.

Build the Carcase. Use glue and 6d finishing nails to join the sides to the bottom and top. Cut the nailing cleats to the dimensions in the Materials List. Glue and nail the nailing cleats in place.

Insert the Back. Use a framing square to make sure the sides are square with the top and bottom. Apply glue to the rabbets in the side and top panels, lay the back in place and secure it with ⅞-inch brads.

Assemble the Stiles and Rails. The rail dimensions in the Materials List will make the stiles flush to the sides of the cabinet. This looks best for an individual cabinet. If you're building a run of cabinets, however, you may want to add ¼ inch to the rail lengths to allow for warped cabinet sides or irregular walls (add ¼ inch to door width, too). Cut the stiles and fasten them with glue

and 6d finishing nails. Then cut the rails to fit between and fasten them the same way.

Prepare the Shelves. Cut the shelf edges to the dimensions in the Materials List. Glue and clamp them to the front edges of the shelves.

Making the Doors

Size the Rails and Stiles. The door dimensions in the Materials List are for a door that overlays the face frame by ⅜ inch on all sides. Cut the stiles to door height. Cut the rails to door width plus the length of the two tenons, less the width of the two stiles. For example, if the door is 16 inches wide with 2-inch-wide stiles, and you want ⅜-inch tenons, you would cut the rails 12¾ inches long (16 + ¾ - 4 = 12¾). Do this work with the miter gauge on the table saw.

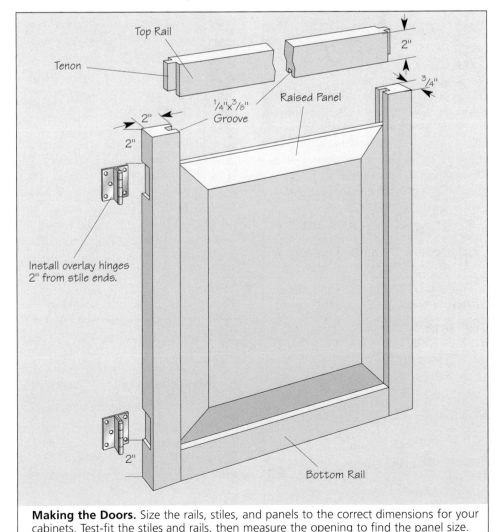

Making the Doors. Size the rails, stiles, and panels to the correct dimensions for your cabinets. Test-fit the stiles and rails, then measure the opening to find the panel size.

Mill Grooves in the Stiles and Rails. Adjust the dado cutter in your saw to a width that matches the thickness of your door panels. Measure the panel to be sure. Position your rip fence to guide the frame member sides when cutting the panel grooves. It's important that the grooves are centered on the frame edges. To test your fence position, turn on the saw and guide a scrap cutoff against the fence and through the cut. Now turn the piece around, and with the groove facing down, guide its opposite side against the fence to make a second pass. If your fence is set correctly, the width of the groove shouldn't increase with the second pass.

Form the Tenons. Each rail tenon is as thick as the door panel and is $\frac{3}{8}$ inch long. Lay out a sample tenon on a piece of rail stock. Adjust the dado cutter's height to $\frac{1}{4}$ inch. Screw a piece of stock to your table saw's miter gauge so it will support stock close to the blade. Clamp a stop block to the rip fence ahead of the blade. Adjust the fence and stop block so that it positions the shoulder layout to the blade. Hold or clamp the rail securely to the miter gauge and slide it past the stop block and over the dado cutter. This way there is no danger of pinching the work between the cutter and the rip fence. Flip the rail over and cut the other side of the tenon. Before cutting the actual rails, cut some scrap wood stock to check the tenon's fit in the groove. Then adjust the stop block or cutter height until you get a perfect fit. Cut the tenons on both ends of each of the rails.

Fit the Panel. The panel in a frame-and-panel door should be $\frac{1}{8}$ inch shorter and narrower than the groove measurements of the frame. The easiest way to determine this is to test-fit the stiles and rails and to measure the opening where the panel is to fit. This will also give you a chance to see how the frame fits together. Square up the frame, then measure the height and width

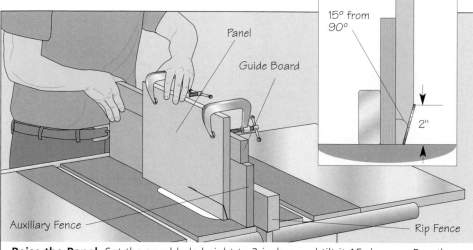

Raise the Panel. Set the saw-blade height to 2 inches and tilt it 15 degrees. Run the panel through the saw using an auxiliary fence and guide board to support the panel.

of each opening. Add $\frac{5}{8}$ inch to each measurement to get the finished dimensions of each panel for a door that has $\frac{3}{8}$-inch grooves. Cut the panel to size, then raise it.

Raise the Panel. You'll need an auxiliary fence tall enough to support the wide panel. Make the fence from a piece of $\frac{3}{4}$-inch plywood or a straight 1x6 or wider board and bolt it onto your saw's fence according to your saw's instructions. Raise the saw blade to about 2 inches. Tilt the blade away from the fence 15 degrees from vertical. Set the fence $\frac{1}{4}$ inch from the blade's near teeth. Back the panel against the auxiliary fence. Select a scrap of 1x3 or 1x4 that is a little longer than the panel. Place this scrap guide board on top of the auxiliary fence and clamp it to the panel as shown in the drawing above. Press firmly on the guide board as you run the panel through the saw. Cut the two bevels that go across the grain first. That way, any tear-out will be eliminated when you cut the bevels that run with the grain.

NOTE: *On most table saws the blade tilts to the right of the operator's side. In this case, you will have to place the fence to the left of the blade.*

Assemble the Door. Glue the tenons and assemble the door around the panel. Be careful not to glue the panel into the groove accidently. The idea is to give the panel freedom to expand and contract with changes in humidity without pushing the frame apart. Draw the stiles against the rails with bar or pipe clamps and let the door stand overnight.

Hanging the Doors

Attach the Hinges to the Door. Overlay hinges come in a variety of styles and finishes. Buy the hinges you like and use them to mark the hinge locations and screw holes on the doors. Drill pilot holes for the hinge screws and install the hinges on the doors.

Attach the Door to the Cabinet. After installing the cabinet or cabinets, set the doors in place with the hinges already attached. With the doors correctly positioned, mark the face frame for the hinge-screw pilot holes. Drill the holes in the face frame, hang the door, and attach the door pulls.

Finish the Cabinet. Apply stain or a clear finish to the cabinet to match the base cabinets. Polyurethane is a good, durable choice for the final finish. Install the shelves, using the adjustable shelf pins and setting them where desired.

Building Your Own Pantry Cabinet

Among the best features of many older houses and a few newer ones is a tremendously practical storage area known as a pantry. Pantries come in many sizes and configurations, ranging from small shelved closets to good-sized rooms with cabinets, shelving, and counter space.

The spacious cabinet featured here has one fixed shelf and four adjustable shelves that rest on supports attached to metal standards. Cut the standards needed for this pantry from eight 42-inch or four 84-inch standards.

The cabinet is designed to give you the convenience of a pantry without taking up much space. It will fit wherever 32 inches of wall space exists, or you can change dimensions to fit larger or smaller spaces.

This unit matches the base and wall cabinets featured earlier and can be installed with existing cabinets where the distance from floor to ceiling or soffit is 84 inches. In the absence of a soffit, you can build the cabinet to match existing cabinets or extend it all the way to the ceiling. To facilitate cabinet placement, allow ½ inch of clearance between the cabinet top and soffit; then conceal the gap with molding.

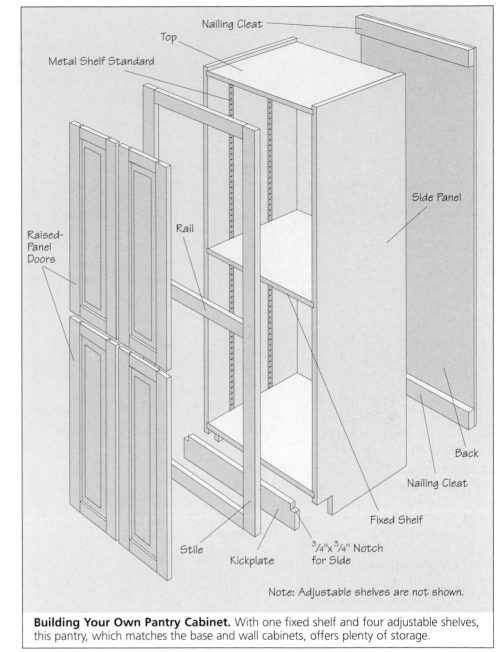

Building Your Own Pantry Cabinet. With one fixed shelf and four adjustable shelves, this pantry, which matches the base and wall cabinets, offers plenty of storage.

Difficulty Level:

Materials List

Quantity	Part	Dimensions
Carcase, shelves, and face frame		
2	Plywood side panels	$\frac{3}{4}$" x 23$\frac{1}{4}$" x 83$\frac{1}{2}$"
3	Plywood top, bottom and fixed shelf	$\frac{3}{4}$" x 23" x 31$\frac{1}{4}$"
4	Plywood shelves	$\frac{3}{4}$" x 22$\frac{1}{8}$" x 30$\frac{1}{4}$"
4	Solid-wood shelf edges	$\frac{3}{4}$" x $\frac{3}{4}$" x 30$\frac{1}{4}$"
1	Plywood back	$\frac{1}{4}$" x 31$\frac{1}{4}$" x 82$\frac{1}{2}$"
2	Solid-wood nailing cleats	$\frac{3}{4}$" x 3$\frac{1}{2}$" x 31$\frac{1}{4}$"
1	Solid-wood kickplate	$\frac{3}{4}$" x 5" x 32"
2	Solid-wood stiles	$\frac{3}{4}$" x 1$\frac{1}{2}$" x 79$\frac{1}{4}$"
3	Solid-wood rails	$\frac{3}{4}$" x 1$\frac{1}{2}$" x 29"

Quantity	Part	Dimensions
Doors (with $\frac{3}{8}$" overlay)		
4	Solid-wood panels	$\frac{3}{4}$" x 11$\frac{3}{4}$" x 34$\frac{7}{8}$"
8	Solid-wood stiles	$\frac{3}{4}$" x 2" x 38$\frac{1}{8}$"
8	Solid-wood rails	$\frac{3}{4}$" x 2" x 11$\frac{3}{4}$"
Hardware		
	4d & 6d Finishing nails	
	$\frac{7}{8}$" Brads	
	#10 x 3$\frac{1}{2}$-inch Wood screws	
4	37$\frac{7}{8}$-inch Metal shelf standards	
4	38$\frac{1}{8}$-inch Metal shelf standards	
16	Metal shelf supports	
4	Door pulls	
8	Self-closing hinges	

Building the Carcase

Cut the parts. Cut the sides, top, bottom, shelves, and back from plywood and the nailing cleats and kickplate from solid wood, all to the dimensions in the Materials List. Then cut the kickplate notches in the bottom edge of each side panel, as shown in the drawing at right.

Cut the Dadoes. Cut three ¾-inch dadoes ⅜ inch deep across the inside surfaces of the side panels. Position the dadoes as shown in the drawing at right.

Cut Grooves for the Standards. Rout ³⁄₁₆-inch-deep and ⅝-inch-wide grooves in the side panels. Locate these grooves as shown in the drawing. Note that the drawing shows one cabinet side. Don't forget to make the other side in a mirror image.

Cut the Rabbets. Cut a ⅜ x⅜-inch rabbet along the rear inside edge of each side panel as shown in the drawing. These rabbets are ⅛ inch deeper than the back panel thickness to create a fitting allowance for less-than-perfect walls. Then use a straight bit to widen the rabbet to 1 inch for 3½ inches below the top dado and 3½ inches above the bottom dado. This accommodates the 1x4 nailers. Square off these widened areas with a chisel.

Assemble the Cabinet. Assemble the top, bottom, and fixed shelf to the sides with glue and four 4d finishing nails into each dado.

Attach the Kickplate and Nailers. Apply glue to the front edges of the kickplate notches, lay the kickplate in place, and secure it with two 4d finishing nails at each end. Apply glue to the widened rabbets in the rear of the side panels, position the nailers between the rabbets, and drive two 4d finishing nails through the side panels into each end of each nailer.

Attach the Back Panel. Apply glue to the rabbets in the rear edges of the side panels, the rear edges of

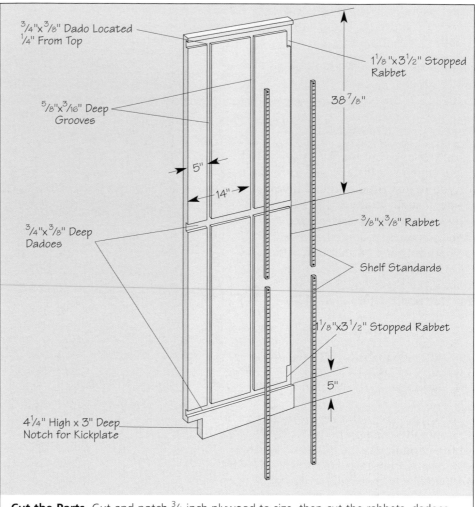

³⁄₄"x³⁄₈" Dado Located ¼" From Top

⁵⁄₈"x³⁄₁₆" Deep Grooves

³⁄₄"x³⁄₈" Deep Dadoes

4¼" High x 3" Deep Notch for Kickplate

1⅛"x3½" Stopped Rabbet

38⁷⁄₈"

5"

14"

³⁄₈"x³⁄₈" Rabbet

Shelf Standards

1⅛"x3½" Stopped Rabbet

5"

Cut the Parts. Cut and notch ¾-inch plywood to size, then cut the rabbets, dadoes, and grooves. Also cut the top, bottom, shelves, back, nailing cleats, and kickplate.

the horizontal panels, and the rear surfaces of the nailers. Lay the back panel in place with its top edge flush to the top of the top panel. Secure the back with ⅞-inch brads.

Building & Installing the Face Frame & Shelves

Cut and Attach the Stiles and Rails. Cut the face-frame stiles to the dimensions in the Materials List and fasten them to the cabinet with glue and 6d finishing nails. Cut the rails to fit between, then glue and nail them with their tops flush to the tops of the top, fixed shelf, and bottom.

Complete the Adjustable Shelves. Cut the solid-wood shelf edges to the dimensions in the Materials List. Glue and clamp the edges to the front of the adjustable shelves.

Install the Cabinet. Before installing the cabinet, sand the solid-wood parts and apply the finish of your choice. Set the cabinet in place against the wall. Make sure the unit is plumb and level, and shim it as necessary beneath the side panels and kickplate. Then attach the cabinet to the wall by driving two #10x3½-inch wood screws through each nailer into each stud (four screws per nailer).

Install the Shelves. Use a hacksaw to trim the metal shelf standards to length. Make all the cuts from the top ends of the standards to keep them in perfect register. Then set the standards in place inside the grooves in the side panels, and secure them with the nails provided. Snap a metal shelf support into each standard for each shelf; then lay the shelves atop the supports.

Build and attach the raised-panel doors as shown in "Making the Doors," page 153.

Cabinet Face Lift

Your existing kitchen may be well designed and the cabinets structurally sound, but perhaps the cabinets' finish is a little worse for wear or you're just tired of them. If you want to keep what you have but update the cabinets' style, you can reface them. Refacing cabinets is a good option if you want a natural or stained wood look. If you want painted cabinets, you'd be better off painting what you have.

Refacing Kitchen Cabinets

Refacing kits generally include new doors, new drawer fronts, and self-adhesive veneer to be applied to the cabinet face frames and sides. You can also buy all new hardware to complete the updated look the of the cabinets.

Difficulty Level:

Tools and Materials

☐ Screwdrivers (flat-bladed and Phillips)
☐ Scraper and sandpaper
☐ Putty knife
☐ Wood putty
☐ Paint and brushes (if necessary)
☐ Utility knife
☐ Veneer (self-adhesive)
☐ Laminate roller
☐ Stain and/or polyurethane
☐ Bristle brush
☐ Hinges
☐ Pencil
☐ Electric drill and assorted bits
☐ Handsaw
☐ Spring and/or C-clamps
☐ 1-inch Wood screws

1 **Strip the Cabinets.** Remove the doors, drawers, and hinges from your existing cabinets. Take any drawer-pull hardware off the drawer fronts. Scrape and sand old peeling finish from the cabinet face frames and sides. Fill all holes, gouges, and scratches with wood

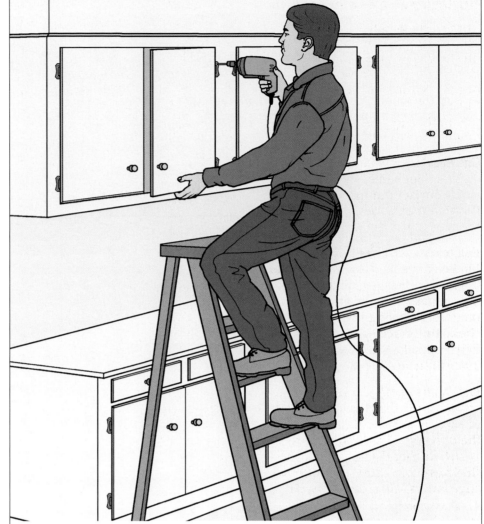

1. Begin by removing the hardware, including hinges, handles, and pulls, as well as the doors and drawers from the wall and base cabinets.

putty. Then sand all the patched surfaces with 150-grit sandpaper. If you intend to paint the cabinet interior, do it now.

2 **Apply Veneer.** Lay the veneer out on a smooth surface. Measure all the surfaces to be covered and add ¼ inch to each dimension. Cut the veneer with a sharp utility knife and steel straightedge. Remove the protective backing and apply the veneer to the sides and the front vertical and front horizontal members, in that order. Carefully trim the veneer with a razor knife and sandpaper after each application. Roll all the veneered surfaces with a laminate or wallpaper roller.

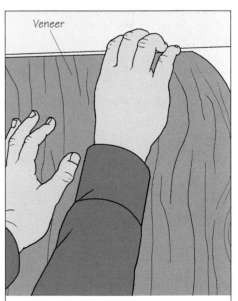

2. Peel the protective backing from the self-adhesive veneer and apply the veneer first to the sides of the cabinets, then to the face frames.

3 Apply Finish to the Cabinets.
Stain the new doors and
drawer fronts, followed by a few
coats of clear polyurethane finish.
Or just apply the polyurethane if
you want to maintain the natural
look of the wood. Also, finish the
sides and face frames to match
the doors. Sand lightly between
the coats of polyurethane for a
total of three coats.

4 Attach the Door Hinges. Lay
the doors on a smooth surface,
set the new hinges 2 inches from
the top and bottom of the doors,
and mark the screw holes. If the
hinges are hidden, lay the door face
down. If the hinges are fully visible,
lay the door face up. Drill pilot
holes and attach the hinges with
the supplied screws. Hold the doors
in the appropriate openings and
mark the hinge locations on the
cabinet face frame. Be sure the
door overlaps the opening by an
equal amount around the perimeter. Leave about a ⅛-inch space
between doors that cover a single
opening. Drill pilot holes in the face
frame and hang the doors. Once the
doors are up, install any handles,
knobs, and catches you may have.

5 Prepare the Drawer Fronts.
Look at your existing drawer
fronts. If they're made from one
piece, clamp them face down to a
work table and cut off the over-
hanging edges with a handsaw. If
they're made from two pieces, with
a decorative false front attached
to the drawer carcass, remove the
front panel and throw it away.

6 Attach New Drawer Fronts.
Lay the new drawer fronts
on a worktable, face down. Set a
prepared drawer box on a panel,
centered with an equal overlap
around the perimeter of the drawer
front. Drill pilot holes through the
front of the drawer into the decorative panel and secure it with
screws. Attach a false front to
the sink cabinet by spanning the
opening from behind with a wood
block and driving screws through

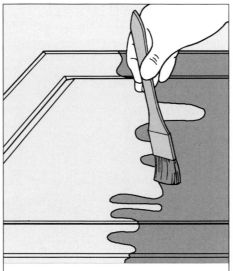

3. Apply stain to the unfinished wood
doors and drawer fronts. Stain the
veneer on the cabinets' sides and
face frames to match.

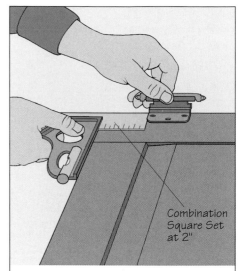

4. Set the hinges on the backs of the
doors, two inches from the top and
bottom. Use a combination square
locked to that dimension as a guide.

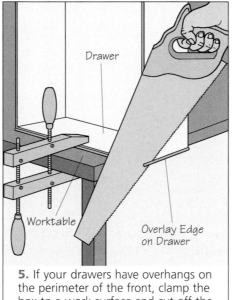

5. If your drawers have overhangs on
the perimeter of the front, clamp the
box to a work surface and cut off the
overhang with a handsaw.

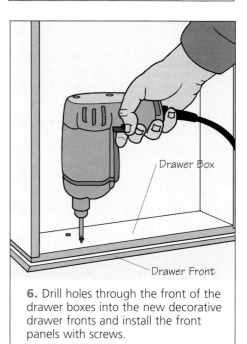

6. Drill holes through the front of the
drawer boxes into the new decorative
drawer fronts and install the front
panels with screws.

the block into the panel. Attach
pulls or handles to all the drawer
and false fronts to complete
the installation.

Cabinet Installation

Wall materials such as plaster and
drywall don't have the strength to
support heavy cabinets. Cabinets
should be supported by framing
inside the wall, which usually means
screwing through the wall surface
into studs. Studs are typically installed on 16-inch centers, so once
you've located one, you can measure along the wall to find and mark
other fastening points.

A magnetic stud finder is one of the
simplest and least expensive ways
to find studs. These nifty gadgets
detect the nails or screws used to
attach the wallboard to the wood.
A bit more expensive but even
better are electronic stud finders,
available in home centers and
hardware stores.

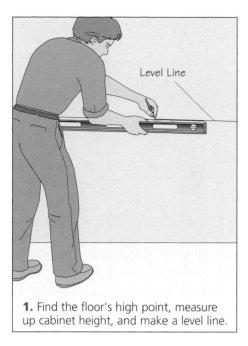

1. Find the floor's high point, measure up cabinet height, and make a level line.

In the absence of a stud finder, probe the wall with a small nail. Make sure that the holes you create will be covered by the cabinet after installation.

Difficulty Level:

Tools and Materials
- ☐ Cabinets
- ☐ Filler strips as needed
- ☐ Stud finder (or nail or awl)
- ☐ 48-inch level
- ☐ Measuring tape
- ☐ Pencil
- ☐ Wood shims
- ☐ Utility knife
- ☐ 2, 2½, 3, and 3½-inch wood screws
- ☐ Handsaw
- ☐ Electric drill with assorted bits
- ☐ C-clamps
- ☐ Screwdrivers (flat-bladed and Phillips)
- ☐ Vinyl or wood kickplates
- ☐ One-by ledger material
- ☐ Quarter-round molding

Installing Base Cabinets

There's no such thing as a perfectly level floor or plumb wall. Even the best walls have a slight ripple; the best laid floor may slope away from the wall imperceptibly. These minor imperfections can ruin a perfectly good finish. Fortunately, it's easy to accommodate for these imperfections during installation.

1 **Scribe a Level Line.** Use a level to find the high spot in the floor where you're installing the cabinet. To do this, set a level on the floor and check whether the floor is level. If it isn't, slide the level along to the high side until the bubble shifts to the other side of the vial. Mark that spot as the high point of your floor.

Measure up the wall from the floor's high point, and make a mark at cabinet height. Use the level to scribe a level line along the wall for the full length of the cabinet or cabinets.

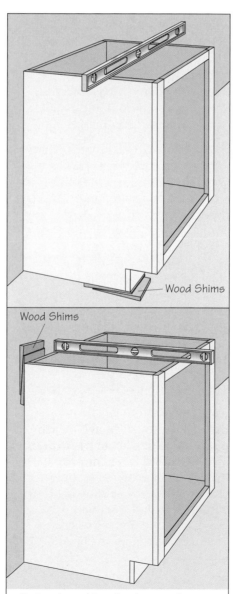

2. Put the cabinet in place against the level line. Use shims to level it, front to back. Do the same side-to-side, then fasten the cabinet to studs.

2 **Install the Cabinet.** Slide the cabinet against the wall, and check it against the level line. Use wood shims at the base of the cabinet to level it from side to side and from front to back. Once the cabinet is level and plumb, attach it to the studs with 3½-inch screws. Trim the shims with a utility knife or chisel.

3 **Install Filler Strips.** If your layout calls for a filler strip at one or both ends of the cabinet run, measure carefully and cut a strip or strips to fit. Then pull the end cabinet or cabinets out, clamp each strip to a stile, and bore two pilot holes for screws through the edge of the stile into the filler. Counterbore these holes so the screwheads won't protrude above the surface. Drive the screws, slide the cabinet or cabinets back into position, and check again to be sure the cabinets are level.

4 **Join the Cabinets.** Secure cabinets to each other by screwing through the stiles, just as you did with the filler strips. Drill and countersink holes for two #8x2½-inch wood screws at each juncture. As you tighten the screws, watch to be sure that the face

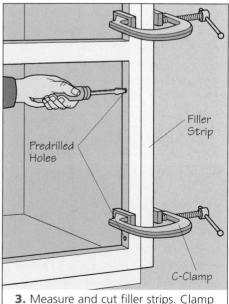

3. Measure and cut filler strips. Clamp the strips to the cabinet's stile and fasten them with screws.

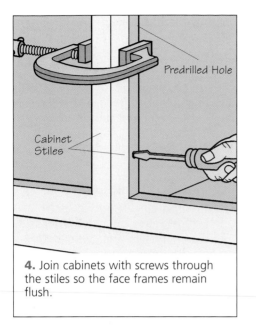

4. Join cabinets with screws through the stiles so the face frames remain flush.

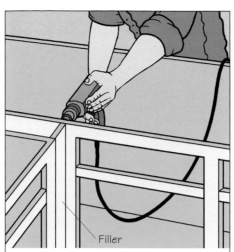

5. Turn a corner by attaching both cabinets to one filler piece. Install one cabinet, attach the filler to the other, then connect them.

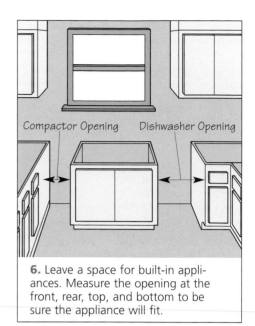

6. Leave a space for built-in appliances. Measure the opening at the front, rear, top, and bottom to be sure the appliance will fit.

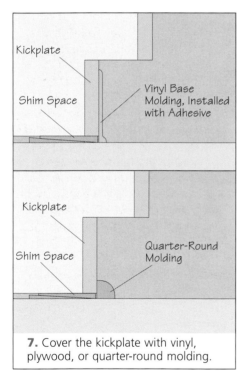

7. Cover the kickplate with vinyl, plywood, or quarter-round molding.

frames remain square and on exactly the same plane.

5 **How to Turn a Corner.** At a corner you'll probably need a filler strip. Install one cabinet, attach a filler to the second cabinet with screws, then butt the two together and drive a second set of screws into the filler. Offset these screws from the first ones.

6 **Leave Space for Appliances.** At points where you want a dishwasher, range, or other built-

in appliance, provide an opening exactly the width called for by the manufacturer. Measure the opening at the front and rear, as well as the top and bottom.

7 **Finish the Kickplates.** There are at least three ways to cover the gaps caused by shimming. An easy and ideal solution for kitchens, where floors will get wet, is to use vinyl base molding. You can attach vinyl molding with construction adhesive or contact cement. It's flexible enough to allow you to press it into place and trim it at the top with a utility knife. You can also face the kickplate with strips of ¼-inch-thick plywood. Or you can add a run of quarter-round molding.

Installing Wall Cabinets

Wall cabinets are a little more difficult to install than base cabinets because they must be hung. Even positioning small units in place can be exhausting unless you have a means of supporting them in place. One of the most basic ways of doing this is to screw a temporary ledger, or rail, along the bottom line of the cabinets.

1 **Install the Ledger.** Using a level, draw a line along the wall indicating the bottom of the wall cabinets. Using 2-inch screws,

secure a temporary ledger along that line. Make sure that you've screwed into studs, and that the board is perfectly level before continuing to the next step.

2 **Hang the Cabinets.** Begin a run of cabinets with an end or corner unit. The first cabinet determines the alignment for the entire run, so be extra careful leveling and shimming it. Lift each succeeding cabinet onto the ledger and position it as close to the wall as possible. Drive two 3-inch

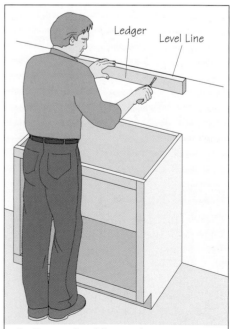

1. Draw a level line at the correct height and attach a temporary ledger.

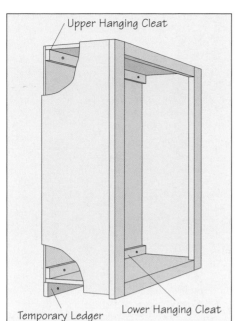

2. Set the cabinet on the ledger; fasten it through the hanging cleats.

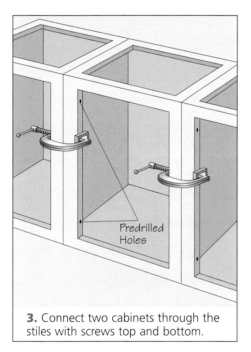

3. Connect two cabinets through the stiles with screws top and bottom.

screws through the hanging cleat just tight enough to hold the cabinet in place. Check for level from front to back. You may have to do a little shimming. Secure the bottom of the cabinet to the wall by driving two 3-inch screws through the lower cleat and into the studs.

3 **Connect the Cabinets.** After you've installed two or more adjacent cabinets, clamp them at their face frames. Bore through the

stiles with a ³⁄₃₂-inch bit and connect them with #6x2½-inch wood screws at the top and bottom.

Depending on how flat and plumb the walls are, there will probably be gaps between the walls and the cabinet. These can easily be concealed by installing quarter-round or other molding along the cabinet.

Trimwork

Besides adding another level of decor to your kitchen, molding can be used to conceal nailholes, screwholes, and other blemishes that are inevitable in construction. Typically, molding is used as a transition piece to cover the gap between a cabinet and a wall, a cabinet and the floor, or a cabinet and another cabinet.

Removing Trim

You'll have to remove any base trim or crown molding from walls or old cabinets before you can install the new cabinets. If you carefully remove this trimwork, you'll be able to reinstall it later.

The best place to start removing trim is where it begins—at a door or corner. If the joint at the corner is coped, remove the coped piece first, then the butted piece. Starting

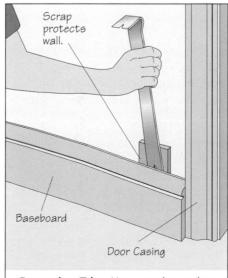

Removing Trim. Use a pry bar to lever molding carefully away from the wall.

at the end, coax the molding away from the wall with a pry bar. Pry as near the nails as possible, and use a thin scrap of wood behind the pry bar to protect the wall. After you've pried part of the the trim away from the wall, move to the next nail. Continue this process until you gradually pry away the entire length of material.

If a strip of molding won't come loose, drive the nails through the piece with a nail set. It's much easier to patch these holes later than to fix broken trim.

■ Nail Safety ■

One of the most common, and most potentially painful, sights around a construction site is a board with a nail (or nails) in it. Remove nails from trim as soon as you remove the trim from the wall. The best way to extract nails from trim without damaging the face of the wood is to pull them completely through the back of the piece. Use slip-joint pliers or end nippers to grab the point of the finishing nail and lever the nail out by rocking the tool. If the molding is damaged or if you're not planning to reuse a piece and you don't want to waste time and energy removing nails, make it a habit to bend the nails over with a hammer.

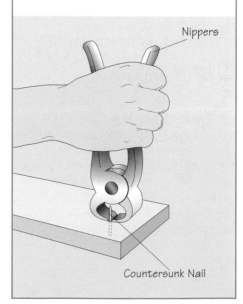

Replacing Trim

Replace any trim you removed earlier, and add new matching trim as required. Wherever possible, use the existing nailholes. Nail removal will have enlarged the holes, so use larger nails during replacement. Fill the exposed nailholes and do any necessary touch up.

When replacing molding, you'll have to fit pieces together around corners. Miter joints are the way to go for outside corners. But for inside corners, it is better to use coped joints. Done properly, a coped joint looks seamless, allowing the profile to continue smoothly through the corner. Coped joints are less likely to open up than inside miter joints.

Making a Coped Joint

Difficulty Level: 🔩 🔩

Tools and Materials
- [ ] Molding
- [ ] Backsaw
- [ ] Combination square
- [ ] Pencil
- [ ] Miter box or power miter saw
- [ ] Coping saw
- [ ] Round file
- [ ] Utility knife or small chisel

1 Miter the Molding. To make a coped joint, first miter the piece of molding as if you were fitting an inside miter. Pencil a 90-degree angle at the top edge of the molding. Then run the pencil along the profile revealed by the miter cut.

2 Cope the Joint. Using a coping saw, back-cut the molding by following the line where the miter meets the front of the molding. If the molding has curves across its entire face, cope all the way across. If it's a molding like a baseboard with a large flat field, you may want to complete the cut with a miter saw. Test-fit your coped piece and fine-tune it with a chisel or small file.

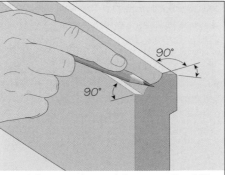

1. Miter-cut the molding; pencil a 90° line along the top and profile.

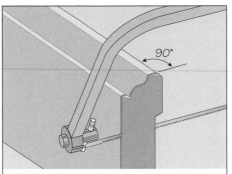

2. Straight-cut the mitered molding, following the lines along the profile.

Once the coped joint is in position, butt the cope against the existing molding and allow the opposite end to run long. Mark the back of the long end and square-cut it to the correct length.

Cutting Crown Molding

Whether you're adding new molding or recutting and replacing molding you removed for cabinet installation, you should have no trouble making the simple cuts with a miter box and backsaw or power miter saw. One kind of molding that might give you some trouble, however, is crown molding. Because of its design, it gets installed differently and must be cut differently.

Crown molding leans at a 45-degree angle from the vertical surface to which it's attached. The trick to cutting crown molding is to lean it in the miter box at that same angle. The easiest way to do this is to turn the molding upside down, so the back faces toward you when it's in the miter box or miter saw. To keep the molding in place when

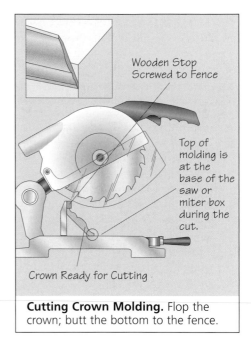

Cutting Crown Molding. Flop the crown; butt the bottom to the fence.

you lean it, attach a stop block to the fence or table. Use a strip of ¾-inch-square stock and screw or clamp it in place.

Installing Crown Molding

Attaching crown molding to a wall is simple—just tilt it into position against the wall and ceiling, and nail it in place. If you're using it on a cabinet, you can install it the same way. You may need to bevel-cut some blocking material and attach that at the top of the cabinet to provide additional support for wider moldings.

Countertops

You'll need to consider countertop options for the new kitchen cabinets. The right countertop will provide you with a convenient and durable work surface.

Plastic laminate is a durable, stain-resistant material that has many applications. Laminate comes in various lengths, widths, textures, and colors to match just about any job and to fit into any project budget. You'll find that the 0.05-inch general-purpose grade is the most common laminate for countertops.

Be extra careful when working with sheets of laminate. The sheets can easily crack or chip before you attach them to a substrate. If you can, have large sheets cut to size at the home center or a cabinet shop.

You can build plastic-laminate countertops in your own shop or you can purchase factory-made countertops, which are available in several standard sizes in most home centers. Some stores can even cut panels to order. These countertops come prelaminated with a special post-forming grade of plastic laminate that can be bent into gentle curves. These "post-formed" counters feature integral backsplashes and curved front edges or no-drip bullnose profiles.

Cutting Plastic Laminate

While it's possible to cut plastic laminate with a saber saw and a special laminate-cutting blade, it's slow work. There's also a chance that you'll damage the material during the cut, or at least not get a smooth finish.

The best tool for cutting plastic laminates is your router and a ¼-inch straight-cutting bit. Use a carbide-tipped bit; plastic laminate will dull a steel-tipped bit in seconds. To guide the router when cutting laminate, make a jig as shown.

When you use the jig, set the laminate on top of a sacrificial piece of plywood. Align the cutting slot to your cutting layout line. Clamp the laminate and the jig to the plywood. Set the router depth to go through the laminate and slightly into the plywood.

Cut edge strips for any project about ¼ inch wider than you need. You'll trim the excess off with a router and a flush-trimming bit after installation. Cut countertops and other flat surfaces about ½ inch larger on all dimensions.

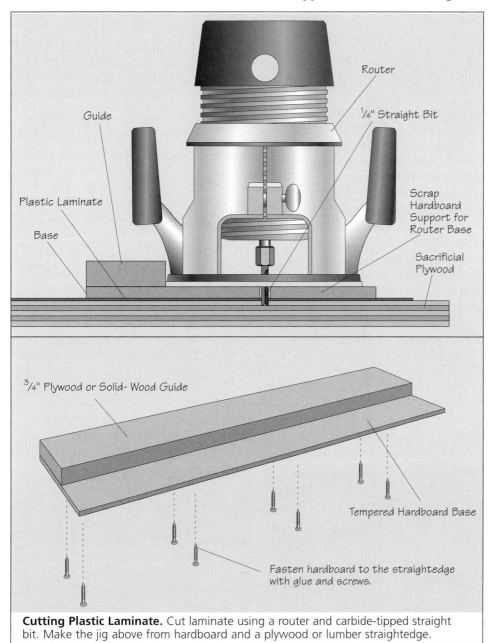

Guide

Router

¼" Straight Bit

Plastic Laminate

Base

Scrap Hardboard Support for Router Base

Sacrificial Plywood

¾" Plywood or Solid-Wood Guide

Tempered Hardboard Base

Fasten hardboard to the straightedge with glue and screws.

Cutting Plastic Laminate. Cut laminate using a router and carbide-tipped straight bit. Make the jig above from hardboard and a plywood or lumber straightedge.

Making a Laminate Countertop

Difficulty Level: 🔩🔩 *to* 🔩🔩🔩

Tools and Materials
- [ ] ¾-inch Particleboard
- [ ] 1¼- and 2-inch Drywall screws
- [ ] One-by hardwood (for edging and backsplash)
- [ ] Basic carpentry tools
- [ ] Miter box or power miter saw
- [ ] 6d Finishing nails
- [ ] Laminate
- [ ] Contact cement
- [ ] Brown wrapping paper
- [ ] Laminate roller
- [ ] Router with carbide flush and chamfer bits
- [ ] Electric drill with assorted bits
- [ ] # 6x2-inch Flathead screws

Cut the Particleboard. Cut two layers of ¾-inch particleboard 23⅜ inches wide and ⅛ inch longer than the run of cabinets. Attach the layers to each other with 1¼-inch drywall screws.

Cut and Attach the Hardwood Edging. Cut ¾-inch-thick hardwood edging strips 1½ inches wide. The side strips should be 27⅞ inches long; the front strips should be ¾ inch longer than the cabinet run. Cut pieces to length with mitered joints at the corner and square

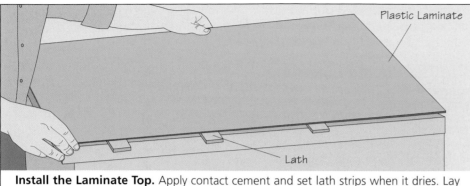

Install the Laminate Top. Apply contact cement and set lath strips when it dries. Lay the laminate on the lath, align it, then remove the strips. Roll the surface.

cuts to meet the walls. Attach the edging with glue and 6d finishing nails.

Install the Laminate Top.
Install the laminate with contact adhesive. Apply contact cement to the horizontal surfaces and the bottom of the laminate. The easiest way to do this is to pour cement directly on the surface and spread it out with a short-napped paint roller, a large brush, or even a scrap of laminate. When the cement is dry to the touch, cover the substrate with plain brown wrapping paper or small strips of lath. Leave about ½ inch of exposed surface along one edge of the substrate. Carefully lay the laminate on the paper or lath. Don't allow the laminate to touch the substrate yet or it will tack immediately.

Align the laminate and press it in place where you left the exposed cement. Gradually remove the paper or lath and press the laminate in place to work out any bubbles. Use a laminate roller or a rolling pin to ensure that the laminate is properly seated. Use a router and flush-trimming bit to trim all four edges of the laminate even with the solid-wood edging.

Chamfer the Side and Front Edges.
Use a chamfering bit in the router to complete the countertop's edge detail. Stop the chamfer 1½ inches from each back corner of the countertop.

Install the Backsplash.
Cut the hardwood backsplash 5 inches wide and to the length needed for your run of cabinets. Bore four equally spaced countersunk pilot holes from the underside of the countertop for the installation screws. Attach the backsplash with four #6 x 2-inch flathead wood screws in countersunk holes.

Countertop Installation

The easiest way to install prefabricated countertops is to have the dealer cut the material to your specifications. Then you need only assemble the pieces and attach them to your base cabinets. The procedures shown here apply to precut counters of post-formed laminate, butcher block, and synthetic marble. If you've decided to construct your own laminate top, see "Making a Laminate Countertop," page 163; to learn about tiling a counter, see "Tiling a Countertop," page 166.

Difficulty Level: 🔨🔨

Tools and Materials

☐ Countertop
☐ 48-inch Level
☐ Shims (if necessary)
☐ Caulking gun and adhesive caulk
☐ Pencil
☐ Electric drill and assorted bits
☐ Wood screws as needed
☐ Tub and tile caulk

Installing Prefabricated Countertops

1 **Check the Cabinets with a Level.** If you've installed new base cabinets as explained on the preceding pages, they should be level. Older cabinets may have settled somewhat, however. Lay a level at several points along the front, rear, and sides to see whether you need to shim under the new counter.

2 **Assemble the Corner Miters.** Precut laminate tops have miter joints at their corners. Lay the pieces upside down on a soft surface. Apply adhesive caulking to the edges of the miters, press them together, slip I-bolts into the slots, and partially tighten the bolts. Check alignment before snugging up each bolt.

3 **Lift the Countertop into Place.** You'll probably need a helper to set the assembled countertop in position. Push the backsplash snugly up against the wall. Temporarily shim underneath if necessary.

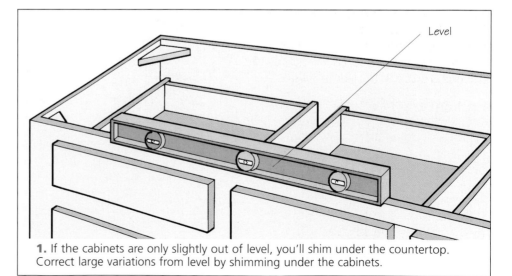

1. If the cabinets are only slightly out of level, you'll shim under the countertop. Correct large variations from level by shimming under the cabinets.

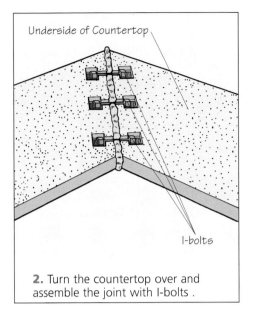

2. Turn the countertop over and assemble the joint with I-bolts .

3. Maneuver unwieldy units carefully to avoid damaging the countertop or cabinets. You'll need a helper or two for a large installation.

4 **Check the Fit at the Wall.** Any high spot on the wall's surface will create a gap between the wall and the backsplash. To identify high spots, hold the shaft of a short pencil against the wall, with the point on top of the backsplash. Pull the pencil along the length of the counter to scribe a line along the top of the backsplash. At any point where the line bows you'll need to sand or file the rear of the backsplash so it will fit flush against the wall.

5 **Level the Countertop.** If the top isn't level, fit shingle shims beneath it at the base cabinets' corner braces. Also, measure to be sure there's at least 34½ inches between the underside of the countertop and the floor. This is the minimum rough-in height for undercounter appliances. If the countertop is less than 34½ inches above the floor or if its front edge interferes with the operation of drawers, you'll have to raise the countertop with riser blocks.

6 **Drive Screws.** Have a helper hold the countertop firmly against the walls while you drill pilot holes up through the cabinets' corner braces into the top's underside. Take care that these holes don't penetrate more than two-thirds of the counter's thickness. Drive #10 wood screws through the braces into the top.

7 **Caulk the Backsplash.** After the top is secured, run a bead of

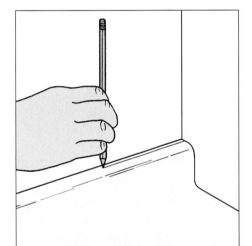

4. Scribe the backsplash with a pencil to find high spots that will create gaps. Sand or file the rear of the backsplash at these points.

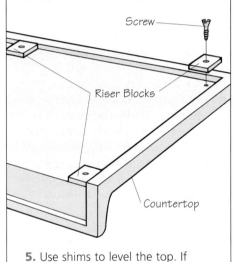

5. Use shims to level the top. If there's less than 34½ inches from the floor to the underside of the counter, lift the top with riser blocks.

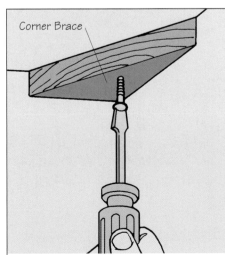

6. Fasten the counter to corner braces with screws. As you tighten the screws, be sure the top is level.

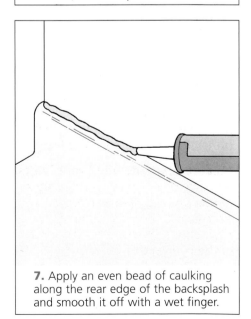

7. Apply an even bead of caulking along the rear edge of the backsplash and smooth it off with a wet finger.

tub-and-tile caulking along the joint between the backsplash and the wall. The sealant keeps moisture from seeping behind the counter.

Installing Other Countertops

Use the same procedure for installing butcher-block and synthetic marble counters. However, these materials are best butt-joined—not mitered—at corners. As with laminate tops, ready-made butcher-block and synthetic marble countertops come with I-bolts or turnbuckles that secure corner junctures.

If you provide them with templates, some countertop suppliers will also cut sink or appliance openings in just about any kind of countertop. To learn about making your own counter cutouts, see "Installing Sinks," page 171.

Tiling a Countertop

You can apply ceramic tile to old tile, plastic laminate, or plywood, but not over particleboard or fiberboard. Roughen old tile and plastic laminate by sanding the surface with 200-grit wet/dry sandpaper before beginning.

Difficulty Level: 🔩 🔩

Tools and Materials

☐ Framing square
☐ Sponge
☐ Tile cutter (rent from supplier)
☐ Tape measure
☐ Tile nippers (rent from supplier)
☐ Hammer
☐ 12-inch 2x4 wrapped with carpet
☐ Rubber float
☐ Masking tape
☐ Tiles
☐ Plastic spacers
☐ Grout
☐ Solvent (as recommended for the adhesive)
☐ Squeegee
☐ Adhesive (type and quantity as recommended by supplier)
☐ Notched trowel (notch size as recommended for the tile and adhesive you want to use)

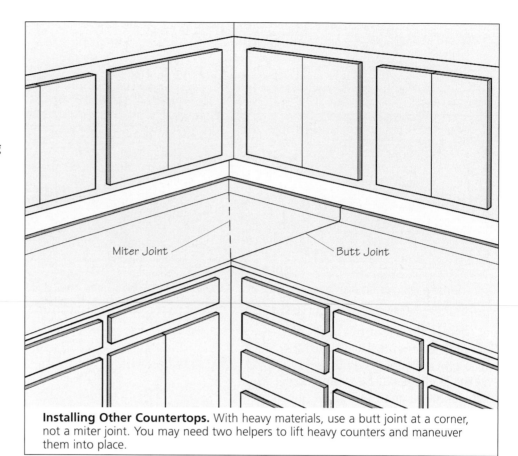

Installing Other Countertops. With heavy materials, use a butt joint at a corner, not a miter joint. You may need two helpers to lift heavy counters and maneuver them into place.

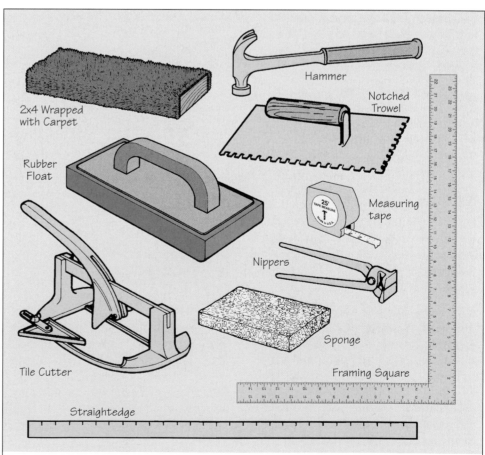

Tiling a Countertop. You can buy most of the tools required to install tile economically. Tile cutters and nippers can usually be rented from the tile supplier.

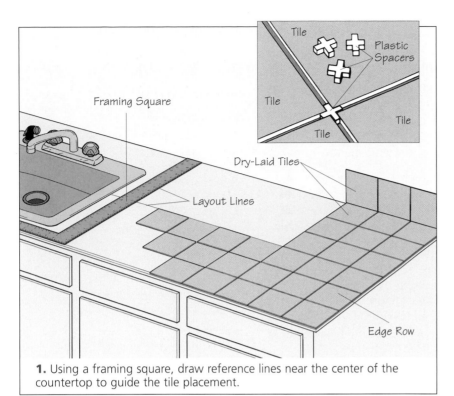

1. Using a framing square, draw reference lines near the center of the countertop to guide the tile placement.

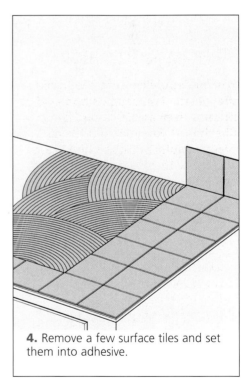

2. Cut large pieces from the tiles with a tile cutter (top). Use the nippers to make small cuts (bottom).

1 **Support and Lay Out the Tiles.** If you are making a new countertop, build a solid base out of two layers of ¾-inch plywood that have been glued and nailed together.

Arrange the tiles on the countertop in the desired pattern. Try to position them so that the amount of cutting is minimized, and you avoid having to make narrow cuts. If your tiles do not come with self-spacers, insert plastic spacers in each corner to set the proper grout-joint widths; they stay in place when tiles are permanently set. Draw joint lines near the center of the top, front to back and side to side, as reference, or work, lines. Mark them with a pencil, using a framing square for alignment.

2 **Cut the Tiles.** Use a tile cutter and nipper to cut tiles to the required size and shape. Cut whole tiles by first scoring the tile with the cutter, then pressing down on the handle to snap the tile in two. Use the nipper to make small cuts and to cut corners and irregular lines, working from the ends toward the middle. Make small nibbles until you get the shape you need.

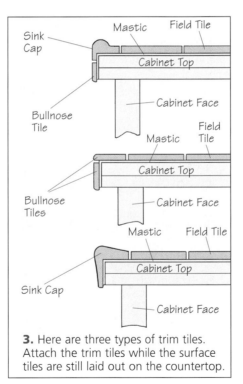

3. Here are three types of trim tiles. Attach the trim tiles while the surface tiles are still laid out on the countertop.

3 **Install the Trim Tiles.** With the dry-laid tiles on the top still in place, adhere the tiles to the front and side edges. Apply adhesive to the edges with the smooth side of the notched trowel, then use the notched side to create ridges of the correct setting depth. Next "butter" the backs of the tiles and position them so they align with

4. Remove a few surface tiles and set them into adhesive.

the loose tiles on the top. Then lay any trim tiles around sink openings or corners.

4 **Install the Surface Tiles.** Lift some of the dry-laid tiles and apply adhesive to the countertop with the notched trowel. Take care not to spread adhesive over too great an area, so that you have time to set the tiles before the adhesive

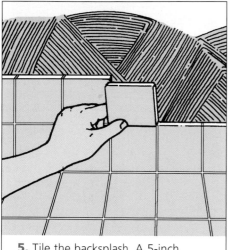

5. Tile the backsplash. A 5-inch backsplash is common, but you can also extend the backsplash to meet wall cabinets or a window.

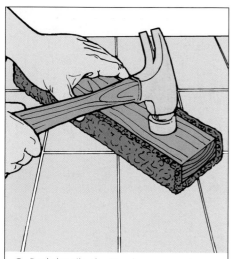

6. Bed the tiles by tapping a carpet-wrapped length of 2x4 over the surface.

7. Press grout into joints with a rubber float.

begins to harden. Press each tile firmly in place with a slight wiggle to ensure a good bond.

5 **Tile the Backsplash.** Apply tiles to the backsplash the same way as the trim tiles. Make sure you turn off the power to any switch or outlet you tile around.

6 **Bed the Tiles.** Use a piece of carpet-wrapped 2x4 to bed the tiles into the adhesive. Tap the 2x4 gently while moving it over the tiles.

7 **Grout the Joints.** First place a strip of wide masking tape along the underside of the front trim tiles to prevent the grout from falling out of the joints. Also mask any surrounding walls or surfaces you want to protect.

Then mix the grout according to the manufacturer's directions (using colorant if desired) and press it into the joints with a rubber float. When the grout is firm, but not dry, clean the surface with a damp sponge. When the grout dries to a hazy residue on the surface of the tiles, clean the haze off with a dry cloth.

Solid-Surface Countertops

Solid surfacing is different from laminate, tile, and synthetic marble in that the color runs all the way through the material. If you damage the surface with a scratch or burn, you can usually repair it by sanding out the defect.

Installing Solid-Surface Countertops

Solid surfacing is not difficult to work with. It can be cut and routed fairly easily with carbide-tipped blades. But the material requires precise measuring, cutting, and joining skills to end up with a high-quality job. For those reasons, many manufacturers recommend that solid surfacing be professionally installed. In fact, some companies back up their products with a

performance and quality guarantee, but only if the product is installed by a professional fabricator.

Difficulty Level: 🔨 🔨 🔨

Tools and Materials

- [ ] Solid surfacing
- [ ] Framing square
- [ ] Pencil
- [ ] 1x4 or ¾-inch Plywood supports
- [ ] Aluminum tape
- [ ] Scribing compass
- [ ] Plywood for template
- [ ] Saber saw
- [ ] Plunge router
- [ ] ⅜-inch Carbide straight bit
- [ ] Electric drill with assorted bits
- [ ] Circular saw with carbide blade
- [ ] Joint adhesive
- [ ] Hand plane (or belt sander)
- [ ] Hot-melt glue gun
- [ ] Spring clamps
- [ ] Putty knife
- [ ] Decorative carbide router bits
- [ ] Caulking gun and silicone caulk
- [ ] Sandpaper
- [ ] Random-orbit sander
- [ ] 220-grit Sandpaper and synthetic wool pad

1 **Measure and Prepare the Cabinets.** Use a carpenter's framing square to create a reference line across the middle of the run of cabinets. The reference line is required because the kitchen walls may not be square. Measure across the front and back, from each side to the middle (A, B, C, D). Also measure the cabinets from front to back (E). Add 1½ inches to the length and width to account for the countertop overhang. Transfer these dimensions to ½-inch-thick solid-surfacing material. Attach supports made from 1x4s or 3½-inch-wide ¾-inch plywood to the tops of the cabinets as shown. Cover the perimeter and surfaces within 3 inches of sink or appliance cutouts with supports. Use aluminum tape where you'll form a joint in the countertop material.

2 **Make a Cutting Guide.** To cut out holes for the sink and/or cooktop, you'll need a template. Mark the outline on a piece of ply-

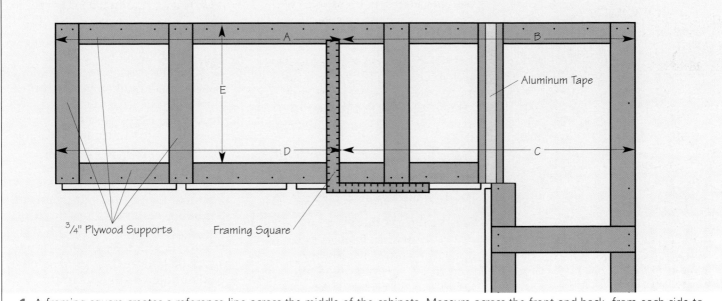

1. A framing square creates a reference line across the middle of the cabinets. Measure across the front and back, from each side to the middle (A, B, C, D). Also measure the cabinets from front to back (E). Attach supports to the tops of the cabinets as shown.

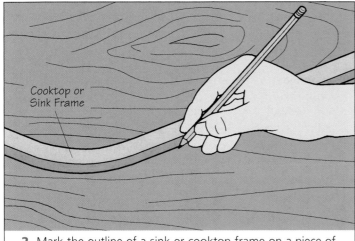

2. Mark the outline of a sink or cooktop frame on a piece of plywood as a template.

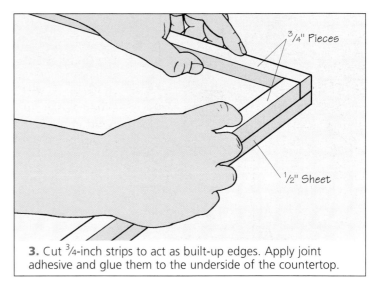

3. Cut ³/₄-inch strips to act as built-up edges. Apply joint adhesive and glue them to the underside of the countertop.

wood. Determine the distance from the edge of the router bit to the edge of the router base and set a scribing compass to this dimension. Trace the template, making a smaller one inside it, with a scribing compass. Cut out this smaller template with a saber saw and use it to make the cutout at the appropriate place on the countertop. Use a plunge router with a ³/₈-inch carbide-tipped straight bit on the solid surfacing material or drill a ¹/₂-inch hole well inside the cutout area as a starting point for a conventional router.

3 **Build up the Edges.** Cut the surfacing material to the dimensions you got in Step 1, using a circular saw with carbide-tipped blade. Also, cut ³/₄-inch-thick solid-surfacing material into ³/₄-inch strips to act as built-up edges. Test-fit the strips for length, butting them at the corners. Apply a bead of solid-surface joint adhesive to one edge of the strips and glue them to the underside of the countertop, flush to the outside edge, using spring clamps to hold them in place. Don't remove any adhesive squeeze-out, and fill any voids you see. After an hour or two, when the adhesive has dried, remove the excess with a block plane and/or belt sander and smooth the edges. Check often with a square to make sure the counter-top edges are perpendicular.

4 **Make the Seam.** You'll need to join at least two lengths of solid surfacing for any but a straight counter. Place the countertop on the cabinets, with a gap of ¹/₈ inch to the walls and a ¹/₁₆-inch joint between the sheets. Shim the sheets if they're not perfectly level. Cut a ¹/₄-inch-deep saw kerf into two strips of scrap wood and secure them on both sides of the seam using a hot-melt glue gun. Insert spring clamps into the grooves to hold the seam together with constant pressure. After about an hour, remove the wood scraps with denatured alcohol and a putty knife and sand the joint with a belt sander and 220-grit paper until you can barely make out the seam.

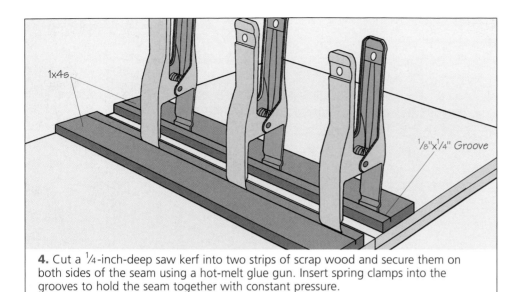

1x4s

⅛"x¼" Groove

4. Cut a ¼-inch-deep saw kerf into two strips of scrap wood and secure them on both sides of the seam using a hot-melt glue gun. Insert spring clamps into the grooves to hold the seam together with constant pressure.

5 **Shape the Edges.** Rout the perimeter of the countertop with a router equipped with a decorative carbide bit like a roundover or ogee bit. Use a bit with a ball-bearing pilot, and move the router slowly. There are a number of decorative edges possible with the use of a router and solid surfacing material. You can get dramatic effects by laminating different colors together, using wood or laminate inlays, and cutting any of a number of different profiles. Once you've finished the edges, lift the countertop off the cabinets, apply silver-dollar-size dollops of silicone caulk or panel adhesive to the

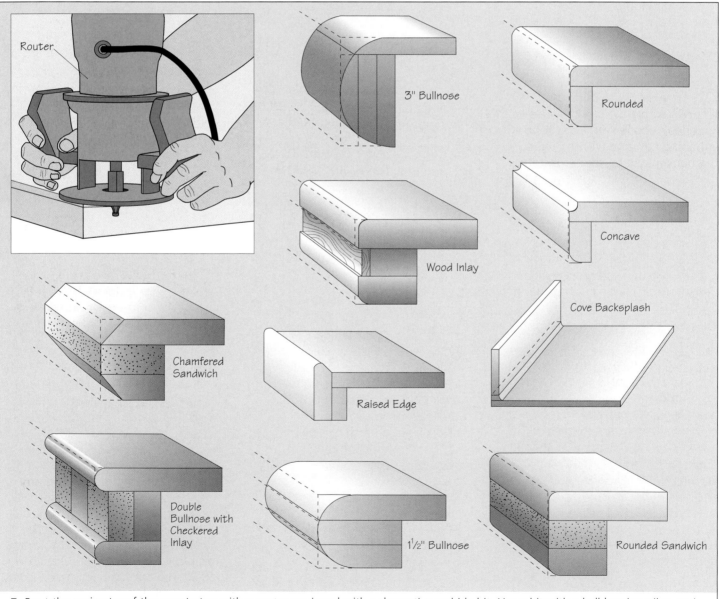

Router

3" Bullnose

Rounded

Wood Inlay

Concave

Cove Backsplash

Chamfered Sandwich

Raised Edge

Double Bullnose with Checkered Inlay

1½" Bullnose

Rounded Sandwich

5. Rout the perimeter of the countertop with a router equipped with a decorative carbide bit. Use a bit with a ball-bearing pilot, and move the router slowly. There are a number of decorative edges possible with the use of a router and solid surfacing material.

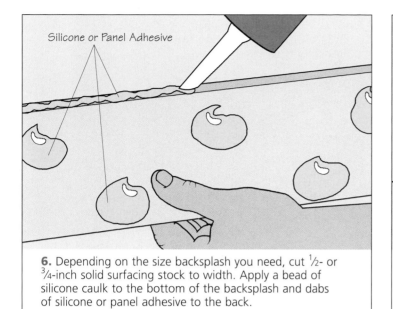

Silicone or Panel Adhesive

6. Depending on the size backsplash you need, cut ½- or ¾-inch solid surfacing stock to width. Apply a bead of silicone caulk to the bottom of the backsplash and dabs of silicone or panel adhesive to the back.

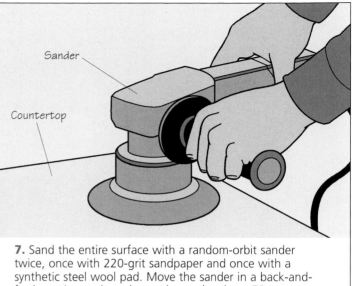

Sander

Countertop

7. Sand the entire surface with a random-orbit sander twice, once with 220-grit sandpaper and once with a synthetic steel wool pad. Move the sander in a back-and-forth motion and overlap each pass by about 50 percent.

countertop supports every 6 inches or so, and replace the countertop, leaving a ⅛-inch gap to the wall.

6 **Make the Backsplash.** Depending on the size backsplash you need (usually 3½ to 5 inches), cut ½- or ¾-inch solid-surfacing stock to width. Clamp the backsplash to your worktable, then round off the top edge with a decorative treatment, if desired, and sand out any saw marks on the bottom edge. Apply a bead of silicone caulk to the bottom of the backsplash and silver-dollar-size dabs of silicone or panel adhesive to the back. Set the backsplash in place with firm, even pressure, then caulk the gap at the wall with silicone.

7 **Finish Off the Countertop.** Sand the entire surface with a random-orbit sander twice, once with 220-grit sandpaper and once with a synthetic steel wool pad. Move the sander in a back-and-forth, rather than circular, motion and overlap each pass by about 50 percent. Keep the sandpaper clean by running it at high speed on a scrap piece of carpet every few minutes. Each sheet of sanding paper should handle about 10 square feet of countertop. Add water and a small amount of detergent when you burnish the top with the synthetic steel wool.

Installing Sinks

Use the following guidelines for installing a kitchen sink into a countertop. See "Installing Faucets in Sinks," page 174, for help with the plumbing. If you must cut a hole in the countertop, it's usually easier to make the cutout before securing the top to the cabinets.

Difficulty Level: 🔧 🔧

Tools and Materials

☐ Saber saw
☐ Drill with bit
☐ Adjustable wrench
☐ Basin wrench
☐ Spud wrench
☐ Screwdriver
☐ Utility knife
☐ Caulking gun
☐ Masking tape
☐ Silicone caulk
☐ Length of rope
☐ 2x4s
☐ Brick
☐ Basin
☐ Countertop

Installing a Sink in a Plastic Laminate Countertop

1 **Position the Basin.** First make a line marking where you want the center of the basin to fall on the countertop. If your basin is self-

rimming, place it upside down, center it over the line you drew, and trace around the outer edge of the rim. Remove the basin and mark the actual cutting line inside the outer line. Determine the dimensions of the cutout from the sink or the manufacturer's instructions. If your basin is metal rimmed, lay the metal trim over the countertop and use it as a template to mark the cutout. Drill ¼-inch holes at the corners to establish the extent of the cutout on the underside of the countertop.

2 **Add Supports.** Install braces below the sides of the sink, unless the countertop consists of two layers of ¾-inch plywood or solid-surface material.

3 **Cut the Opening.** Use a saber saw to make the cutout.

4 **Install the Sink.** The specific method of installation depends on the type of sink.

• Self-Rimming Sinks. You can install a self-rimming sink on any countertop, after cutting a hole smaller than the outer rim (see Step 1). Place a bead of silicone caulk over the countertop where the rim will go. Then position the sink in the opening and press it into the sealant. Install the four metal clips that come with the sink on the

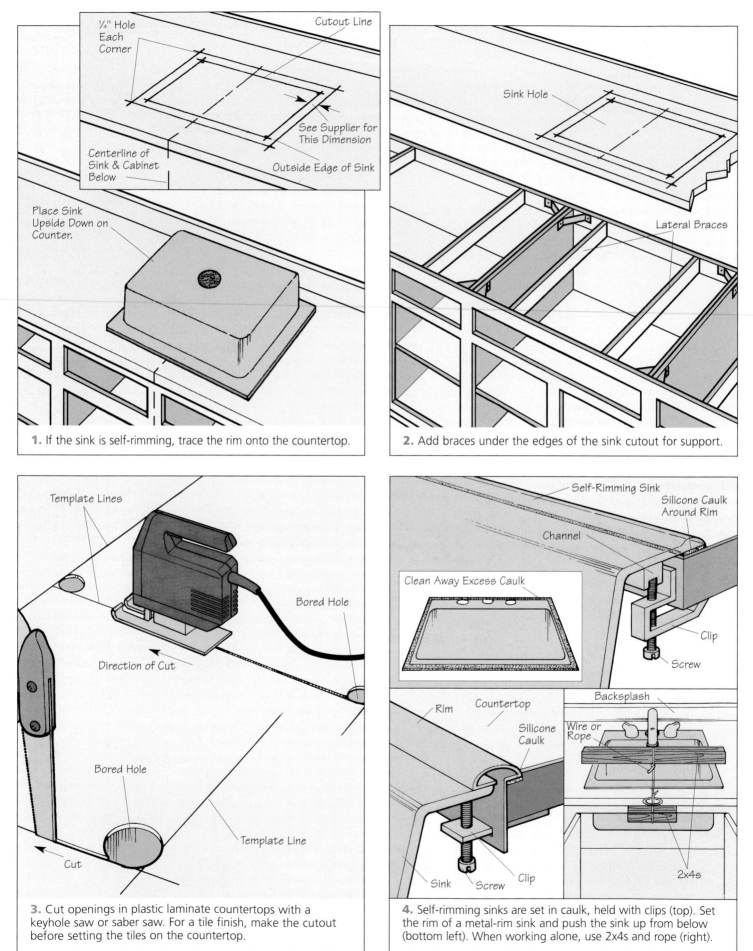

¼" Hole Each Corner

Cutout Line

See Supplier for This Dimension

Outside Edge of Sink

Centerline of Sink & Cabinet Below

Place Sink Upside Down on Counter.

1. If the sink is self-rimming, trace the rim onto the countertop.

Sink Hole

Lateral Braces

2. Add braces under the edges of the sink cutout for support.

Template Lines

Bored Hole

Direction of Cut

Bored Hole

Cut

Template Line

3. Cut openings in plastic laminate countertops with a keyhole saw or saber saw. For a tile finish, make the cutout before setting the tiles on the countertop.

Self-Rimming Sink

Silicone Caulk Around Rim

Channel

Clean Away Excess Caulk

Clip

Screw

Rim   Countertop

Silicone Caulk

Backsplash

Wire or Rope

Sink   Screw   Clip

2x4s

4. Self-rimming sinks are set in caulk, held with clips (top). Set the rim of a metal-rim sink and push the sink up from below (bottom left). When working alone, use 2x4s and rope (right).

underside and tighten each clip's screw snugly but not all the way. Gradually tighten the screws enough to hold the sink firmly. Finally, run your finger around the edge to shape the caulk, then remove any excess sealant from the countertop.

• Metal-Rimmed Sinks. Lay a bead of silicone caulk around the cutout and place the metal rim into the caulk. Have a helper push the sink up from below to meet the trim and allow you to tighten the clips. If you have to work alone, suspend the sink into position, held in place by a 2x4 across the top and another across the bottom, with a rope connecting the two. Before tightening the rope, place a bead of caulk between the sink edge and metal trim. Then tighten the rope by twisting a screwdriver in the rope, to pull the sink up to meet the metal trim. Finally, tighten the setscrews on the clips below and clean off any excess caulk.

Installing a Sink in Tile

There are three ways to install a sink in a tile countertop:

• Drop the sink into the opening after tiling the countertop. To do this, set the sink into a bed of caulk and secure with clips from below.

• Install the sink in the cutout first, then tile up to the sink's trim edge.

• Rout out a recess for the sink rim in the countertop to allow the rim to set flush with the untiled surface. Then install the sink in the countertop before tiling. Install tile over the edge of the sink.

Installing a Sink in a Solid-Surface Countertop

If the sink is not an integral part of the countertop, you can mount a self-rimming sink into the cutout. Order the countertop piece with the cutout already made, if possible. If you have to cut it yourself,

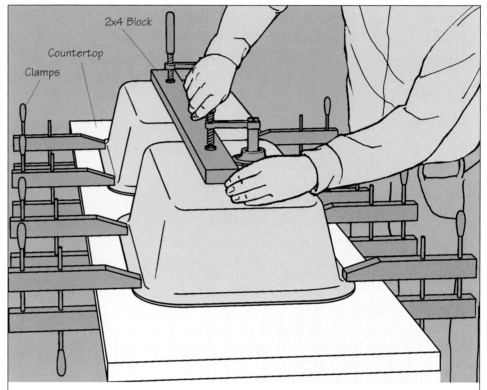

Installing a Sink in a Solid-Surface Countertop. Glue the sink to underside of solid-surface countertop, then apply pressure by clamping through the drain hole, using wood blocks to protect around the edges and sink's underside.

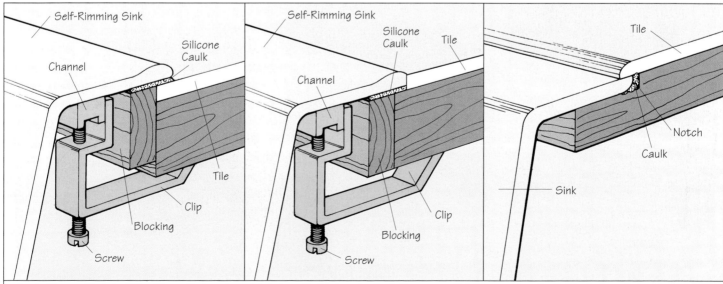

Installing a Sink in Tile. The self-rimming sink is installed into a bed of silicone caulk laid over the tile (left). Or install the sink in the countertop, then tile up to the sink's edge (middle). If you want the tile to overlap the sink, rout out a notch or recess in the countertop so the sink's edge is flush with the untiled surface (right).

mark the cutout, drill a pilot hole along the line, and cut the opening with a saber saw equipped with a carbide-tipped blade. Apply adhesive to the sink's rim, place it upside down on the underside of the top, and clamp it in place.

Installing Faucets in Sinks

A visit to a home center will give you a good idea of the wide array of faucets available. In addition to the old tried-and-true dual-lever faucet with replaceable washers, you'll see single-lever types in a variety of styles. You can have handles that incorporate wood or ceramic. Spouts and bases come in chrome, brass, and many colors of enameled metal. Naturally, prices range to suit the level of luxury. To find your way through the options, it will help to have some idea of the basic faucet types.

Your first decision is whether to select a dual- or single-lever faucet. Faucets control water flow in various ways. Compression-type faucets depend on rubber washers or diaphragms to open or close down the water flow. Newer types use means other than compression to control the water flow, such as cartridges, balls, or disks. Cartridge faucets regulate water flow with a movable cartridge and rubber O-rings. Ball faucets use a slotted plastic or brass ball atop a pair of spring-loaded rubber seats. The single lever rotates the ball to adjust the water temperature and flow. Disk faucets contain a pair of plastic or ceramic disks that move

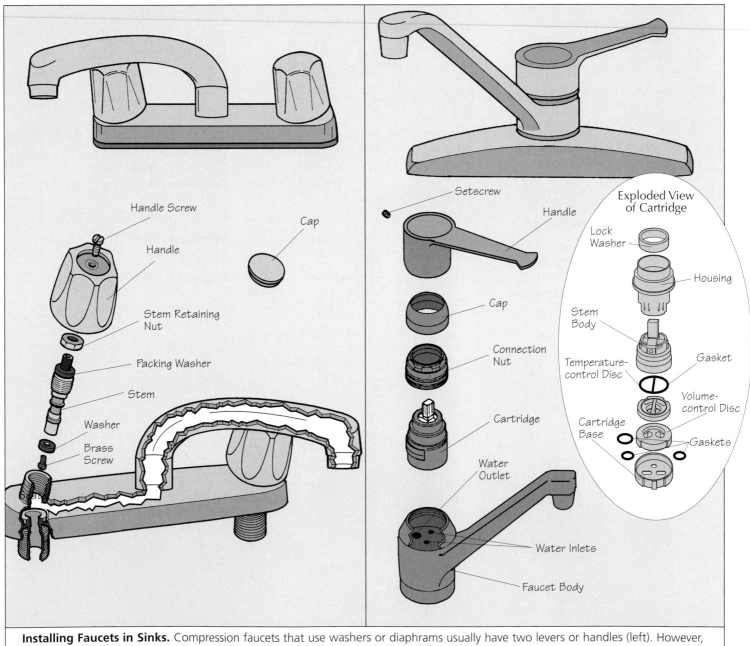

Installing Faucets in Sinks. Compression faucets that use washers or diaphrams usually have two levers or handles (left). However, disk faucets can also have two levers, although they usually have a single handle (right).

up and down to regulate the volume of the flow, and rotate to control the temperature.

The following steps describe how to work with various types of water-supply tubing and how to replace an old faucet or install a new one. Before you buy a faucet set, be sure its offset (the distance, center to center, between the hot and cold taps) matches the spacing of the holes in the sink. Check this by measuring the distance between the center of the hot and cold supply risers from under the sink.

Working with Copper Tubing

Copper tubing is much easier to install than old-fashioned galvanized steel. You can choose between 20-foot-long lengths of rigid tubing or coils of flexible tubing. The advantage of flexible tubing is that you can bend it to snake through curves in existing walls and floors without making joints. The downside is that curves have to be gentle and without kinks; making the bends requires a little practice. By contrast, each turn in rigid tubing requires a joint with a soldered or threaded coupling. Couplings can be easily made if you can get access to the joint, but they're hard to make in places with cramped access.

Copper tubing is made in four grades, according to the thickness of the walls: K, L, M, and DWV. Find out which types your local code accepts. Very likely, they will be

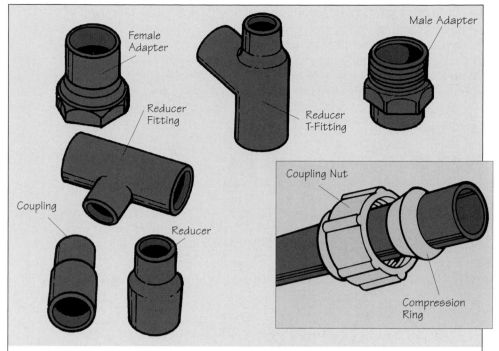

Couplings. Copper couplings for soldered joints or compression-ring assemblies are available to suit any joint requirement in water-supply piping.

type M or L for water-supply piping. Both type M and type L are available in rigid and flexible tubing.

Couplings

You can join both rigid and flexible copper tubing with soldered joints or compression couplings. Soldered connections may be less prone to leakage over time, but they can't always be made. Joining copper tubing to a pipe or fitting of another material, such as brass, has to be made with compression couplings. Compression couplings become watertight when you tighten the threaded nut, drawing a flange against the end of the pipe.

Couplings are available with threaded nuts on both ends or with one end threaded and the other straight, to be soldered.

Cutting Copper Tubing

Difficulty Level:

Tools and Materials
- [ ] Basic plumbing tools
- [ ] Wire brush
- [ ] Emery cloth or multipurpose tool

1 Cut the Pipe. Cut the pipe with a tubing cutter or hacksaw. If using a tubing cutter, gradually tighten the cutting blade against the pipe as you rotate the

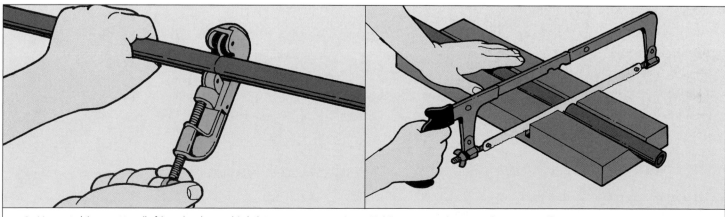

1. Use a tubing cutter (left) or hacksaw (right) to cut copper pipes. Tubing cutters leave a cleaner cut line.

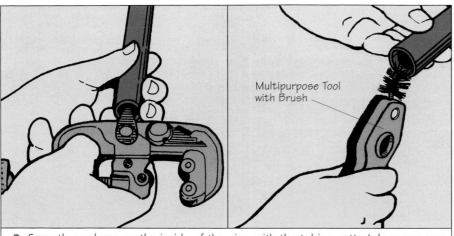

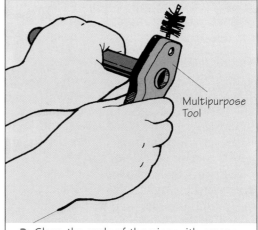

2. Smooth any burrs on the inside of the pipe with the tubing cutter's burr remover (left). Clean inside the pipe and fitting with a wire brush (right).

3. Clean the ends of the pipe with emery cloth or a multipurpose tool before soldering.

tool several times until the pipe snaps apart. If using a hacksaw, place the pipe in a grooved board or miter box for easier cutting.

2 **Remove the Burrs from Inside the Pipe's End.** After cutting, remove the burrs from the inside of the pipe. Some tubing cutters contain a burr remover. Use a wire brush to clean the insides of the pipe and fitting that the pipe will be joined to.

3 **Clean the Outside of the Pipe's Ends.** Before soldering, clean the ends of the pipe with emery cloth or a multipurpose tool that contains an abrasive for cleaning the outside of the pipe and a brush for the inside.

Soldering Connections

Difficulty Level:

Tools and Materials

☐ Basic plumbing tools
☐ Small brush
☐ Solder
☐ Flux

From a home center or hardware store, get a small torch that screws to a disposable propane canister. Also, buy a good self-cleaning flux and solder. Use only lead-free solder (nickel or silver) for pipes that carry potable water. When soldering with a torch you can endanger both your body and your house. Protect your eyes with goggles and your hands with gloves. Get a 12x12-inch piece of sheet

metal to insert between the joint to be soldered and any nearby wood, to protect your house from catching fire.

1 **Apply the Flux.** Use a small brush or toothbrush to coat the joint ends with flux.

2 **Join the Pipes to the Fittings.** Slide the fitting over the pipes' ends so that half of the fitting is on each pipe.

3 **Apply the Solder.** Light your torch and heat the joint by running the flame over the pipe and fitting, taking care to avoid burning the flux. When the pipe is hot enough to melt the solder, take the torch away and feed solder into the joint until it won't take any more. Heat the pipe for about 5 seconds.

1. Coat the ends of the copper pipe with a generous amount of flux.

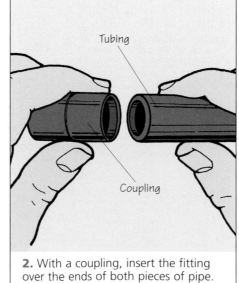

2. With a coupling, insert the fitting over the ends of both pieces of pipe.

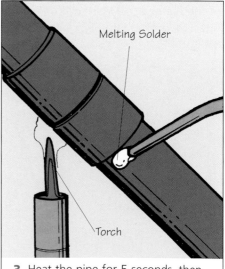

3. Heat the pipe for 5 seconds, then the fitting as you solder the joint.

4. To prevent fire, place a piece of sheet metal between the soldering area and any combustible material.

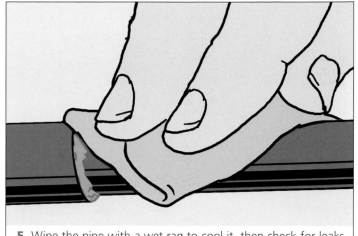

5. Wipe the pipe with a wet rag to cool it, then check for leaks. Stop leaks with more solder; if that doesn't work, redo the joint.

Then move the torch to the fitting as you feed more solder into the joint. Continue until the joint stops drawing the solder in and there are no gaps in the solder. If the solder around the rim of the joint stays puddled and does not draw in as it cools, reheat until the solder lique-fies, then try again. Practice with some scrap pipes and connectors, until you feel confident to solder your new supply lines.

4 **Protect Surfaces.** If you're soldering near wood or other combustible materials, place a piece of sheet metal between the soldering area and the material to prevent fire.

5 **Clean the Joint and Test for Leaks.** Cool the pipe with a wet rag, then test the joint for leaks. If more solder doesn't stop the leaks, melt the joint apart and start over.

Cutting and Joining Plastic Pipe

Difficulty Level: 🔩 🔩

Tools and Materials

☐ Basic plumbing tools
☐ Solvent cement
☐ Primer (PVC piping)
☐ Rubber gloves
☐ Compression clamp fittings (if joining to cast iron)

Lightweight plastic pipe ranges in diameter from 1 ½ to 6 inches. Most plastic DWV lines can be installed with just a few simple tools. Making connections is easy and straightforward, but requires a little practice to do with ease. After cutting the pipe with a handsaw, clean the ends to be joined, apply solvent cement, and join the pieces. Be sure to match the solvent cement to the type of plastic used in the pipe (PVC or ABS). You can even join a new section of plastic pipe to an existing cast-iron waste line with compression clamp fit-tings consisting of flexible gaskets and metal rings that screw-tighten.

Plastic waste piping is made of ABS (black) or CPVC (white) plastic. Check with your local plumbing

inspector to find out which type is acceptable for your project. Make sure to match the solvent to the type of piping material.

1 **Cut the Pipe.** Measure the lengths required, allowing for the fittings. Assume the pipe will fit all the way inside the sleeves of the fittings. Unless you are cutting piping already in place, put the lengths to be cut in a miter box. Cut the pipe with a backsaw or hacksaw. Use a utility knife and/or emery cloth to remove burrs from the cut ends and to dull the outer cut edge so that it will slide smoothly into the fitting.

2 **Test the Fit.** After cutting the pipes, test-fit the parts that are to be joined. If the new pipe is

1. Hold the plastic pipe firmly in a miter box while cutting it to length.

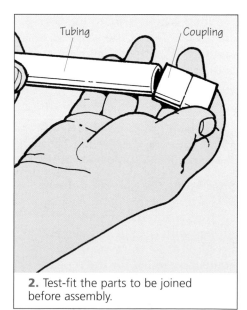

2. Test-fit the parts to be joined before assembly.

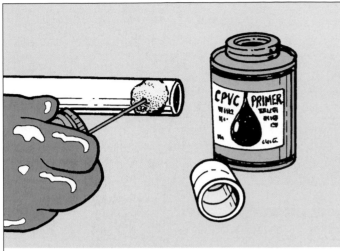

3. Using primer, clean and prepare for cement the outside ends of the pipe and the inside surface of the fitting.

4. Coat the ends of pipes on the outside and the insides of the fittings with solvent cement.

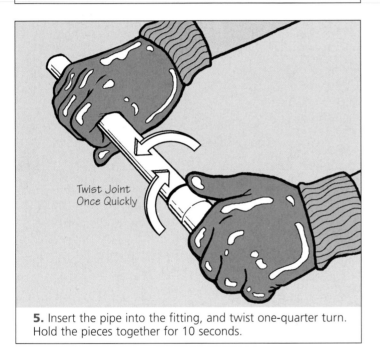

Twist Joint Once Quickly

5. Insert the pipe into the fitting, and twist one-quarter turn. Hold the pieces together for 10 seconds.

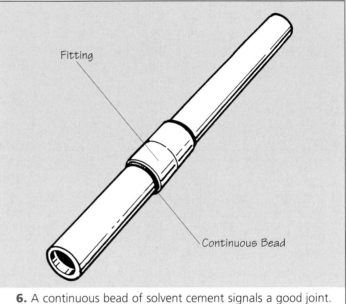

Fitting

Continuous Bead

6. A continuous bead of solvent cement signals a good joint. Wipe off any excess with a rag.

too long, simply trim to the correct size. If the pipe is too short to fit completely in the fittings, cut another piece of pipe, which can be added to the first piece, or start over with a new section of pipe.

3 **Clean the Ends of the New Pipe.** Use PVC primer to clean the ends of PVC pipe and fittings.

4 **Apply the Solvent Cement.** Thoroughly coat the ends of each pipe and the insides of the fittings with the solvent cement. Be sure to use the type of solvent cement intended for the type of plastic pipe you are using.

5 **Join the Pipe to the Fitting.** Immediately after applying solvent cement, insert the pipe into the fitting and twist the two parts against each other about one-quarter turn. Hold the pieces together for about 10 seconds.

6 **Wipe Off Any Excess Solvent Cement.** If the joint is formed properly, the solvent cement will form a continuous bead around the joint. Wipe off any excess cement around the pipe and fitting with a cloth.

Removing the Old Faucets

Difficulty Level: 🔨 *to* 🔨🔨

depending on the accessibility of the faucet mounts

Tools and Materials
☐ Basic plumbing tools
☐ Putty knife
☐ Plumber's putty or silicone sealant
☐ Flashlight
☐ Braided stainless-steel risers
☐ Caulking gun

1 **Close the Shutoff Valves.** Begin by shutting off the valves in the hot- and cold-supply pipes below the

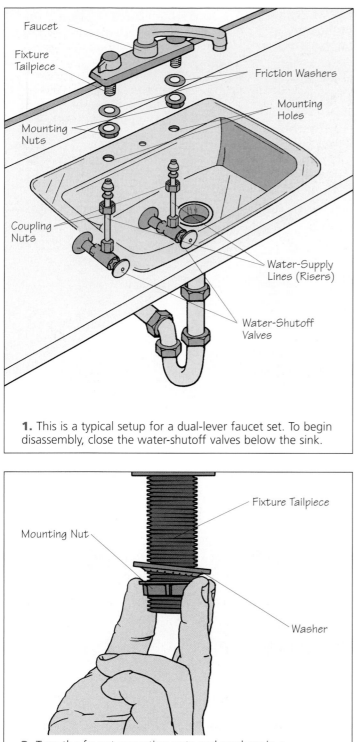

1. This is a typical setup for a dual-lever faucet set. To begin disassembly, close the water-shutoff valves below the sink.

2. Disconnect the faucet tailpieces from the supply risers with a basin wrench.

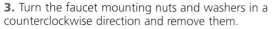

3. Turn the faucet mounting nuts and washers in a counterclockwise direction and remove them.

4. Coax the faucet off the sink by inserting a putty knife under the baseplate, if necessary, and clean the sink.

sink. If there are no valves, shut off the water supply at the main, which is probably in the basement.

2 **Disconnect the Tailpieces from the Risers.** Set up a flashlight to shine on the piping below the sink, then use a basin wrench to disconnect the faucet tailpieces from the supply risers.

3 **Remove the Mounting Nuts and Washers.** Remove the faucet mounting nuts and washers by turning them counterclockwise. On single-lever faucets, the supply piping converges at the center and the unit is held in place by mounting nuts at the sides and a nut and retaining ring in the center. Use

whichever tool fits: adjustable pliers, adjustable wrench, or basin wrench.

4 **Pry the Faucet off the Basin.** If the faucet won't budge easily, coax it by inserting a putty knife under the baseplate. Then use the putty knife to remove any caulk or adhesive from the sink.

Installing the New Faucet Set

1 **Install the Gasket or Sealant.** After cleaning the surface of the sink in the area in which the new faucet will sit, install the gasket. If your faucet set came without a gasket, put down a bead of silicone sealant or plumber's putty around the lip of the faucet baseplate. Insert the faucet tailpieces into the mounting holes of the sink and press the faucet down into the sealant, if used. Wipe off any excess sealant with a rag.

2 **Tighten the Mounting Nuts.** Put the washers and mounting nuts (if any) onto the tailpieces and tighten. Do not overtighten.

3 **Attach the Risers.** Attach braided stainless-steel risers to the faucet and to the water

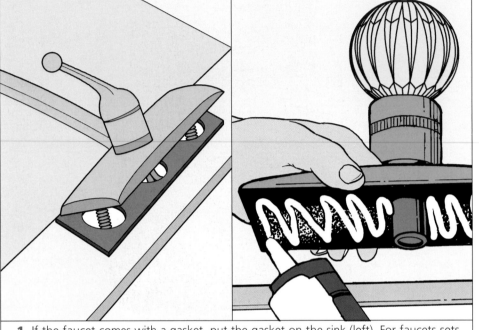

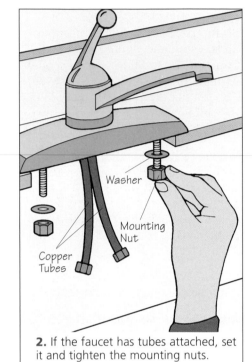

1. If the faucet comes with a gasket, put the gasket on the sink (left). For faucets sets without gaskets, place silicone sealant on the faucet baseplate (right).

2. If the faucet has tubes attached, set it and tighten the mounting nuts.

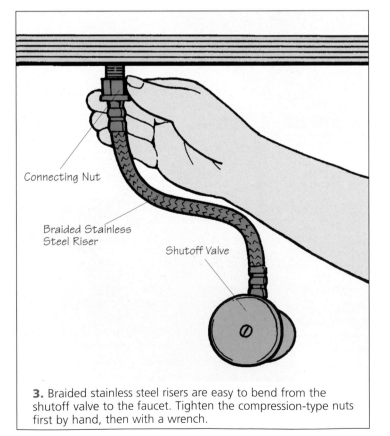

3. Braided stainless steel risers are easy to bend from the shutoff valve to the faucet. Tighten the compression-type nuts first by hand, then with a wrench.

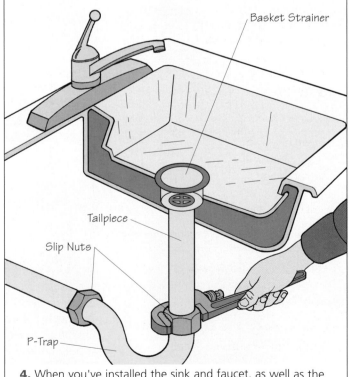

4. When you've installed the sink and faucet, as well as the basket strainer, connect the drainpipe. Attach the tailpiece to the strainer, then connect the trap to the drain with slip nuts.

shutoff valves. This type of riser is flexible, unlike chrome-plated copper, making it easier to adjust when connecting. Tighten the nuts without overtightening.

4 **Install the Drain Fittings.** With the sink and faucet installed, it's time to hook up the drainage system—the P-trap and drainpipe. Set the basket strainer in the sink and tighten the locknut. Connect the tailpiece to the strainer with a slip nut, then install the trap. The long end of the trap goes over the tailpiece. Tighten the slip nuts on each end of the trap.

When you've assembled all the parts of the faucet and drainage system, turn the shutoff valves on and check all the connections for leaks. If a connection is leaking, turn the nut a little at a time until the leak stops.

Waste-Disposal Units

Attached to the drain of the sink, waste-disposal units make quick work of kitchen scraps, plate scrapings, and other organic garbage. They act like powerful blenders, grinding up vegetable matter and even chicken bones with strong cutting blades and sending them down the drain.

Connecting a Waste-Disposal Unit

Difficulty Level: 🔨

Tools and Materials

☐ Waste-disposal unit
☐ Plumber's putty
☐ Screwdrivers (flat-bladed and Phillips)
☐ Plastic wire connectors
☐ Pliers

1 **Prepare Sink Opening.** Run a bead of plumber's putty around the underside of the sink flange and slip the sleeve into the sink hole. Press down on the sink flange to make sure it's seated.

2 **Attach the Mounting Assembly.** Slip the fiber gasket and metal mounting ring over

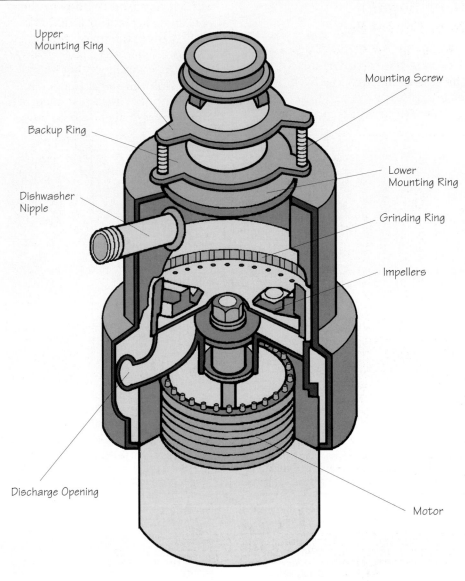

Waste-Disposal Units. A batch-feed disposer, controlled by a wall switch, is the safest and most efficient to use. It's installed on a sink with hardware that includes a sink flange, gasket, and mounting rings, and connected to the sink's drainpipe through the discharge tube.

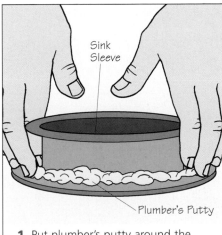

1. Put plumber's putty around the underside of the flange and drop the sink sleeve into the hole.

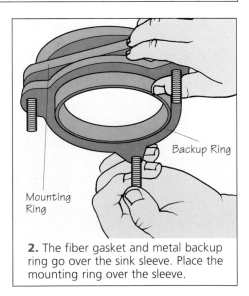

2. The fiber gasket and metal backup ring go over the sink sleeve. Place the mounting ring over the sleeve.

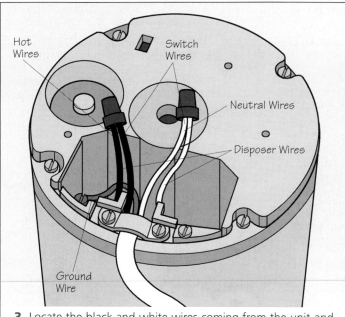

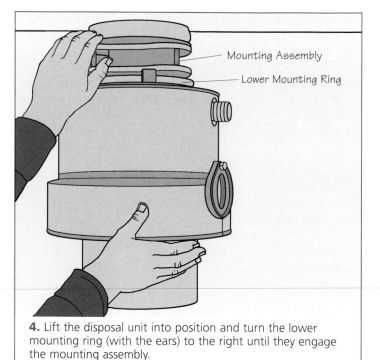

3. Locate the black and white wires coming from the unit and from the appliance cord and connect them, white to white and black to black.

4. Lift the disposal unit into position and turn the lower mounting ring (with the ears) to the right until they engage the mounting assembly.

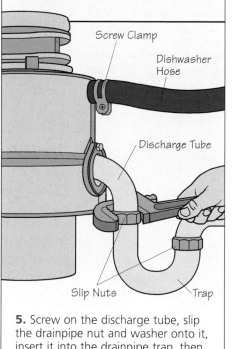

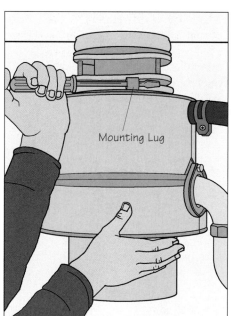

5. Screw on the discharge tube, slip the drainpipe nut and washer onto it, insert it into the drainpipe trap, then tighten the slip nut.

6. Insert the tool supplied with the disposal unit (or a screwdriver) in the lug and turn it until the disposer is fully engaged in the locking notch.

coming from the appliance cord to the unit's ground screw. Tuck the wires in place and replace the cover.

4 **Connect the Unit and Mounting Assembly.** If you plan to install a dishwasher, turn the disposer unit on its side and knock out the molded drain plug in the dishwasher nipple. Lift the disposer unit into position, lining up the unit's mounting ears with the mounting screws on the sink assembly. Turn the unit's lower mounting ring (with the ears) to the right until the ears engage the flanges on the upper mounting ring.

5 **Attach the Discharge Tube and Drain Trap.** Find the discharge opening on the disposal unit and screw the discharge tube to it using the metal flange and rubber gasket. Rotate the unit to align with the drain trap. Slip the drainpipe nut and washer onto the discharge tube, insert the tube into the drainpipe trap, then tighten the slip nut onto the trap. If you're installing a dishwasher, attach the dishwasher's drain hose to the unit's nipple with a screw clamp.

6 **Secure the Disposer.** Insert the tool supplied with the disposal unit, or a screwdriver, into

the sink sleeve and push them up to cover the sink flange. Place the backup ring and its three screws over the sink sleeve, push it up toward the mounting ring, and pop the snap ring into place on the groove of the sink sleeve. Tighten the three screws so the mounting assembly is seated firmly and evenly with the sink.

3 **Make the Electrical Connections.** Remove the electrical cover plate from the disposal unit and locate the black and white wires coming from the unit and from the appliance cord. Connect the white wire from the appliance cord to the unit's white wire with a wire connector and the black wire to black. Attach the ground wire

the left side of one of the disposal unit's lugs. Turn the lug counterclockwise until the disposal unit is fully engaged in the locking notch. To check for leaks, set the sink's stopper and fill the sink with water. Once you have a few inches of water, let the sink drain, observing the drain line to make sure no water drips from the connections.

Built-in Dishwashers

Built-in dishwashers are designed to slide into a 24-inch-wide space under a standard 36-inch high counter. Dishwashers require hookups for hot water, drainage, and electricity.

Installing a Dishwasher

Difficulty Level: 🔧 *to* 🔧🔧

Tools and Materials

☐ Dishwasher
☐ Compression T-fitting
☐ Compression-fitting shutoff valve
☐ Tubing cutter
☐ Copper tubing (³⁄₈-inch or larger)
☐ Adjustable wrench
☐ Bucket
☐ Rubber or plastic drain line
☐ Air gap
☐ Hose clamps
☐ 12-gauge Electric cable
☐ Basic electrical tools
☐ Wire connectors
☐ 1-inch Wood screws

1 Prepare the Opening. If you're installing all new cabinets, leave space for the dishwasher near the sink and span this opening with the countertop. If you're installing the dishwasher in an existing kitchen, you'll have to sacrifice a 24-inch section of base cabinet. Test-fit the dishwasher in the space intended for it and make any adjustments that may be needed. Now pull the machine out and make an opening in the side of the cabinet between the dishwasher and the under-sink compartments. This opening should be large enough to accommodate the water-supply and drain lines.

2 Provide a Hot-Water Line. Because a dishwasher is usually located adjacent to the sink, that's the most likely place to tap into a hot-water line. You can also bring one up from the basement or through the wall behind the machine if that suits your situation better.

Regardless of where you go for water, you'll need a T-fitting, a shutoff valve, and enough copper tubing to reach from the connection at the pipe to the connection at the dishwasher. Use compression fittings for these connections. The dishwasher installation manual will specify the tubing size you need, usually ³⁄₈ inch.

Turn off the water supply and drain the line. Cut the supply line and attach the T-fitting with compression nuts and rings. Turn the connectors by hand until they're tight, then give an additional quarter-turn with a wrench. Don't overtighten the connectors or you'll deform the compression ring and/or the tubing, causing a leak.

Attach the shutoff valve for the dishwasher to the T-fitting and run a water line to the front of the dishwasher compartment.

Place a bucket under the supply line, turn on the water, and check your connections for leaks. Shut off the water and tighten the connections as needed.

3 Provide a Drain Line. The drain line consists of a rubber or plastic hose that's resistant to high temperatures. Run the line through the opening in the cabinet.

Local codes may or may not require an air gap, but it's a good idea to provide one anyway. Otherwise, if your sink drain becomes obstructed, dirty water may back up into the dishwasher. You may either purchase a prefabricated air gap or loop the hose as high as possible under the sink cabinet so waste water will not back up.

Make drain-line connections with hose clamps. If you have a waste disposer, it has a drain nipple for this purpose. If not, purchase a

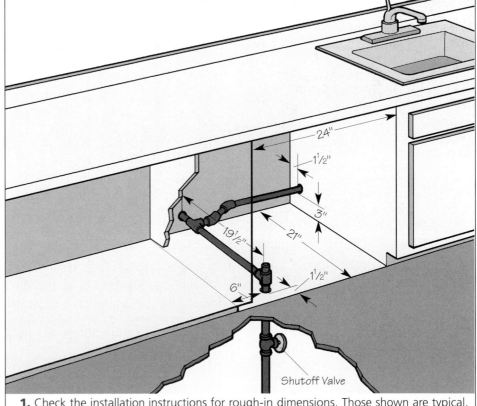

1. Check the installation instructions for rough-in dimensions. Those shown are typical. Note that the water line can come from below.

waste T-fitting and install it above the sink trap as shown.

4 **Provide Power.** A dishwasher requires its own 20-amp grounded circuit. Shut off the electricity and run a cable from a convenient junction box to the front of the dishwasher compartment.

5 **Finish the Installation.** Now remove the front panel at the bottom of the dishwasher and slide the unit into place. Manufacturers provide space underneath the machine to clear water, waste, and power lines and to make the final connections. Level the dishwasher by turning levelers on each front leg. Secure the machine by driving wood screws through holes at the top into the countertop.

Use wire connectors to make the final electrical connections from the circuit wire to the unit: black wire to black, white wire to white, green ground wire to the grounding screw. Connect the water line to the fill connection in the machine. Again, take care not to overtighten the compression fittings. Attach the drain line to the waste connection with a hose clamp.

Turn on the water and the electricity to the special circuit for the dishwasher and run the unit through one cycle. Check for any leaks. Install the kickplate cover that hides the plumbing and electrical connections.

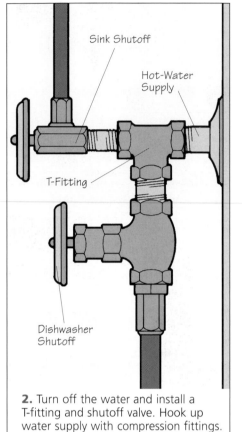

2. Turn off the water and install a T-fitting and shutoff valve. Hook up water supply with compression fittings.

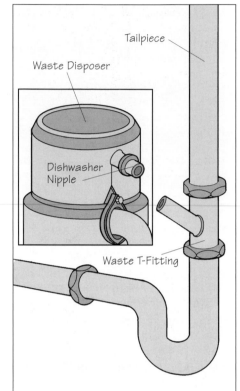

3. The drain line from the dishwasher may connect to a new fitting in the sink drain line or to a waste disposer.

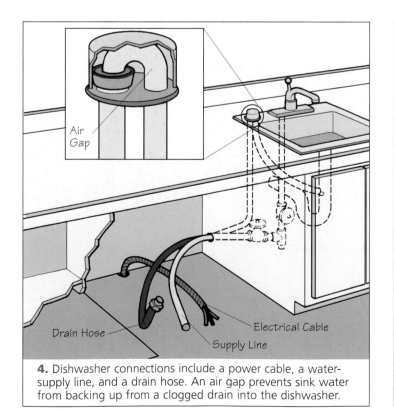

4. Dishwasher connections include a power cable, a water-supply line, and a drain hose. An air gap prevents sink water from backing up from a clogged drain into the dishwasher.

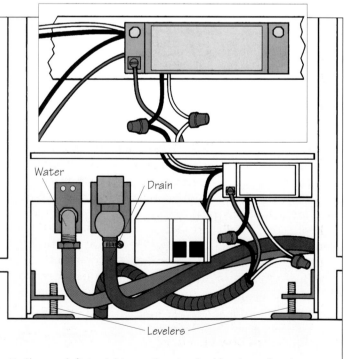

5. Shown, left to right, are the standard hookups for the water supply, drain line, and power. Note the fittings and hookup of each. The wire attached to the screw is the ground wire.

Range Installation

Electric ranges plug into a special receptacle (see "120/240-Volt Receptacles," page 100) through an appliance cord you wire to the range's connection block. Gas ranges require a gas line (see "Bringing Gas to a Range," page 94) and a 120-volt receptacle for an electric cord to bring power to the clock, lights, and electronic ignition devices.

Preparing for Installation

Check with the local building department for applicable codes before hooking up either a gas or electric range if you're changing what you already have. With electric ranges, codes specify the type and length of appliance cord you must install. With gas ranges, most codes permit use of special flexible brass tubing from the gas-line shutoff to the range; a few, however, require that this connection be made with rigid iron gas pipe.

Attach the Appliance Cord. Read and follow the manufacturer's instructions for the electric range. Typical 120/240-volt installations require four connections. There are terminals for black and red "hot" wires, the white neutral wire, and the green grounding wire. You remove the cover and knockout from the range's connection block, secure the cord's wires to the terminals specified, and replace the cover. Some ranges are "hard-wired" to a junction box instead of an appliance cord.

Install the Flexible Gas Connector. For a gas range, purchase a flexible connector that's only slightly longer than you need. Don't plan to run the line through walls, cabinets, or anywhere it could be damaged. To hook up the connector, coat the threads on the shutoff with pipe joint compound or wrap them with plumber's tape, and thread one of the connector's nuts onto the shutoff. Turn the nut down hand-tight, then using one wrench to hold the shutoff and the other to turn the nut, tighten about a quarter-turn more.

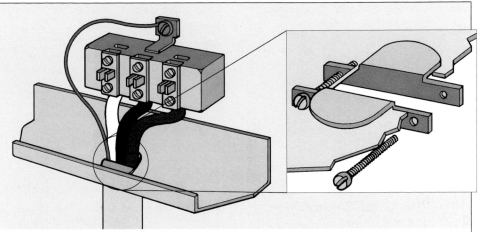

Attach the Appliance Cord. Screw the cord's wires to terminals on the range's connection block. A strain reliever, shown at right, takes stress off the cord.

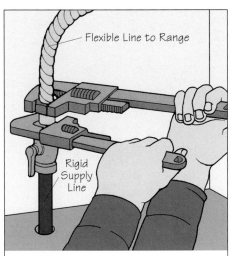

Install the Flexible Gas Connector. Thread the connector's compression nut onto the shutoff valve. Use two wrenches; don't overtighten.

Flexible Line to Range

Rigid Supply Line

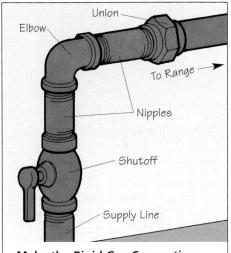

Make the Rigid Gas Connection. Assemble the pipes and fittings as shown. Seal all connections before tightening them with wrenches.

Union

Elbow

To Range

Nipples

Shutoff

Supply Line

CAUTION: Overtightening can crack soft brass gas fittings, causing a dangerous gas leak.

Make the Rigid Gas Connection. If the local code requires that you use rigid pipe for a gas hookup, you'll need a couple of short lengths of pipe, called "nipples," elbow and union fittings, and enough pipe to reach the range's gas inlet. Seal all connections with pipe joint compound or plumber's tape. Check the connections for leaks by brushing them with soapy water.

Sliding the Range into Place

With slide-in ranges, you remove the broiler or drawer in an electric model to provide access to hookups. As you

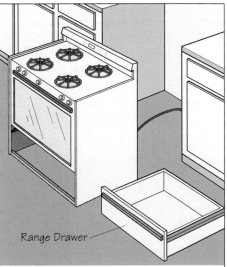

Sliding the Range into Place. Remove the broiler or drawer and ease the unit into position. Don't collide with the connections underneath.

Range Drawer

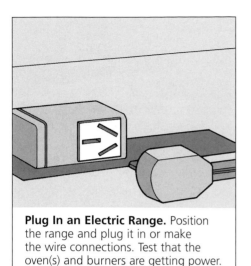

Plug In an Electric Range. Position the range and plug it in or make the wire connections. Test that the oven(s) and burners are getting power.

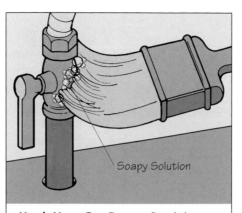

Hook Up a Gas Range. Bend the flexible connector but don't crimp it. Turn on the gas. Test all connections by brushing them with soapy water.

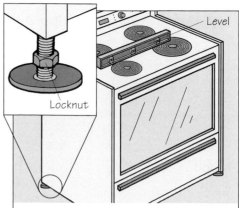

Leveling the Range. To raise the front or rear of a range, unscrew one of its leveling legs. Check for level by placing a 24-inch level across the unit's top.

push the unit into place, check to be sure it clears the connections.

Plug In an Electric Range. Plug the range's appliance cord into an outlet at floor level or wire it directly to a junction box. Replace the drawer, making sure it clears the cord.

Hook Up a Gas Range. After plugging in the power cord to a gas range and sliding the range into place, secure the flexible connector or rigid pipe to the range's gas inlet. Before replacing the broiler, turn on the gas and test all connections by coating them with soapy water. If the solution bubbles, gas is escaping; tighten the leaking connection slightly and test it again.

Leveling the Range

If the rangetop is not even with adjacent cabinets, you can adjust the leveling legs at the front and rear of the unit. Check that the range is level by placing a 24-inch carpenter's level across the top of the range. Once you're satisfied, tighten the locknuts on the legs.

Installing Drop-In Units and Wall Ovens

Follow similar procedures with built-in cooking units. With some of these, however, you may need to wire the appliance directly to an electrical junction box. Many codes don't allow plug-in connections for ranges considered more permanent than slide-in units.

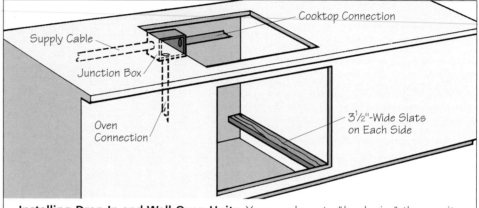

Installing Drop-In and Wall-Oven Units. You may have to "hard-wire" these units, or permanently connect them to an electrical junction box. Check with the local building department and follow the installation instructions that come with the unit.

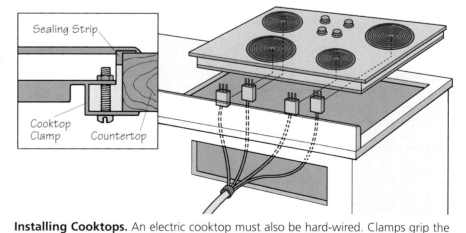

Installing Cooktops. An electric cooktop must also be hard-wired. Clamps grip the countertop around the perimeter of the opening, similar to those in sink installation. The sealing strip blocks grease and moisture from running into the opening.

Installing Cooktops

Cooktops also require permanent electrical connections. These units clamp to the countertop in much the same way a kitchen sink does (see "Installing Sinks," page 171).

To learn about installing a range hood, see "Range Hood Installation," page 106.

Now that all the built-ins are installed, you can install your other appliances and enjoy your new kitchen.

MAINTAINING SURFACES

	ROUTINE CARE	SPOTS AND STAINS	LONG-TERM CARE
COUNTERS			
Plastic	Wipe with a sponge dampened in detergent solution.	Rub with nonabrasive household cleaner.	Seal with auto or appliance wax.
Wood	Lightly sponge and wipe dry. Don't let water stand.	Rub lightly with fine sandpaper or steel wool.	Rub in mineral oil every few months.
Tile, Granite	Sponge with sudsy water. Buff with a soft cloth.	Treat with a degreaser or tile cleaner.	For tile, periodically reseal grout.
CABINETS			
Laminates	Wipe with a sponge dampened in detergent solution.	Rub with nonabrasive household cleaner.	Revive dull finishes with automotive or appliance wax.
Wood	Wipe with a damp sponge or cloth.	Rub with appliance cleaner/wax.	Restore gloss with furniture polish.
FLOORS			
Resilient	Dust mop. Damp mop.	Scrub with mild detergent or nonabrasive cleaner. Scrape carefully with a sharp knife.	Seal older types with paste wax, newer ones with liquid wax. Use special dressing for no-wax flooring.
Wood	Dust mop. Damp mop lightly and dry.	Rub lightly with fine sandpaper or steel wool.	Clean with solvent-base polish; buff with electric polisher.
Ceramic Tile	Dust mop. Damp mop.	Treat with degreaser or tile cleaner.	Some types need periodic sealing.
SINKS AND APPLIANCES			
Baked Enamel	Wash with detergent and water.	Treat with chlorine bleach or nonabrasive household cleaner.	Polish with appliance wax.
Porcelain	Scrub with detergent and hot water.	Use chlorine bleach or mild scouring powder.	Stay away from abrasive cleaners; they dull porcelain finishes.
Stainless Steel	Wash with hot, sudsy water.	Use fine steel wool or nonabrasive cleaner.	Restore dull finishes with silver polish or stainless-steel cleaner/polish.
Aluminum	Rinse with hot water, polish with a soft cloth.	Use scouring pads, rubbing in one direction only.	Treat with aluminum cleaner/polish.

MAINTAINING APPLIANCES

Dishwashers Wipe down the control panel with a lightly dampened cloth. Clean the door with appliance wax. Interior surfaces take care of themselves. Check the air gap (if any) monthly. Never use a sudsing detergent in a dishwasher. To remove suds from the tub, open the door and let the suds evaporate. Then add one gallon of cold water to the tub, and run the rinse cycle to pump out the water.

Microwave Ovens Opening the oven door a few minutes after cooling helps air out the interior. An occasional wiping with a solution of baking soda and water keeps the interior fresh. Never use commercial oven cleaner. Also, don't operate an oven with a bent door, broken or loose hinges or latch, or faulty door seals—you could be exposed to harmful radiation.

Ranges Mop up spills right away, especially acidic foods such as fruit juices, tomato, or vinegar, which can damage the finish. To clean under a slide-in range, remove the broiler or bottom drawer. Built-up soil in drop pans under burners can catch fire, so clean these often. Both gas and electric burners can be easily removed for access to drip pans.

Refrigerators Dirt that accumulates on a refrigerator's condenser impairs its efficiency. Twice a year, remove the grille at the bottom and vacuum the condenser. While you're down there, slide out the defrost pan and clean it with detergent and water. For efficient energy use, be sure that the refrigerator is level and ventilation around the front grille isn't blocked. Also, check door seals occasionally for air leakages at the top, bottom, and sides.

Vent Hoods Grease impairs the efficiency of a hood and can cause a fire. Clean the filter frequently; many can be washed in a dishwasher. At least once a year, wash grease off the fan and clean inside the duct as far as you can reach.

Waste Disposal Units Learn what your disposer can and can't handle. Don't feed it cornhusks, seafood shells, artichokes, wood, glass, paper, metal, or plastic. Also, don't pour chemical drain cleaner into a disposal unit. Periodically clean away grease by grinding up ice cubes or small bones.

KITCHEN SAFETY

Open flames, an abundance of electrical appliances, sharp knives, potentially lethal cleaning compounds, and a variety of other hazards make the kitchen one of the most dangerous rooms in your home. Observe these do's and don'ts to ensure that you're not harbor-ing an accident in the making.

FIRE HAZARDS
- Do not plug appliances into lightweight extension cords. Use only heavy-duty types that are no more than 12 inches longer than you need.
- Do not let grease build up in hoods, vents and flues.
- Do not keep cloth and paper near the range.
- Do not use aerosols or other flammable substances in cooking or baking areas.
- Do not wear clothing with loose sleeves when you cook.
- Do invest in a suitable fire extinguisher. (See Putting out Fires, at right.)
- Do replace any worn plug or frayed cord.

SHOCK HAZARDS
- Do take care always to keep water and electricity away from each other.
- Do not clean or service appliances while they are still plugged in.
- Do not keep a coffee maker, radio, or other electrical device near the sink. It could fall in and give you a dangerous shock.
- Do not attempt to pry bread from a toaster with a knife or other metal utensil.

OTHER HAZARDS
- Do not leave cabinet drawers open.
- Do not let pot handles protrude from the side or front of the range.
- Do not use a chair or wobbly step stool to reach high places.
- Do not use scatter rugs with slippery backings.
- Do provide safe storage for sharp knives. Just tossing them in a drawer not only invites cuts, it also dulls their edges.

PUTTING OUT FIRES
When a fire breaks out, keep calm and react quickly. Small fires can be extinguished in a matter of seconds, before they develop into bigger ones.

By all means invest in a fire extinguisher. Fire extinguishers are rated according to the types of fires they can put out: A, B, and/or C. Class A fires happen with ordinary combustibles such as wood and paper; water puts out these. Class B includes flammable and combustible liquids; Class C are electrical fires . Most kitchen fires begin as Class B or C, so a Class B-C extinguisher is the one to buy.

Locate your fire extinguisher in the path of exit from the kitchen so you can escape if the fire gets out of hand. Make sure all family members read and understand the operating instructions for your extinguisher and know what to do in an emergency.

If a small pan on top of the stove catches fire, turn off the burner under it and smother the flames with a tight-fitting lid or a cookie sheet. A mixture of baking soda and salt will also often put out a pan fire. Do not use water; it will spread the flames and make the fire worse.

If fire breaks out in the broiler, turn off the heat and close the door. Wait a few minutes, and open the door a crack. If the flames haven't died down, spray them with a fire extinguisher and close the door.

Glossary

Backsplash The vertical part at the rear and sides of a countertop that protects the adjacent wall surface. It is at least 4 inches high.

Base cabinet A 24-inch-deep cabinet that supports a countertop.

Bearing wall A wall that provides structural support to framing above. Joists rest on the top plate of a bearing wall. See Joist.

Butcher block A counter or tabletop material composed of strips of hardwood, often rock maple, laminated together and sealed against moisture penetration.

Caulking A waterproof, adhesive filler material that remains flexible so that it will not pop or flake out of seams and cracks.

Chalkline A cord that is rubbed with or drawn through chalk and stretched taut between two points, just above a surface. It is pulled up in the center and released so that it snaps down, leaving a straight line marked on the surface between the end points.

Circuit The electrical path that connects one or more outlets (receptacles) and/or lighting fixtures to a single circuit breaker or fuse.

Circuit breaker A device that protects an electrical circuit against overcurrent demand and short-circuit conditions just as a fuse does, by opening to break the flow of electricity.

Cleanup center The area of a kitchen where the sink, waste disposer, trash compactor, dishwasher, and related accessories are grouped for easy access and efficient use.

Convection oven An oven in which hot air is circulated by natural flow assisted by a small fan. A convection oven does not radiate external heat to the degree that a conventional oven does, and is more energy-efficient.

Cooking center The kitchen area where the cooktop, oven(s), and food preparation surfaces, appliances, and utensils are grouped.

Cooktop A unit containing a group of burners—gas, electric, or magnetic-induction—and perhaps a grill or ventilator. See Range.

Countertop The work surface of a counter, island, or peninsula, usually 36 inches high. It may be wood, plastic laminate, ceramic tile, marble, slate, or solid surface (acrylic).

Dado A square groove cut into a board to receive and support the end of another board, such as the end of a shelf. See Rabbet.

Drywall Sheets of gypsum sandwiched between a low-grade backing paper and a smooth-finish front surface paper that can be painted. Also called wallboard and, improperly, Sheetrock (a trade name).

Fishtape A long flexible metal tape about ¼ inch wide with a loop at the lead end, used to pull wires through existing walls.

Framed cabinets Cabinets with a full frame across the face of the cabinet box.

Frameless cabinets European-style cabinets without a face frame.

Framing The skeleton structure of studs and joists that supports walls, ceilings, and floors. See Joist, Stud.

Furring Strips of wood attached to a wall to provide support and attachment points for a covering such as hardboard paneling.

Galley kitchen A layout in which counters and appliances are arranged in a straight line along one wall, or along two facing walls, as on the opposite sides of a narrow room.

GFCI Ground-fault circuit interrupter: A special circuit breaker, especially in a GFCI receptacle, that reacts to an abnormal electrical condition in a fraction of a second.

Grout The fine-particle cement filler in the seams between ceramic tiles. It is available either ready-mixed or as dry powder that is mixed with water, and comes in a wide range of colors to match or complement any tiles.

Header A horizontal structural member that runs across the tops of window or door openings or between ceiling joists to support the ends of intermediate joists that butt into it.

Hot-water dispenser A sink accessory that keeps a small tank of water heated to near-boiling so that hot water is instantly available through its separate faucet.

Island A base cabinet and countertop unit that stands free, not touching any walls, so there is access from all four sides.

Jamb The vertical (side) and horizontal (top) pieces that cover the wall thickness in a door or window opening.

Joint compound The plaster material used to fill small holes and seams in drywall.

Joint tape Paper or synthetic mesh tape about 3 inches wide that is used to bridge the seams between drywall panels.

Joist A floor or ceiling support member that rests on the top plates of bearing walls.

Lazy Susan Axis-mounted shelves that revolve. Also called carousel shelves.

Microwave oven An quick-cooking appliance that uses high-frequency electromagnetic radiation, which penetrates food, to cause internal heat and cook from the inside out.

NKBA National Kitchen and Bath Association, an educational trade organization of the kitchen industry that, among other things, tests and certifies kitchen designers.

Non-bearing wall An interior wall that provides no structural support for any portion of the house above it. It usually runs parallel to ceiling joists and can be removed without concern for the overhead structure.

Pantry A storage room or large closet for packaged foods.

Particleboard A material composed of wood chips and coarse fibers bonded with adhesive into large sheets from ½ to 1½ inches thick. It is commonly used as the support for countertops and for cabinet construction.

Peninsula A countertop, with or without a base cabinet, that is connected at one end to a wall or other counter and extends outward, providing access on three sides.

Plastic laminate A hard-surface, thin material made from melamine under high pressure and used for the finished surfaces of countertops, cabinets, and furniture.

Rabbet A square L-shaped groove cut into the edge of a board to receive the edge of another board and form a corner joint. See Dado.

Range A unit that combines one or more ovens and a cooktop.

Range hood A ventilator set above a cooktop or the burners of a range.

Sheetrock See Drywall.

Shim A thin wedge-like insert used to adjust the spacing between adjacent materials.

Soffit A short wall or filler piece between, for example, the top front edge of a wall cabinet and the ceiling above.

Solid surfacing A countertop material made of acrylic plastic and fine-ground synthetic particles, sometimes made to look like granite.

Stud A vertical framing member of a wall

Task lighting Light aimed directly onto a work area, such as a sink or a cooktop.

Trash compactor A mechanical device for squeezing trash into a compact bundle.

Underlayment Sheet material—usually plywood—placed over a subfloor to provide a smooth, even surface for new flooring.

Wainscoting Paneling that extends 36 to 42 inches or so upward from the floor level, over the finished wall surface. It is often finished with a horizontal strip of molding mounted at the proper height and protruding enough to prevent the top of a chair back from touching a wall surface.

Wall cabinet A cabinet, usually 12 inches deep, that's mounted on the wall a minimum of 12 inches above a countertop.

Wallboard See Drywall.

Waste disposal unit An electrically powered unit that mounts below a sink drain and grinds food waste into tiny particles that can be carried away by the flow of drain water.

Work triangle The area bounded by the lines that connect the sink, range, and refrigerator.

Index

Have a home improvement, decorating, or gardening project? Look for these and other fine Creative Homeowner books wherever books are sold. . .

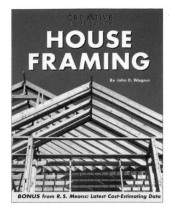

Designed to walk you through the framing basics. Over 400 illustrations. 240 pp.; 8¹/₂"×10⁷/₈"
BOOK #: 277655

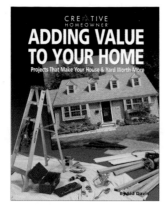

Advice for improving the value of your home. Over 400 illustrations. 176 pp.; 8¹/₂"×11"
BOOK #: 277006

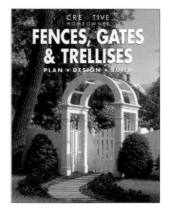

Step-by-step instructions & projects. Over 395 color illustrations. 160 pp.; 8¹/₂"×10⁷/₈"
BOOK #: 277981

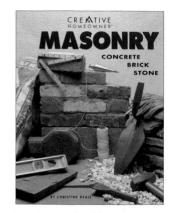

How to work with concrete, brick, and stone. Over 500 Illustrations. 176 pp.; 8¹/₂"×10⁷/₈"
BOOK #: 277106

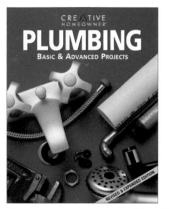

Take the guesswork out of plumbing repair. More than 550 illustrations. 176 pp.; 8¹/₂"×10⁷/₈"
BOOK #: 277620

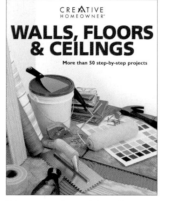

How to replace old surfaces with new ones. Over 500 illustrations. 176 pp.; 8¹/₂"×10⁷/₈"
BOOK #: 277697

Step-by-step deck building for the novice. Over 500 color illustrations. 176 pp.; 8¹/₂"×10⁷/₈"
BOOK #: 277180

How to convert unused space into useful living area. 570 illustrations. 192 pp.; 8¹/₂"×10⁷/₈"
BOOK #: 277680

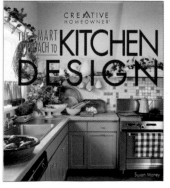

How to create kitchen style like a pro. Over 150 color photographs. 176 pp.; 9"×10"
BOOK #: 279935

How to work with space, color, pattern, texture. Over 300 photos. 256 pp.; 9"×10"
BOOK #: 279667

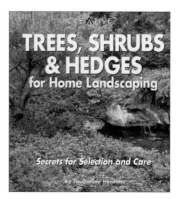

How to select and care for landscaping plants. Over 500 illustrations. 208 pp.; 9"×10"
BOOK #: 274238

Create more beautiful, healthier, lower-maintenance lawns. Over 300 illustrations. 160 pp.; 9"×10"
BOOK #: 274359